PRAISE FOR

CHOOSE FREEDOM

"Bruce Eberle has written the book I've been searching for! In fact, I'm going to give copies to a few young friends so that they will understand why it's an incredible blessing to be an American. Bruce beautifully demonstrates how the principles of America's Founders are just as important today as they were to the founding of our great free republic."

–REBECCA HAGELIN, AUTHOR AND COLUMNIST

"This book is an indispensable resource for any student interested in becoming a stronger conservative and better leader. We'll use it extensively with the next generation of conservative women students we're preparing to lead America"

–MICHELLE EASTON, PRESIDENT, CLARE BOOTHE LUCE
CENTER FOR CONSERVATIVE WOMEN

"*Choose Freedom* is addressed to students, yet a compelling read for every American."

–RON ROBINSON, PRESIDENT EMERITUS, YOUNG AMERICA'S FOUNDATION

"The oldest two of my four daughters recently began asking serious questions about government and policy. *Choose Freedom* is a great presentation of real history and current events. This book is well timed to inform and equip my daughters (and others) for the task at hand. Thank you, Bruce!"

–BILL MEIER, PRESIDENT AND CEO, KINGDOM WORKERS

"*Choose Freedom* is the right book for encouraging young conservatives in high school and college to get involved in the Conservative movement. Give one to a young person today."

–ALAN GOTTLIEB, FOUNDER, CITIZENS COMMITTEE FOR THE RIGHT TO KEEP AND BEAR ARMS, SECOND AMENDMENT FOUNDATION

"Bruce Eberle's latest book, *Choose Freedom*, not only tells the story of the modern Conservative movement but also explains why conservatives and so-called 'progressives' disagree on virtually every issue. *Choose Freedom* is a hopeful book and a must-read for every high school and college student, as well as every American who cherishes freedom and the exceptional legacy of our Founding Fathers."

–GARY BAUER, PRESIDENT, AMERICAN VALUES

"It seems that more and more the fundamental philosophy of the founding is being lost in American education today, and Bruce Eberle here has written a great and necessary correction, calling attention to the need to cultivate virtue, faith, and duty and to understand how good government and policy flow from those things. Bruce issues a call to America's youth to restore the spirit of the founding to today's society and government."

–DR. AARON PALMER, CHAIRMAN, SCHOOL OF HUMANITIES, WISCONSIN LUTHERAN COLLEGE

"Want to save this country from Karl Marx and his acolytes? Read *Choose Freedom* with the author's simple and convincing solution: a return to God, the Founding Fathers, and the Constitution."

"I love the book! So many times when I read conservative columnists, they just tell me things I've read a dozen times elsewhere. But in your book, I find myself over and over again thinking, 'I didn't know that.'"

"When someone with Bruce Eberle's amazing reputation writes a book, we should all give pause and read. The topics and principles that he discusses are eternal and have great value, especially in these difficult and challenging political times. We would all do well to hear his wisdom on freedom, virtue, liberty in the economy, and the great need for all of us who cherish this freedom to stand up and defend it! I hope you enjoy this book and appreciate the author and the principles discussed as much as I do."

"Your book is an eloquent clarion cry to push back and expose the imminent threat of socialism with its dangerous, false façade, which threatens the very founding principles of America. *Choose Freedom* is so historically and thoroughly researched with marvelous references and quotes of extraordinary examples of conservatism—its leaders, ideals, practices, principles, and precepts."

"*Choose Freedom* tells an old, fundamental story about society and faith: how Christian faith undergirds politics and what happens in society when faith wanes."

"Know what you believe and why you believe it? Bruce Eberle's essential book helps young people answer this most important question!"

–**BECKY NORTON DUNLOP**, RONALD REAGAN DISTINGUISHED FELLOW, HERITAGE FOUNDATION

"*Choose Freedom* is a clarion call for a new generation of leaders in this movement. Eberle shows the way yet again."

–**BRENT BOZELL**, FOUNDER, MEDIA RESEARCH CENTER

"Bruce Eberle's book is a remarkable compendium of the issues challenging America today and a compelling 'call to action' for a new generation of Americans whose future and freedom depend on their action. I highly recommend it."

–**JAMES LACY**, NATIONAL CHAIRMAN, YOUNG AMERICANS FOR FREEDOM, 1978-1983

"God gave us the precious gift of freedom, and Bruce Eberle provides the owner's manual that helps us understand the magnificence of His offering. *Choose Freedom* is a marvelous work, not only for its authoritative history but because the author has a deep and deserved faith in high school and college students who bear the responsibility for defending freedom and bestowing it on future generations. This book will restore your hope for America's future."

–**TOM KILGANNON**, PRESIDENT, FREEDOM ALLIANCE

"*Choose Freedom* should be read by every promising and literate mind in our high schools and colleges. It's blunt. It's honest. It takes no prisoners."

–**RON DOCKSAI**, NATIONAL CHAIRMAN, YOUNG AMERICANS FOR FREEDOM, 1969-1975

"In *Choose Freedom* Bruce demonstrates that freedom is what has made America the greatest country in human history. The book eloquently describes the blessings that freedom has given us, the growing threats to our freedom, and what we must do to save and preserve it."

—JAMES ROBERTS, FOUNDER AND PRESIDENT, RADIO AMERICA

"Bruce Eberle articulately and succinctly elucidates the perennial options between which we must each choose. In the end, we side with the Gnostic dreamers whose vision of heaven on earth justifies a lust for power and glorification of the state or we link arms with the conservatives who understand that man is bestowed with God-given rights and an inherent yearning to fulfill a just and virtuous life on earth before an everlasting judgment. *Choose Freedom* provides the key that will unlock the truth for a new generation of Americans seeking a genuine understanding of human nature and the laws that govern the universe."

—CHRISTOPHER LONG, PRESIDENT, INTERCOLLEGIATE STUDIES INSTITUTE (2011-2016) AND NATIONAL DIRECTOR OF YOUNG AMERICANS FOR FREEDOM (1986-1988)

"*Choose Freedom* highlights the biblical and moral core of true conservatism, written by one of its most respected leaders."

—WILLIAM OLSON, CONSTITUTIONAL ATTORNEY

"*Choose Freedom* provides a thought-provoking and alternative view regarding the virtues of freedom at a critical moment in time for our blessed country."

—DR. DANIEL W. JOHNSON, PRESIDENT, WISCONSIN LUTHERAN COLLEGE

CHOOSE FREEDOM!

EMBRACE IT. UNDERSTAND IT. DEFEND IT.

By Bruce Eberle

REPUBLIC

BOOK PUBLISHERS

CHOOSE FREEDOM!

First Edition

Copyright 2023 by Bruce Eberle

ISBN: 978-1-64572-088-1

Ebook: 978-1-64572-089-8

For inquiries about volume orders, please contact:

Republic Book Publishers

editor@republicbookpublishers.com

Published in the United States by Republic Book Publishers

Distributed by Independent Publishers Group

www.ipgbook.com

Book designed by Mark Karis

Printed in the United States of America

Dedicated to the one hundred young men and women who met at Sharon, Connecticut, September 9–11, 1960, and ignited a liberty movement that not only changed the trajectory of America but also the world for the better. We remain in your debt. Thank you.

CONTENTS

FOREWORD

YEARS AGO, I visited Ronald Reagan Elementary School in New Berlin, Wisconsin, on the president's birthday. The school officials asked me to share my thoughts on why I admired our fortieth president.

In addition to talking about Reagan's character and leadership, I also mentioned some of his successful accomplishments. As you would imagine, talking about tax policy with a roomful of fifth graders was not easy. So, I tried to connect in terms they would understand at their age.

I asked the students to think about going over to their grandparents' house to do some chores—like raking leaves. When they finish, their grandparents give them each $10 for their work. But when they return home, their parents take $7 from them for "room and board."

One of the fifth graders yelled out, "That's not fair!" Another shouted out, "Why would we even work?" Even in elementary school, these young people understood the fundamentals of a free-market economy versus the oppressive taxation needed for government-run socialism.

As conservatives, we too often think and talk with our heads. Liberals tend to think and talk with their hearts. We should not concede the logic of our minds but share it in ways that have an emotional appeal.

Young people today are drawn to fairness and authenticity. Bruce Eberle makes a compelling case to Choose Freedom using authentic examples that promote true fairness. He understands that we are created equal with certain unalienable rights given to us by God, not the government. The fundamental role of government is to protect these rights.

Dr. Martin Luther King Jr. had a dream that his "four little children will one day live in a nation where they will not be judged by the color of their skin but by the content of their character." Eberle rightly notes that radicals are turning that dream upside down with programs that judge people based on their race like critical race theory (CRT) and the 1619 Project. Race is but one of the many important topics covered in *Choose Freedom*.

As a young man, Eberle was drawn to the fundamental truths laid out in the Sharon Statement. This is the founding document of Young Americans for Freedom, adopted by the students who gathered at the home of William F. Buckley Jr. in 1960. Their inspiration came from the founding document of our beloved republic—the Declaration of Independence.

In addition to describing the foundation of the Conservative movement, Eberle covers a wide range of issues facing society, and particularly young people, today. In each example, he spells out the difference between those of us who put our faith in the individual, family, and ultimately God versus those who put their faith in the government and the elites who run it.

For young people, the contrast could not be clearer.

Those on the Left put their faith in the government. They want to tell you what to do, when to do it, and how to do it. They think they know better than you.

We put our faith in you. As long as you don't threaten our health and safety or that of our neighbor, we believe that you should be able to do your own thing, live your own life, and pursue your own dreams.

History is filled with failed regimes based on socialism, communism, and Marxism. Their false prophets promised power to the people, but most end up in poverty with control in the hands of the elite. It failed for those living in the former Soviet Union and those under Soviet influence in the past. And it is failing in places like Cuba and Venezuela today.

In America, Marxism was not successful because we do not live in a class-based society. Ronald Reagan spent most of his childhood in Dixon, Illinois, living in five different homes rented by his family. He went to a local college, then worked as a radio announcer before heading to Hollywood to be a second-tier actor. Yet he became one of the most consequential leaders of the twentieth century, proving that class is not a barrier to success in our country.

Unfortunately, Marxists are making another run in America these days. Instead of just focusing on income, they seek to divide us based on race, sex, and gender. As president of Young America's Foundation, I see it frequently with students on campus and even in schools. Those on the Left are the ones seeking division—pitting one group against another in our country.

Colleges, once havens for free thought and expression, have put up some of the most significant roadblocks to free speech for conservative students and speakers on campuses across the nation. Amazingly, even things like putting up flags for each of the 2,977 innocent victims of the attacks on September 11, 2001, are now considered divisive and blocked at many schools.

It has been said that if colleges and universities were to close again, it would do more to stop the spread of communism than of COVID. Ironically, communist officials in other countries routinely suppress freedom of speech for their political opponents. Sadly, we are seeing that in American culture today.

Radicals engaged in a long-term plan to take over the institutions of higher education. They then moved on to overtake the teachers' unions and seek control of the government-run schools. Woke thought has even made it into private schools. They dominate traditional media, culture, and social media. The only thing keeping them from total domination is that we have the truth on our side.

As conservatives, our counter to the radical Left should be talking about our love for America. We love this country so much that—regardless of age, race, sex, ethnicity, religious beliefs, income, or age—we want the same liberties and opportunity available to them that was passed on to us by previous generations.

Simply put, we *Choose Freedom*.

–SCOTT WALKER, GOVERNOR OF WISCONSIN, 2011-2019

PREFACE

WHEN I JOINED YOUNG AMERICANS FOR FREEDOM in 1962 it gave
me an opportunity to be part of a great cause: the cause of defending
and preserving freedom. This book is about choosing freedom over
socialism, a choice that your generation must make. I wrote it as my way
of passing along the joy of loving and understanding the foundational
principles of a free society. My goal is to help you not only appreciate
the freedom you have inherited as an American citizen but also embrace
it, enjoy it, and take an active role in preserving it for yourself and for
those who come after you.

I believe your generation has within its power the ability to not
only preserve and protect the freedom we enjoy in this great country
but also to pass the torch of freedom to those generations yet unborn.

I have every confidence that you, like those freedom lovers who preceded you, will rise to this challenge and successfully repel the efforts of those among us to seduce your generation into believing the phantom promises of socialism.

Those who subscribe to an anti-freedom, far-Left ideology seek to replace free speech with censorship that leads to tyranny and despotism. They call themselves progressives, but the only "progress" they seek is to grow the power of government and limit your freedom and opportunity. Progressives want government to look after you, care for you, and make decisions for you from cradle to grave. They want you to choose hatred based on the color of a person's skin rather than love for and harmony with your fellow Americans. They want you to embrace an Orwellian state instead of the individual freedom bequeathed to you by America's Founders. They want you to choose socialist subservience rather than free enterprise and opportunity.

But I have good news. While those in today's Progressive movement insist that their ideas are ascendant, they are actually in decline, as evidenced by their acts of desperation and panic, as well as by their rejection by the American people. Yes, the anti-freedom Progressive movement is still powerful, well-funded, and intent on eliminating and replacing the fundamental principles of individual freedom upon which this nation was founded. But I believe your generation—young adults of all races and ethnic backgrounds—seeks freedom and opportunity, not the regimentation and economic misery that socialism always brings. However, you and I must remember that if you don't truly cherish freedom and defend it, but instead take it for granted, it will disappear quickly. As Ronald Reagan reminded us,

> Freedom is a fragile thing and it's never more than one generation away from extinction. It is not ours by way of inheritance; it must be fought for and defended constantly by each generation.[1]

Just as those who founded Young Americans for Freedom sought to pass their love of liberty along to future generations, it is up to you and your generation to pass along the principles and the love of freedom to the generations that follow you. This is your opportunity, your challenge, and your time, just as it was for America's Founders and for those who began the modern Conservative movement in the early 1960s. Now is your time to advance the cause of liberty in this God-blessed land.

It starts with truth and honesty, as George Washington said in his Farewell Address on September 19, 1796, after serving two terms as our first president:

> I hold the maxim no less applicable to public than to private affairs, that honesty is always the best policy.[2]

Indeed, without honesty and truth undergirded by faith in God, our nation will not prosper and survive. I remember listening to my father and mother talk about God and country and the importance of government being small and letting each American be free to live their own life as they chose. Each evening after finishing our dinner, my two brothers and I were expected to sit quietly and listen to Fulton Lewis Jr. on the radio. His program was broadcast Monday through Friday over the Mutual Broadcasting System, then the largest radio network in the United States. Lewis, who was the Rush Limbaugh of his time, reflected the conservative views of my parents and their love for this land of freedom.

I mention this because the love of freedom as personified by the Conservative movement didn't really begin with William F. Buckley Jr., with his founding of *National Review,* or even with the founding of Young Americans for Freedom. In fact, it has really existed in a continuous line of Americans since George Washington and the Founders who understood and championed the important idea of limited government being essential to the preservation of liberty.

Fulton Lewis Jr. championed that idea when I was young, and Rush Limbaugh carried its banner into the twenty-first century. After the death of Buckley, Rush was rightly recognized as the philosophical leader of America's Conservative freedom movement. Now that Rush is gone, Ben Shapiro and others serve in that role, explaining and promoting the same ideas that motivated our Founders to create the first true republic, the first truly free society in the history of the world.

Of course, the foundation of freedom, the rule of law and limited government, can be traced back to England. And free markets can be traced back to the Pilgrims and their leaders, William Bradford and John Winthrop, who landed in 1620 at Plymouth Rock. Ronald Reagan spoke often of Winthrop's view of America[3] as a "shining city on a hill,"[4] seeing this vision of America not only as it was for Winthrop and the Pilgrims, but also for Americans of our times. That vision was also a major theme of President Reagan's Farewell Address to the American people (see Appendix A, page 187).

The free-market principles and the emphasis placed on the need for public virtue by Bradford and Winthrop, as well as the Founders of our Republic, were critical to the success of our free society. It is that foundation upon which today's modern Conservative movement is built. God willing, each generation, including yours, will not only stay true to that foundation but also make its own imprint upon it in ways that will preserve and advance liberty in your lifetime and beyond.

Some would say that the Conservative movement is divided into two camps: an intellectual side that is concerned with understanding and propagating the fundamental principles of freedom, not only on campuses but also in think tanks and in the pages of conservative publications, websites, and books; and the other generally defined as the activist side, those who focus primarily on the advancement of conservative principles in all spheres of society, including campus activism, and in the political arena. However, it would be inaccurate to suggest that those who focus primarily on the intellectual sphere are uninterested in the application of conservative principles in society and in politics, just as it would be inaccurate to say that those who think of themselves as activists have no interest in having a deep understanding of the principles that are necessary for a free society to exist. Those who identify themselves as activist conservatives but do not fully understand the foundational principles of a free society easily succumb to undertaking projects and supporting policies that are not conservative at all. Similarly, those intellectual conservatives who have no understanding of how policy is implemented are ineffectual at best.

It is my hope that you will not only gain a deep understanding of the principles that animated America's Founders but also of today's Conservative movement. But, more than just an understanding of those principles, I hope that you will follow those principles when you consider policies, ideas, and candidates for public office, regardless of their political party. I hope you will be a principled American first, last, and always before loyalty to a political party. Remember, political parties are simply political vehicles that have been created for the practical purpose of winning elections. Candidates may be conservative or progressive, but historically, political parties bend with the winds of public opinion.

Individual conservatives and progressives work though political parties and endeavor to make them bend to their beliefs, but conservative youth groups like Young Americans for Freedom, Campus Reform, the Intercollegiate Studies Institute, and Turning Point USA steer clear of political endorsements, overt political activity, and direct political activism. Nevertheless, their individual members are often engaged in political activity supporting conservative causes and conservative candidates. Neither political party has always nominated presidential candidates (or candidates for other offices) who stayed true to the small-government, pro-freedom vision of America's Founders. Moreover, the idea of preserving individual freedom and sustaining a free society must not be limited to politics or even primarily focused on it. It must be spread to the academy, to literature, to our culture, and throughout the fabric of America if your generation is to preserve freedom for yourself and future generations. That's what today's Conservative movement, America's freedom movement, is all about.

In politics, as I have experienced in my own lifetime, political leaders have too often failed to heed the wise words of George Washington in his Farewell Address to avoid foreign allegiances, but they have instead foolishly engaged in wars that were not in the best or just interests of the United States. Presidents have misguidedly acquiesced to demands that the U.S. act as policeman to the world. Democrat and Republican presidents have engaged in ghastly deficit spending and have gone far beyond the enumerated powers of the United States Constitution. It is good, even important, to be involved in politics, but remember, the Conservative cause and its principles stand firm while politicians sway with the political winds. In reality, the Conservative movement is about committed individuals who understand and appreciate the necessary order, structure, and composition of a free society and apply those elements to government today.

You and I need to understand the bedrock upon which the principles held by America's Founders stand. It is the same foundation upon which the principles of today's Conservative movement stand. We could simply refer to these principles and values as common sense, and that would be true. But it is far more accurate and important to understand that these principles, these eternal verities are derived from God. It is the embrace of godly wisdom that is the unshakable link from America's Founders to today's Conservative movement.

That reliance on God and the moral values enumerated in the Ten Commandments is not only recognized in our Declaration of Independence but also in the Sharon Statement adopted by the hundred student leaders who formed Young Americans for Freedom over September 9–11, 1960, on the grounds of the Buckley estate in Sharon, Connecticut.

In 2015 *The New York Times* recognized the Sharon Statement as a "seminal document" of the Conservative Movement, and it is widely regarded by historians and thought leaders as one of the most important declarations in the history of American conservatism.[5]

Neither the Declaration nor the Sharon Statement were perfect for the obvious reason that they were written by imperfect humans; yet even with their failings,[6] the young conservatives who gathered at Sharon captured the essential limited government philosophy that was necessary to preserve a free society. *National Review* publisher William Rusher, who was present as a senior Conservative observer at the founding of Young Americans for Freedom, said of the Sharon Statement:

> Nowhere else, for many years, did anyone attempt so succinctly and comprehensively, let alone so successfully, to describe what modern conservatism was all about.[7]

And, since it can be argued that the formation of Young Americans for Freedom was the founding organization of the modern Conservative movement, in this book I pay close attention to the Sharon Statement as it applies to the current challenges our nation faces.

In addition to providing the historical background of the beginning of the Conservative movement, I have endeavored to elaborate on where the Conservative movement stands on important issues of the day and why conservatives take those positions. Similarly, I have provided information on the founding of the American Progressive movement in the 1890s and where their ideology has taken them. But, perhaps most important, I have pointed out the fatal error of progressivism and why that misunderstanding means that Conservatives and Liberals will always be at loggerheads on each and every policy and issue. It is this fatal flaw that has led progressivism to keep moving leftward, away from fundamental truth and godly wisdom.

It is important for me to point out that when I use the term "progressive" in this book I am referring to dedicated leftists who used that term for self-identification beginning in the late 1800s and do so again today. I am not referring to those who may have been duped into supporting progressive candidates and their programs because they have heard only one side of the story in the classroom, online, or in corporate media. Those who have fallen for the false progressive narrative and do not understand its consequences are not true progressives; they are well-meaning, yet mistaken and uninformed. Many of them can be persuaded to accept the wisdom of America's Founders if we patiently take the time to lead them in that direction. They, too, can become freedom lovers and defenders.

I should also point out that this book is not intended to be a full and comprehensive presentation of each and every aspect of today's Conservative movement or of the Progressive movement. Nor will it necessarily reflect the views of every leader of today's Conservative movement. In fact, I am quite certain that there will be many of my friends who will argue that I left out important points or that my conclusions are not consistent with their own beliefs. The bottom line is that I take full responsibility for the views expressed herein, which are what I believe to be aligned with those of America's Founders, as well as with the founders of the modern Conservative movement.

–BRUCE EBERLE, VIENNA, VIRGINIA, NOVEMBER 23, 2022

1

WHY THIS BOOK?

YOU MAY NOT BE INTERESTED in the history of today's Conservative or Progressive movements, and that's fine, but don't you want to know the reason that conservatives and progressives differ on every single issue? You'll find the answer in chapter five.

In school, if you are identified as a conservative, you may be called a Nazi, fascist, racist, or White supremacist—even by your teacher or professor—but in this book you will find out that those descriptions more closely describe progressive liberals from their beginning . . . and even still today. And, as far as being called a Nazi is concerned, that charge doesn't hold water. Conservatives believe in limited government, but Nazis and communists and progressives believe in big, powerful government—as this book proves using their own words and documents.

You will also find out why America's Founders—not just the ones who wrote the Declaration of Independence and the Constitution but also the Pilgrims at Plymouth—understood that a free republic like the United States cannot exist if the citizens do not possess what the Founders called "virtue." But what did they mean by "virtue"? You'll find that explanation in chapter four.

This book also identifies the reason that today the United States is involved in seemingly endless wars across the globe, something that George Washington urged Americans to avoid. See chapters fourteen and fifteen to understand Washington's prescient logic.

Discover how critical race theory is just a stepchild of "critical theory" originally proposed by Karl Marx. It's just another means of pitting Americans against each other to bring Marxist progressives to power. Chapter ten.

But, perhaps most important of all, in this book you'll learn how you can make a hugely positive impact as an individual on the future of the United States. One courageous person with knowledge of the truth and dedicated character can truly change the course of history. And don't assume you will be joining the losing side. When you read this book, you may be surprised to learn that the Progressive movement is dying, not growing and expanding. It's in panic mode, so the progressives are fighting dirtier all the time.

To protect your opportunities for the future and the freedom you enjoy, you can become an important part of the Conservative movement. You'll find out that there is a bright, bold line that runs from the freedom philosophy of America's Founders to today's Conservative movement, and a depressing, dark line that runs from the early segregationist founders of the Progressive movement to today's Marxist Progressive movement. There are so, so many opportunities for you to play an instrumental role in preserving the greatness of America, "the last, best hope for freedom" as President Ronald Reagan described the United States.

You may be thinking, "I already know what I believe, and I'm ready to roll." If that's the case, then you will be most interested in chapters twenty-one to twenty-five: "They Want You to Shut Up," "Persuade Others to Your Point of View," "To Win, You Have to Stay on Offense!" "Know the Facts—Have the Answers," and "This Is Your Time!"

That's fine, but if you're going to advance the conservative cause, you need to be fully prepared to stand up to the progressive Left. That's why I wrote this book. You may be thinking, "But, why should I read everything in this book? I don't really care who created the Conservative movement or why they did it." If that's your perspective right now, that's okay . . . but you are missing out on a great American story!

If you must, skip chapter two, "Today's Conservative Movement," but you might want to briefly stop at chapter three. The Sharon Statement discussed there is important because it had a deep impact on developing the early Conservative movement. It also still rings true today and provides a north star to navigating the future. That's why I mention it often.

Also in chapter three, I explain why the late Andrew Breitbart's comment that "politics is downstream from culture" is true, but I argue that his formulation is incomplete. Why is it incomplete? Why is that important? And what is our culture downstream from? You will want to know the answer to these questions in order to stay on course and be effective.

In chapter four I discuss the one bedrock principle that enabled America's Founders to write the Declaration of Independence and create the United States Constitution. Without this understanding the Founders' creation of the world's first true republic would have been impossible. Thanks to the Founders, you and I enjoy a breadth and depth of freedom that really doesn't exist in any other country in the world.

Whatever you do, please do not skip chapter five. If you have ever wondered why conservatives and progressives disagree on every issue and how to solve problems, chapter five answers that question clearly and definitively. Understanding why conservatives and progressives can never come to a common ground is extremely important if you want to know what we are up against. When you do, it's like a lightbulb being turned on in your head. It certainly helps in understanding the laughable and strange way progressives think, as epitomized by my progressive friend whom I write about in chapter seven. As my wife likes to say, the minds of progressives just aren't wired right.

You're probably aware of the fact that progressives like to virtue signal. They really believe that they are ethically superior to conservatives like you and me. As I relate in chapter six, you will learn that progressives and the Progressive movement have a very dark past filled with racism and White supremacy that continues to this day. They not only were the ones who justified and instigated segregation first in the South (then all across the nation), but they also supported the sterilization of black women as a means of reducing the black population. It's also a key reason for their virulent, and sometimes violent, support of abortion.

In chapters eight through seventeen I argue that the choice of your generation is between freedom and socialism (chapter eight); why free markets are the only way to get (and keep) people out of poverty (chapter nine); where critical race theory originated (chapter ten) and why it is so dangerous (chapter eleven); who those folks are who attend the annual economic summit in Davos, Switzerland (chapter twelve); how one of America's worst presidents, Woodrow Wilson created "the Swamp" (chapter thirteen); how creating a foreign policy that always puts American interests first is essential to our survival as a nation (chapters fourteen and fifteen); and the critical importance of the Right to Life and the Second Amendment (chapters sixteen and seventeen).

You may already know some aspects of these topics, but consider what one of this book's early reviewers wrote:

> I love the book! So many times when I read conservative columnists, they just tell me things I've read a dozen times elsewhere. But in your book, I find myself over and over again thinking, "I didn't know that."[1]

Even if you decide to skim chapters eight through seventeen, please give a decent read to chapters eighteen, nineteen, and twenty: "Climate

Change," "Progressive 'Compassion,'" and "Doing Good." You'll find data in the climate chapter that you are very unlikely to hear in school or from traditional media.

In chapter nineteen you'll find solid evidence that while progressives *claim* to be compassionate and frequently accuse conservatives of being "hard-hearted," their self-description doesn't match their actual generosity. You may also be surprised to learn, in the chapter titled "Doing Good," that too often the best intentions of presidents and other government officials to use the power of government to "do good" ends up causing far more harm to those they intended to help.

In the final chapter, I point out that you and I and all patriotic Americans need to remember that being a citizen of America is a great privilege. Of course, with that privilege comes the responsibility of not only doing our job as citizens to preserve individual freedom but also sharing an understanding of the principles of freedom with those around us and future generations. Being a freedom-loving American has nothing whatsoever to do with where your family came from, the color of your skin, or whether you were born rich, poor, or somewhere in between.

It is the responsibility of each of us—and especially your generation—to make sure that those who follow you understand and appreciate the blessing it is to be an American. Today's Conservative movement is the American freedom movement, and this is your opportunity—no matter your background—to share and defend the precious principles of freedom bequeathed to us by America's Founders. You have an opportunity to play an important role in the movement that seeks equal justice, unlimited opportunity, and maximum individual freedom for all Americans.

Welcome to the freedom team!

2

THE CONSERVATIVE MOVEMENT

THE PRINCIPLES OF LIMITED GOVERNMENT, individual freedom, individual responsibility, reliance on God, and free markets have been with us since the beginning of our nation in 1776 when the Founders signed the Declaration of Independence. Yet, by the turn of the twentieth century, those principles were under attack by a cadre of dedicated progressives who advocated a new approach by government that minimized the value of individual freedom and maximized the importance of a large, centralized government.

This group of progressives made great inroads into our political system and our educational system, so much so that by the 1950s it was the dominant political philosophy of our nation with little effective pushback by conservative political leaders or by limited government advocates on campus. Providentially, William F. Buckley Jr. launched *National Review* in 1955 with the sole purpose of rolling back the suffocating tide of big government liberalism. And in 1960, with Buckley's encouragement, a conservative youth group was launched on the Buckley family estate in Sharon, Connecticut.

From September 9 to 11, nearly one hundred students from colleges and universities all across the United States met to launch a Conservative movement—initially on campus and then throughout society. What they did there truly changed the course of history. It eventually led to the election of Ronald Reagan. The young conservatives that met for three days at the Buckley estate not only adopted the Sharon Statement—a declaration of conservative values and principles that is still recognized today as one of the most clear, concise recitations of those principles—but they also launched the modern Conservative movement on college and university campuses across the nation. Although little celebrated or recognized at the time, this gathering is now widely acknowledged as the beginning of the attempt to restore the priceless values and principles that guided America's Founders as they created the American Republic.

The invitation to attend the gathering at Sharon went to a list of 120 conservative activists involved in various student groups.[1] Under the guidance of Marvin Liebman, Doug Caddy arranged for the organizational meeting of this new group.[2] A letter went out under Caddy's signature to those young conservatives who were interested in giving conservatism an active voice on campus and in the political arena. The invitation letter began with these words:

> America stands at a crossroads today. Will our Nation continue to follow the path towards socialism or will we turn towards Conservatism and freedom? The final answer to this question lies with America's youth. Will our youth be more conservative or more liberal in future years? You can help determine the answer to this question.[3]

Traveling at their own expense, conservative student leaders from forty-four colleges came to Sharon. Those attending made it clear that they had no desire to replace or compete with the Intercollegiate Society of Individualists (ISI)[4] that had been in existence for a number of years and was working toward "a conservative intellectual revival on campus."[5] Instead these young men and women were interested in not only challenging liberal dominance on campus but also in achieving success in the political arena.

During the three-day meeting they adopted the Sharon Statement, elected Robert Schuchman as the first national chairman of YAF, and selected Doug Caddy as the executive director of the new organization. Subsequently, Caddy opened up an office in New York City with the able assistance of Marvin Liebman. The fledgling organization raised money, started YAF chapters on college and university campuses across the United States, and then, just one year later, boldly held a rally in New York City's Manhattan Center which, according to the *Harvard Crimson*, consisted of a

> shouting, cheering throng [that] filled every inch of sitting and standing room [in] bedecked Manhattan Center on 54th St.[6]

In his book *Revolt on Campus,* Sharon Statement author Stan Evans wrote of the event,

> The meeting had a powerful impact, one way or another, on all who attended. As one mirthful conservative remarked, it was the sheer audacity of the enterprise which made it so enjoyable. It was, indeed, an audacious undertaking, so much so that it excited wide coverage in the New York papers, on the wire services, and in *Time* magazine.[7]

Neither was the event ignored by prominent liberals such as Murray Kempton of the then quite far Left *New York Post* who snarkily opined,

The Young Americans for Freedom are only five months old yet they were able to put four thousand children into Manhattan Center Friday for an "Homage to Barry Goldwater Night." . . . We must assume that the conservative revival is the youth movement of the sixties.[8]

The national media also took notice of the rally.

The New York Times put its story about the rally on page one. Hundreds of articles and columns were generated. Television networks carried film clips the following evening. In one night Young Americans for Freedom became a national institution, and has remained one to this day.[9]

The large, rambunctious rally in the heart of Manhattan was indeed an audacious introduction on the national scene for YAF, but it was only the beginning. There was much work to be done recruiting students to the organization and raising the funds needed to finance the goals of the ambitious YAF leaders.

On March 7, 1962, less than two years after its founding, the fledgling organization upped its game, holding a massive rally in Madison Square Garden calling for world victory over communism. Again, the rally featured Barry Goldwater, who by this time was drawing the attention of conservatives all across the nation as a possible 1964 presidential candidate. The Garden was filled to the rafters with some 18,000 young conservatives.[10] Outside were hundreds of protesters including communists, Nazis, and other leftwing cranks protesting the event. The rally drew so much attention nationwide that even in my hometown of St. Joseph, Missouri, I was able to hear long excerpts from the speeches by Brent Bozell Jr., Senator John Tower of Texas, and Barry Goldwater over my local radio station.

Shortly thereafter I responded to a YAF ad in *National Review* and enthusiastically became part of a great movement to protect, preserve, and defend freedom in America. Along with other national YAF members in my area, we quickly started a local YAF chapter and then worked to build a strong YAF organization across Missouri. Others around the nation were doing the same thing, making Young Americans for Freedom members a force to be reckoned with on campus and in the political arena.

As for the one hundred founders of Young Americans for Freedom, they dedicated themselves to advancing the conservative cause, the cause of individual freedom, the rule of law, and the principles of America's Founders. At just twenty-six years of age, M. Stanton Evans was already the youngest editor of a major newspaper in the United States, the *Indianapolis News*. Evans maintained his ties with YAF throughout his life, writing several dozen books, including *Revolt on Campus*, the story of the young men and women who created Young Americans for Freedom. Later, he founded the National Journalism Center, which trained talented young conservative writers for positions in the news media.

Jameson Campaigne Jr., who was also at Sharon, was a long-time member of the YAF national board of directors and worked for the Henry Regnery Company. Campaigne later teamed up with YAF Treasurer James Linen IV to purchase and run six daily newspapers in the Chicago area. Eventually, Campaigne started his own publishing house, Greenhill Publishers, which has published more than fifteen million conservative books. He continues today in his support of Young Americans for Freedom and the Conservative movement. Also attending the conference at Sharon was future editor and publisher of *Human Events*, Allan Ryskind. In the early days, *Human Events* was the weekly lifeline of conservatives all across the nation.

Prior to the gathering at the Buckley estate where YAF was founded, Carol Dawson was a national leader in the College Republicans and attended the 1960 GOP convention in Chicago. Dawson played a key role at that convention in the Youth for Goldwater for Vice President campaign. Dawson also served on the committee that drafted the Sharon Statement and then as secretary of the national organization.

At just twenty-eight, Lee Edwards was the oldest participant at the founding of YAF at Sharon. Edwards went on to serve as the head of public affairs in the office of Senator Goldwater, served in a similar role in the Draft Goldwater for President campaign, and subsequently in the official campaign. Edwards later wrote a highly regarded biography of Senator Goldwater.[11] Edwards was also the editor of the *Conservative Digest,* published by Richard Viguerie for ten years. Although Viguerie served as executive secretary of Young Americans for Freedom following Doug Caddy, he was not at Sharon. Nevertheless, as the recognized father of political direct mail fundraising, Viguerie has made a huge impact on YAF and many other conservative organizations, raising hundreds of millions of dollars for the Conservative movement and its candidates.

Since the founding of YAF, other excellent conservative groups have made their mark on the Conservative movement as noted above. To be sure, it is young conservatives like yourself who are the future of the Conservative movement and the hope of our nation. I am confident you will be up to the task.

3

THE SHARON STATEMENT

WHEN WILLIAM F. BUCKLEY JR. founded *National Review* and served as midwife to the founding of Young Americans for Freedom, he sought to create a movement that not only preserved America's founding principles but that would also be successful in spreading its views of limited government and maximum individual freedom to a wider audience. How better to do this than through a group of young men and women on college and university campuses across the nation? It was a wise strategy, and it worked.

Buckley not only hosted the founding meeting of Young Americans for Freedom at his family estate but continued to personally nurture the organization throughout his life. It is worth noting that while Buckley and other senior conservative leaders (then only in their thirties!) were present at the founding of YAF, they did not participate in the proceedings.[1]

As noted, the Sharon Statement remains to this day, more than sixty years later, the most concise and clear statement of the values and purpose of not only Young Americans for Freedom but also of today's conservative movement. It reads as follows:

> In this time of moral and political crises, it is the responsibility of the youth of America to affirm certain eternal truths.
>
> We, as young conservatives, believe:
>
> That foremost among the transcendent values is the individual's use of his God-given free will, whence derives his right to be free from the restrictions of arbitrary force;
>
> That liberty is indivisible, and that political freedom cannot long exist without economic freedom;
>
> That the purpose of government is to protect those freedoms through the preservation of internal order, the provision of national defense, and the administration of justice;
>
> That when government ventures beyond these rightful functions, it accumulates power, which tends to diminish order and liberty;
>
> That the Constitution of the United States is the best arrangement yet devised for empowering government to fulfill its proper role, while restraining it from the concentration and abuse of power;
>
> That the genius of the Constitution—the division of powers—is summed up in the clause that reserves primacy to the several states, or to the people, in those spheres not specifically delegated to the Federal government;

That the market economy, allocating resources by the free play of supply and demand, is the single economic system compatible with the requirements of personal freedom and constitutional government, and that it is at the same time the most productive supplier of human needs;

That when government interferes with the work of the market economy, it tends to reduce the moral and physical strength of the nation; that when it takes from one man to bestow on another, it diminishes the incentive of the first, the integrity of the second, and the moral autonomy of both;

That we will be free only so long as the national sovereignty of the United States is secure; that history shows periods of freedom are rare, and can exist only when free citizens concertedly defend their rights against all enemies;

That the forces of international Communism are, at present, the greatest single threat to these liberties;

That the United States should stress victory over, rather than coexistence with, this menace; and

That American foreign policy must be judged by this criterion: does it serve the just interests of the United States?

Although issues that came along later could not be addressed in the Sharon Statement, this document is still very timely today. At one point, after the fall of the Berlin Wall, it might have been thought that communism had been vanquished, relegated to the ash heap of history, but not so. Still today, the greatest foreign threat to our nation is the Communist regime of China with its allies and outposts in Cuba, Vietnam, Venezuela, and Nicaragua. Equally dangerous, or perhaps even more so, is the Marxist ideology that has taken deep root in America's colleges and universities and even in high schools and elementary schools. Such places of learning are too often populated by Marxists teachers and professors who seek to indoctrinate, not teach.

But there is much more to the Sharon Statement than identifying the threat of communism, including the important recognition of "eternal truths" that never change regardless of the age. Like those clear-minded and courageous Americans who signed the Declaration of Independence, the young conservatives of 1960 and young conservatives today recognize that the true author of liberty is the God who created us. Together with the Founders these young conservatives realized that "liberty is indivisible, and that political freedom cannot long exist without economic freedom." They fully understood that socialism is totally incompatible with a free society.

They also recognized that "the purpose of government is to protect" individual freedom, not to limit it, and that when government "accumulates power," individual freedom is endangered. The Sharon Statement reminds us that "we will be free only so long as the "national sovereignty of the United States is secure."

Consider how consistent the Sharon Statement is with the views of the Founders who believed that unless the citizens of our nation are well-informed and educated in the principles of a free society, and have the virtue (moral character) necessary to live in and maintain a free society, it cannot survive.

One of the most respected signers of the Declaration of Independence, although today one of the least noted, was Dr. Benjamin Rush. In fact, at the time of his death in 1813 he was considered second only to George Washington and Benjamin Franklin as to his leadership in the new republic. Rush wrote,

> The only foundation for a useful education in a republic is to be laid in Religion. Without this there can be no virtue, and without virtue there can be no liberty, and liberty is the object and life of all republican governments.[2]

The Father of our nation, George Washington emphasized the necessity of a government that depended on the favor of God to succeed, and he noted that "virtue . . . is a necessary spring of popular government."[3]

John Adams wrote, "Religion and virtue are . . . the only foundations of republicanism and all free governments."[4]

Even Thomas Jefferson asked the rhetorical question, "Can the liberties of a nation be thought secure when we have removed their only firm basis, a conviction in the minds of the people that these liberties are a gift of God?"[5]

Jefferson along with a majority of other Founders recognized the critical importance of a strong consensus of citizens striving for godly virtue as essential to the preservation of a free society. It was not an expectation or desire that virtue would flow from government but that a consensus of virtue among the people and those they elected would animate their decisions within the guiderails of the United States Constitution. Why was such moral character so critical to the existence of a free society in the views of the Founders? Why does it matter at all?

Just a few years ago the late Andrew Breitbart made the astute observation that "politics is downstream from culture." By culture, Breitbart was referring to generally accepted American norms and standards in regard to life, family, marriage, sex, public speech, and public behavior. In other words, he was talking about what American society has traditionally believed to be appropriate, acceptable, and respectable moral and ethical conduct. He recognized that these attitudes and practices drove political outcomes. Breitbart was correct, and his observation helped the Conservative movement recognize a need to focus on the culture of our society, not just on political ideals or political outcomes. However, I believe that Breitbart's formulation was incomplete.

Yes, politics is downstream from culture, meaning that it is the culture of a society that influences politics, not politics that influences culture. Breitbart's point was that if conservatives only focus on elections and ignore culture, they will fail. Of course, elections are important, but if the culture of society has changed, politics will bend in observance to the culture, not vice versa. Early on, the Sharon Statement author, Stan Evans, realized that

> the real sickness of modern society . . . is relativism gone wild. For it is relativism which refuses to allow the existence of any objective standards, either moral or aesthetic.[6]

But that begs the question, where did this relativism come from that influences culture? The answer is the prevailing consensus of faith in our society. It is not necessarily faith in the God of the Bible, but it is faith in something that has become the accepted god of a majority of Americans.

And, just how does this faith influence culture?

4

THE ESSENTIAL FOUNDATION

COMING TO AMERICA IN THE 1830s, Alexis de Tocqueville observed about Americans and their faith,

> In the United States, when [Sunday] arrives, the commercial and industrial life of the nation seems suspended; all noise ceases. A deep repose, or rather a sort of solemn meditation, follows; the soul finally comes back into possession of itself and contemplates itself.
>
> During this day, places devoted to commerce are deserted; each citizen surrounded by his children, goes to a church; there strange discourses are held for him that seem hardly made for his ears. He is informed of the innumerable evils caused by pride and covetousness. He is told of the necessity of regulating his desires, of the delicate

enjoyments attached to virtue alone, and of the true happiness that accompanies it.

Once back in his dwelling, one does not see him run to his business accounts. He opens the book of the Holy Scriptures; in it he finds sublime or infinite magnificence of the works of God, of the lofty destiny reserved for men, of their duties, and of their rights to immortality.[1]

What de Tocqueville recognized in the 1830s and America's Founders understood fifty-four years earlier when they drafted and signed the Declaration of Independence, is that faith in God and seeking to practice Judeo-Christian virtue is absolutely necessary to the existence of a free republic.

Not too surprisingly, nearly half of the men who signed the Declaration had some seminary training[2] and most read the Bible. The Founders also understood the critical importance of the institution of the Church, in its many denominations and forms, to sustaining a free republic. For it is from the Church that the moral character of the citizens of a republic must be renewed and refreshed regularly. Thus the Church is one of the often unheralded yet essential foundations upon which our free country is built. The Founders understood, as Stan Evans wrote,

> Self-government required observance of the moral law, respect for rights of others, restraint upon the passions. Virtue was thus a necessary precondition to a regime of freedom, and a nation that lost its religions moorings was considered ripe for tyranny.[3]

It is understandable therefore why reference to God was mentioned four times in the Declaration of Independence, as "Creator" and as "Judge" of the universe, as a loving and caring God they called "Divine Providence," and as the "God" of nature who rules the earth. The Founders—and later de Tocqueville—realized that if the United States doesn't have an enduring moral culture based on godly truth, a republican form of government could not be sustained. That's precisely what

Benjamin Rush, Benjamin Franklin, John Adams, George Washington, Thomas Jefferson, and many other Founders were referring to when they spoke of and wrote about the need for public virtue. They made it clear that they understood that a consensus of faith in God was essential to the ongoing health and continuance of a free society. Nevertheless, the Founders were nearly universally opposed to a state religion, viewing it as an unnecessary and dangerous avenue that would lead to disunity and conflict as it often did in Europe.

The Founders also understood that if the citizens of a nation do not exercise self-restraint, if there is no true compassion, no personal generosity, no sense of duty and honor, no self-sacrifice, no integrity, no honesty, no hunger for equal justice, no love for your neighbor, no forgiveness, and no accountability to God, a republic like that of the United States would not succeed. They knew that only if the people were seeking to be virtuous could liberty flourish and survive. They agreed that a consensus of Americans who valued integrity and were honest in their dealings, hardworking, humble, compassionate, forgiving, and self-restrained were essential to the success of our new nation. Conversely, they knew that freedom could not exist if the people themselves were greedy, corrupt, and immoral. When people are corrupt and refuse to exercise self-restraint, are dishonest, or fail to exercise personal compassion and charity toward others, then of necessity the power of government will grow and individual freedom will diminish. Intuitively, they knew that

> America is great because it is good, and if America ever ceases to be good, it will cease to be great.[4]

The Founders also understood that such good character did not exist in a vacuum; it came from faith in God and from striving to conform to the virtues enumerated in the Bible. But were the Founders themselves men of faith? Some weren't Christians but, like Jefferson, fully accepted the moral teachings of the Bible, specifically the Ten Commandments.

Other Founders were Christians, including George Washington who, according to this description by a contemporary, was a man who

respects God's Word, believes in the atonement through Christ, and bears himself in humility and gentleness.[5]

Other Founders put their trust in God, including John Hancock, who wrote shortly before the American War for Independence,

In circumstances dark as these, it becomes us, as men and as Christians, to reflect that, whilst every prudent measure should be taken to ward off the impending judgement . . . all confidence must be withheld from the means we use; and reposed only on that God who rules in the armies of Heaven, and without, whose blessing the best human counsels are but foolishness—and all created power vanity.[6]

Another Founder, John Adams, wrote,

The only foundation of a free Constitution is pure virtue, and if this cannot be inspired into our people in a greater measure than they have it now, they may change their rulers and the forms of government, but they will not obtain a lasting liberty.[7]

In a similar vein, Patrick Henry, the trumpet of the American Revolution and five-time governor of the Commonwealth of Virginia, wrote,

Righteousness alone can exalt . . . a nation. Reader! Whoever thou art, remember this, and in thy sphere practice virtue thyself, and encourage it in others.[8]

The importance of virtue to the Founders is also noted in the fore-word of a bestselling American history textbook used in private schools and by parents who home school:

Honor counted to founding patriots like Adams, Jefferson, Washington, and then later, Lincoln and Teddy Roosevelt. Character counted. Property was also important; no denying that, because with property came liberty. But virtue came first.[9]

. . . As Americans, we alone remain committed to both the individual and the greater good, to personal freedoms and to public virtue, to human achievement and respect for the Almighty. Slavery was abolished because of the dual commitment to liberty and virtue— neither capable of standing without the other."[10]

Yes, virtue counts in everyday life, in marriages, at work, at play, and especially in those who have been elected to public office at the national, state, and local levels. Yet, progressives can and do justify anything to advance toward their unreachable utopia. Such men have already done so by justifying slavery, segregation, gulags, and concentration camps.

Whittaker Chambers, a former atheist and underground Soviet courier who was totally committed to the triumph of worldwide socialism as envisioned by the Soviet Union, described himself and other communists as believers in the world's second faith[11]: "You shall be like God."[12] Chambers only broke with his long-time communist faith when he realized that "religion and freedom are indivisible. Without freedom the soul dies. Without the soul there is no justification for freedom."[13] He then correctly declared that "faith is the central problem of this age."[14]

President Ronald Reagan put the importance of faith in God as the foundation of our society this way

> Without God, there is no virtue, because there's no prompting of the conscience. Without God, we're mired in the material, that flat world that tells us only what the senses perceive. Without God, there is a coarsening of the society. And without God, democracy will not and cannot long endure.[15]

5

THE IRRECONCILABLE DIVIDE

WHAT IS THE FUNDAMENTAL, irreconcilable division that stands between conservatives and progressives? What is the one thing that divides conservatives and liberals on every issue? What is the single truth that the Left rejects, causing them to always reach the wrong conclusion, no matter the issue?

Put simply and accurately, the fundamental difference between conservatives and liberals is their understanding of human nature. Consider the way that a progressive author described the early progressive view of human nature that originated with the Social Gospel movement and that still defines the Progressive movement today:

Those following the Social Gospel movement declared that the Kingdom of God is to be on earth. Christians' efforts should be directed towards perfecting society rather than concentrated on securing individual salvation. Recognizing the concept of evolution, the followers of Social Gospel believed that social order is gradually improving. In time it will evolve into the Kingdom of God on earth.[1]

He continued,

The Social Gospel movement rejected the orthodox Christian position that man is innately sinful. It maintained that human nature is essentially good. Evil results from a corruption of that nature under external pressure from a corrupt society. Hence, to improve society one should attempt to reorganize and reform the social order in a way that will permit the better side of human nature to emerge.[2]

The progressive's belief in the upward moral trajectory of human nature is strikingly similar to the view of the atheist founder of communism, Karl Marx. However, it stands in stark contrast to that of America's Founders and of conservatives who understand that every person born is imperfect and has no ability to change human nature, he can only temper it by trusting in God and seeking to do His will. Conservatives also recognize that history shows that too much power in the hands of an imperfect human being always leads to disaster for themselves and severely damages those others over whom they exert power.

While early American conceptions of national government had carefully circumscribed its power due to the perceived threat to individual liberties, [early] progressives argued that history had brought about an improvement in the human condition [human nature], such that the will of the people was no longer in danger of becoming fractious.[3]

Progressives continue to believe that their own human nature is improving and getting better all the time. They believe that human nature will continue to advance for those who are the most intelligent and well-educated. Moreover, because of this "progress," those who consider themselves to be among the "intellectual elite" believe they are not only qualified to make the best decisions for everyone else in society but it is in fact their ethical responsibility to do so.

As the historical record shows, those who identify themselves as progressives follow an ideology that comes directly from the German Philosopher Georg Wilhelm Friedrich Hegel (1770–1831), the man to whom Karl Marx repeatedly stated his indebtedness for the development of his radical reorientation of society.[4]

Accordingly, the approach to government of these two camps, progressives and conservatives, will always and forever be in conflict. There is no compromise available because at the bottom line, it is a choice between a society that rejects the God of the Bible and one that seeks to be in sync with and faithful to that God. It is a choice between good and evil, right and wrong. Those who believe in God seek to follow His moral precepts and understand that man lives in a fallen state and can therefore never create the perfect society that progressives and Marxists fervently believe is possible. Accordingly, conservatives will always and forever disagree with those who reject God and believe their own created moral values are superior to God's moral values.

If progressives, who are captive of this dangerous utopian outlook, successfully create a government of unlimited power, then all freedom, all democracy, all equal justice, all freedom of speech, all freedom of religion, and certainly your right to own a firearm will quickly vanish. Progressives reason that if you have not—like *they* have—progressed to a higher ethical state, there is no reason for you to have free speech, worship what they believe to be a false God, or to own a firearm, all of which are dangerous to their creation of a utopian socialist state.

However, the reality is that if you don't fear big government as the Founders did, if you embrace it and see it as the solution to all problems, then you have made government your god. If you convince yourself that through the agency of government you can finally create a utopia, a perfect society, you are on a very dangerous road that leads to a human nightmare. The Left understands that

> religion itself—and indeed any dependence on a Creator—is a direct contradiction to the progressive conception of man as changeable and perfectible.[5]

The mistaken certainty that man can achieve perfection or even near-perfection leads progressives to believe that for the first time in human history they can use technology and "science" to alter human nature for the better. As Professor Ronald Pestritto wrote of progressive theoretician Herbert Croly in his book, *America Transformed,*

> In contradistinction to *The Federalist,* which thought men capable of self-government but carefully circumscribed the scope of popular government due to the permanent inclination to factiousness within man's nature, Croly made a more utopian assumption about the perfectibility of human nature.[6]

Croly, along with other leading lights of the Progressive movement believed that democracy "must stand or fall on a platform of human perfectibility."[7]

Accordingly, progressives believe they can bring about world peace and universal prosperity, but to do so they must first overcome and suppress those who have not reached their level of clarity and ethics. They see the restraints of the Constitution as being no longer necessary in this enlightened world; in fact, they see such limitations as a hindrance to the advancement of mankind.

On the economic side, progressives believe that a top-down command economy (socialism) is the only way to bring equity and justice to our nation. They foolishly believe this even though, tried time after time, there has never been a successful socialist society. Nevertheless, they insist that progressive leaders of years past had not previously evolved to the higher ethical plane that *today's* progressives have achieved. Now, they insist, having reached a higher ethical plateau, they not only have the opportunity but also the obligation to do whatever is necessary to create this nirvana.

This self-delusion has already driven progressives to publicly propose "re-education camps"[8] for Americans who voted for Donald Trump so that these misinformed Americans can be "de-programmed."[9] They also believe that due to their higher ethical plane they should be allowed to censor free speech or, as they call it, engage in "content moderation or content screening,"[10] especially when it comes to college campuses and social media platforms like Twitter, Facebook, and YouTube. Content moderation or screening is, of course, simply censorship of free speech. It was one of the very first steps taken by socialist dictators like Hitler[11] and Stalin[12] to make sure their citizens only heard what they wanted them to hear. Dictators always use nonthreatening language such as this taken from the 1920 Nazi platform (Plank 23) that sounds innocuous but leads to total censorship of free speech:

Newspapers which violate the public interest are to be banned.[13]

Who would want newspapers or radio or television or social media to "violate the public interest"? No one wants to "violate the public interest," but the problem is who is it that gets to decide what is in the public interest? Who is it that decides it's okay to let the Ayatollah, Vladimir Putin, Louis Farrakhan, Richard Spencer, and terrorists across the globe use Twitter,[14] but a president of the United States, Donald Trump, must be banned? Of course, if you believe that utopia can be achieved, censorship is the right thing to do; in fact, it is totally justifiable.

It is not hard to see where this is going. As Bill Buckley said of such utopianism, it "inevitably . . . brings on the death of liberty."[15] And, as Ben Shapiro observed,

Those systems of thought, in the absence of God, end with the gulags, they end with the gas chambers. They end in terrible places.[16]

Sadly, it is clear that today's Marxist progressive leaders have more in common with utopians like Robespierre, Lenin, Hitler, Mao, Pol Pot, and Castro than they do with past progressive/liberal leaders such as Hubert Humphry, John Kenneth Galbraith, or Arthur Schlesinger Jr. Sadly, today's progressives are similar in outlook to early turn-of-the-twentieth-century progressives who used their belief that they had reached a higher ethical plane to justify the segregation of Black Americans from White Americans.[17] It was the same flawed logic that progressives used to impose literacy tests and poll taxes on Black Americans to keep them from voting[18] because they judged them to be inferior.

> From the Age of Enlightenment onward, Western intellectuals have adopted various manifestations of "rationalism" to dismiss all forms of religious or nationalist convention. They claim that their reasoning alone can build a superior morality and a brave new world.[19]

It is clear to the most casual observer that today's progressive leaders promote a virulent form of progressivism that does not tolerate any dissent from their political and cultural doctrines. They have not only rejected the God of the Bible[20] and the imperfection of man, they have made government their god, with Barack Obama, Hillary Clinton, Bernie Sanders, and Alexandria Ocasio-Cortez serving as their demigods. It is clear that progressives also worship themselves as individuals who have achieved a higher ethical state than other mortals. Again, as the devil told Adam and Eve, "You will be like God,"[21] and radical progressives believe just that. Indeed, the headline of a *New York Times* editorial, "In This Time of War, I Propose We Give Up God,"[22] clearly reflects the attitude of today's far-Left Progressive movement. The only god they have room for in their lives is themselves and government.

In sharp contrast, as previously noted, America's Founders and today's conservatives realize that man is imperfect and thus incapable of perfection or creating a perfect society. Understanding this, conservatives justifiably fear all-powerful government. They recognize, as Lord Acton said, that "power tends to corrupt and absolute power corrupts absolutely."[23] The reality is that human nature makes it very difficult for a person who has great power to resist imposing their judgment and their beliefs on others.

Conservatives realize that the United States is not a perfect nation, nor will it ever be. That is why, with the Founders, they understand that freedom is fragile and can only exist when government power is limited and people recognize their imperfect condition yet seek to be virtuous and put their trust in God. That understanding was emphasized by those who preceded us who put God in our pledge of allegiance, our national anthem, and our national motto. They also put "In God We Trust" on every dollar and on every coin. The Founders and subsequent generations of leaders did their best to remind Americans that their freedom and success ultimately relies on God.

> Who has accomplished this? Who has determined the course of history from the beginning? I, the Lord, was there first, and I will be there to the end. I am the one![24]

Even in the early days of the Conservative movement, its leaders understood the danger of rejecting God and the deadly implications of such rejection to the existence of a free society. That was the essence of Bill Buckley's first book, *God and Man at Yale*, in which he wrote,

> The duel between Christianity and atheism is the most important in the world.[25]

Similarly, it was the author of the Sharon Statement, Stan Evans, who wrote of the centrality of the Bible as the source for a principled understanding of freedom.[26]

When there is no faith in or reverence for God, no belief in redemption and no accountability to God, there can be no self-restraint, no compassion, no forgiveness, no self-sacrifice, no humility, no honesty or integrity, no rule of law, and thus no individual freedom. Instead, there is only a lust for power, greed, human slavery, and a total disregard of godly morality, leading to child sacrifice and all sorts of debauchery.

This is the direction that today's Left seeks to take our nation. For example, the primary political home of progressivism, the relentlessly Left-moving Democratic Party, recently passed a resolution which proudly noted that

> religiously unaffiliated Americans overwhelmingly share the Democratic Party's values, with 70% voting for Democrats in 2018, 80% supporting same-sex marriage, and 61% saying [illegal] immigrants make American society stronger; and [that] . . . the religiously unaffiliated demographic represents the largest religious group within the Democratic Party, growing from 19% in 2007 to one in three today.[27]

The resolution went on to herald the "value, ethical soundness and importance" of such Americans! Today's progressive Left has rejected the God Franklin D. Roosevelt called upon to bless American soldiers and sailors on D-Day in World War II. In a national radio address that day, FDR said in part,

> Almighty God: Our sons, pride of our Nation, this day have set upon a mighty endeavor, a struggle to preserve our Republic, our religion, and our civilization, and to set free a suffering humanity. Lead them straight and true; give strength to their arms, stoutness to their hearts, steadfastness in their faith. And, O Lord, give us faith. Give us faith in thee; faith in our sons; faith in each other.[28]

Freedom flourishes in a virtuous society, but what happens when the leaders of society think of freedom as virtue itself? The answer is the French Revolution. To its ideological leader, Jean-Jacques Rousseau,

> freedom meant liberation from the forms and institutions of society—family, church, class, and local community. The state, in fact, would be the liberator.[29]

Instead, however,

> Rousseau's philosophy of radical and unbounded freedom spawned the most oppressive regimes of the modern world, inspiring revolutionaries like Robespierre, Marx, Lenin, Hitler, and Mao.[30]

The lesson is that without the guardrails of faith that produce virtue, a free society simply cannot exist. Only when our faith rests in God, not man, as the old hymn "America"[31] proclaims, is our republic and our freedom truly secure:

Our fathers' God to Thee, Author of liberty, To Thee we sing.
Long may our land be bright, with freedom's holy light,
Protect us by Thy might, Great God our King!

6

RANCID ROOTS FROM 1800s

WHILE THE MODERN CONSERVATIVE MOVEMENT began with William
F. Buckley Jr., who founded *National Review* in 1955,[1] and with the
formation of Young Americans for Freedom at the Buckley estate in
1960, the American Progressive movement began in the late 1800s and
was led by well-educated men like Richard T. Ely. Ely was a voracious
writer who authored more than twenty books between 1883 and 1941.
A neo-Hegelian, Ely studied in Germany like many of his progressive
contemporaries.[2] As a founder of the American Economic Association,
no one was more instrumental in promoting a progressive approach to
government and to economics than Ely, who was very influential in
both the progressive era of Woodrow Wilson and during the New Deal
of Franklin D. Roosevelt. It is noteworthy that his first book was titled

French and German Socialism in Modern Times.

It can be reasonably argued that Professor Ely, who taught Wilson at Johns Hopkins University, was instrumental in swaying his student to his neo-Hegelian, progressive point of view. Beginning with America's first progressive president, Woodrow Wilson, progressives expressed their disagreement with the way that government was established by America's Founders. In fact, they fundamentally disagreed with the founding principles that inspired the Declaration of Independence and upon which the United States Constitution is based.

Another progressive contemporary of Ely, W. W. Willoughby, argued that government is in

> possession of omnipotent rulership over all matters that arise between itself and the individuals of which it is composed.[3]

From the beginning, progressives not only believed that they are ethically and morally superior to all others in society but also that they were entitled and even obligated to *impose* their superior understanding on others for the betterment of society.

Another student of Ely, progressive economist John R. Commons, an advocate of the Social Gospel movement[4] and who was offered a position in the Wilson administration,[5] showed his true racist colors, writing that

> after many thousand years of savagery and two centuries of slavery, [Black Americans were] suddenly let loose into the liberty of citizenship and the electoral suffrage. The world never before had seen such a triumph of dogmatism and partisanship . . .. [A] theory of abstract equality and inalienable rights of man took the place of education and the slow evolution of moral character.[6]

Clearly incensed, Commons continued, "suffrage [the right to vote] must be earned, not merely conferred."[7] Commons argued against

Black Americans having the right to vote until they developed enough "intelligence, manliness and cooperation,"[8] which he believed should be determined by a literacy test.

Progressives were not only the originators of segregation and Jim Crow laws but also of literacy tests and poll taxes[9] that were used for decades to deny Black Americans the right to vote that they were guaranteed under the Fifteenth Amendment to the U.S. Constitution.

Progressives then and progressives today, such as Barack Obama, have an attitude of superiority, a contempt for those they consider to be their lessors. Obama sees himself as a "philosopher king"[10] who arrogantly believes that he knows better than Americans themselves what is best for them. As Charlie Kirk wrote in *Human Events* of the elitist Left's view of American citizens,

> It is a way of looking at humanity and saying, "You poor uneducated and huddled masses. You are so incapable of making the right choices for yourselves. Let me (us) help you. I am educated. I am thoughtful. I am wise. I have the best interests of all in mind."[11]

It is because of this superiority attitude that progressives believe they have the right to use the power of government to impose their vision of a rightly ordered society on everyone. That's why progressive teachers object when parents have the temerity to suggest that they should decide what their children should be taught when it comes to values and truth.[12] The cancel culture that pervades our society today is reminiscent of the terrible injustice wreaked upon Black Americans by progressives in the late 1800s, which continues unto this day.

When today's progressives use the power of government to insist that everyone must use politically correct terms in our public discourse and must adhere to their standards of speech and policy, they are simply following the "ethical ideal"[13] of their ideological founders. Today's efforts to stifle free speech, to silence any voices of dissent on the Internet and on television and radio are "justified" by their progressive ideology. When you know the "truth," why should you allow anyone to challenge you or engage in speech that is counter your "truth"? From their perspective, free speech is a bad idea and dangerous to advancing their mistaken ideology.[14]

As Professor Tiffany Jones Miller put it in *National Review,*

> For the progressives, government, as the agent of moral progress, is not only not obliged to secure to individuals the legal right to make decisions about their own lives, but is obliged to *condition* all such rights upon consideration of whether private decision-making conduces to their own and others' fullest possible development. From this point of view, even severe restrictions upon certain people's ability to govern their own affairs, and participate in the selection of their rulers, would not injure their freedom but advance it.[15]

In other words, from the perspective of a progressive, American citizens are entitled to make their own decisions, govern their own affairs, and enjoy individual freedom of choice only so long as the choices they make are agreeable with decisions that will benefit them and society as defined by progressive elites! This is a complete and total revision of the Founders' belief that the genius of America lies with its citizens,[16] who in their own wisdom choose elected officials who support policies that are agreeable to them. It also stands in stark contrast to the first principle of the Sharon Statement:

> That foremost among the transcendent values is the individual's use of his God-given free will, whence derives his right to be free from the restrictions of arbitrary force.[17]

The founders of the Progressive movement of the late 1800s, however, felt no constraint from America's Founders who stressed that individual freedom was only possible when government power was limited. In fact, these progressives led the first significant movement to challenge the legitimacy of the underpinnings of the American Republic. It began in the South with the suppression of the rights of Black Americans and then spread across the land.

> Beginning in 1890, a wave of disenfranchisement swept through Dixie as every southern State enacted literacy tests, poll taxes and other restrictions making it virtually impossible for black men to vote.[18]

While historians have argued that the advent of these and other restrictions on Black Americans was coincidental to the advent of the Progressive movement, it was not. In fact,

> The very same [progressive] reformers who championed minimum wages, maximum hours, social insurance, and other labor reforms not only generally opposed extending the suffrage [voting rights] to blacks, but also "promoted a policy of segregation" for blacks and "various degenerates"' including the feeble minded, epileptics, and "unemployables." And, they did so not in spite of the principles animating their economic reforms, but precisely because of them.[19]

Since the time of America's first progressive president, Woodrow Wilson, progressives have expressed their disagreement with the way that government was established by America's Founders. In fact, they fundamentally disagreed with the founding principles that inspired the Declaration of Independence and upon which the United States Constitution is based.

Whereas America's Founders sought to limit the power of government as a means of protecting individual freedom for all, the early founders of the modern Progressive movement like Richard T. Ely, Edward A. Ross, and Woodrow Wilson believed that government should have unlimited power. As Ely put it,

There is no limit to the right of the State [i.e., the government, to do whatever it chooses to do].[20]

. . . The progressives believed in "progress," in short, because they believed that history, as a process of moral growth, has an upward trajectory.[21]

Ely, Ross, Wilson, and the early progressives believed in the ability of enlightened humans (i.e., men and women such as themselves) to move up to a higher ethical and moral plane than others in society. Not only did they believe that ethics and morality had an upward trajectory, but they accordingly believed that those more advanced along this trajectory had not only a right but an *obligation* to move others up this path, by government force if necessary.

In a 1907 Independence Day address, future president Woodrow Wilson stated that "each generation must form its own conception of what liberty is"[22] and said,

Mr. Jefferson and his colleagues in the Continental Congress prescribed [the meaning of liberty] . . . for no generations but their own.[23]

To press his point home, Wilson added,

We are not bound to adhere to the doctrines held by the signers of the Declaration of Independence, we are as free as they were to make and unmake governments.[24]

Accordingly, it should not be a surprise when we hear today's radicals disrespect America's Founders, tear down monuments,[25] rename schools[26] and other public institutions after progressive heroes, and generally impose their "politically correct" views upon their fellow Americans. Apparently, progressives are oblivious to the fact that they live in a glass house and should not throw stones because their political founding father, President Woodrow Wilson, was a racist who used the power of the presidency to spread segregation and racism all across our land. Yes, Wilson dressed it up

in pseudo-scientific theories, [making it] perhaps more pernicious than that of the old tribal racists of the South, given that it was not regionally centered and was professed to be fact-based.[27]

It was not fact based, of course—that was just window dressing—but there should be no argument that in the current political atmosphere

[Ku Klux] Klan membership certainly should be a disqualifier of public commemoration. Why [then] are there public buildings and roads still dedicated to the late Democratic Senator Robert Byrd, former "exalted cyclops" of his local Klan affiliate, who reportedly never shook his disgusting lifelong habit of using the N-word? Why is 20th century Supreme Court Justice Hugo Black, once a Klansman, still honored as a progressive hero? . . .[28]

What about progressive heroes Ruth Bader Ginsburg and Margaret Sanger?

Sanger was an unapologetic racist and eugenicist who pushed abortion to reduce the non-white population.[29]

Even with the benefit of 21st-century moral sensitivity, Ginsburg still managed to echo Sanger in a racist reference to abortion ("growth in populations that we don't want to have too many of").[30]

In the early twentieth century, Sanger and virtually the entire Progressive movement were not only advocates for abortion (especially of Black Americans) but also of the pseudoscience of eugenics,[31] which justified their efforts to limit the black population via sterilization. Even more shocking, Sanger maintained a close and admiring relationship with Nazi eugenicist Dr. Ernst Rudin,[32] who wrote to Sanger,

> We can hardly express our efforts more plainly or appropriately than in the words of the Fuhrer, "Whoever is not physically or mentally fit must not pass on his defects to his children. The state must take care that only the fit produce children."[33]

It was only after these radical positions were exposed to the public "in the mid-20th century [that] their racist/fascist agenda was rejected."[34] So, in order to distance themselves from their Nazi inclinations, the progressives rebranded themselves as liberals, a title they clung to until the early twenty-first century.

> In the national political debates of the 1980s the term "liberal" had become a dirty word, and thus in the new millennium those who once called themselves "liberals" embraced the term "progressive" instead. This embrace went deeper than a mere re-packaging: progressive politicians pointed to the original Progressive Era as the source of their principles.[35]

It was Hillary Clinton who instigated and encouraged the change from liberal back to progressive. When

> asked whether she was a "liberal"; she distanced herself from that term . . . and described herself instead as a "progressive." . . . She made clear that she meant by this term to connect herself to the original Progressives from the turn of the 20th century.[36]

Apparently assuming that no one would remember the rancid legacy of the early progressives, Hillary relabeled herself a progressive. Today's progressives project their racism onto conservatives, not realizing that their own twisted ideology indicts themselves.

Progressives of today have now moved so far Left that there is hardly any daylight between what they believe and what Karl Marx advocated as America's parents have found out. Accordingly, those parents who participated in school board meetings to express their concern about their children being indoctrinated in racist Marxist dogma like critical race theory have been investigated and "tagged" by the FBI[37] as potential domestic terrorists. Along those same lines, freedom of speech was to be regulated by President Biden's Orwellian "Truth Ministry," that is, the Disinformation Governance Board[38] (temporarily on hold as of the time this book was written). There is little doubt that it will return at some point in the future if progressives have their way.

Today, in the progressive world, we are told that if you believe the Bible you are misguided. If you believe in the Constitution as written, you are misinformed. If you own a gun, you are dangerous. In fact, if you believe and share anything that is contrary to the dictates of the woke Left, you are spreading disinformation. The bottom line is that you are simply not entitled to your full rights as an American citizen if you do not adhere to the wishes of the ruling progressive elites. Of course, that's not freedom. That's tyranny.

7

ODD PROGRESSIVE VIEW OF REALITY

I HAVE A FRIEND who identifies himself as a progressive. He has a PhD in history and served as vice president for advancement (fundraising) of a large public university. Not surprisingly, his parents were very far Left, and in fact, his grandfather on his mother's side was a card-carrying communist. When his mother was growing up and other children were going off to summer camp for fun, she was sent to a Young Communist League camp for indoctrination. You might say that my friend was a red diaper baby once removed.

You may meet progressives similar to my friend. They are charming, well educated, and pride themselves on their intelligence and their power of reason. They reject what they consider to be sophomoric ideas, and instead insist that only through human reason can we really understand the world. My progressive friend is a very nice person, but he sometimes expresses ideas that make you want to roll your eyes. For instance, when we were talking about young Black men in the cities of our nation who engage in crime and killing, he said, "They're hopeless" (echoing Hillary Clinton's "super predator"[1] remark).

Now, I happen to know these young men are not hopeless because my wife and I have been involved for many decades with a Christian organization[2] that takes in boys (and more recently at-risk girls) who have committed crimes like carjacking, drive-by shooting, assault with intent to kill, arson, drug dealing, and more. The organization runs a home for at-risk boys who have done all these things and more. Yet amazingly, the success rate of the home is more than 84 percent. In other words, of the boys who come to the home, 84 percent are never again arrested for committing a crime.

More important, these truly reformed young men break the cycle of crime and poverty in their family, becoming productive members of society. Our "graduates" have a track record over nearly four decades of becoming good husbands, good fathers, and good citizens. They have become outstanding members of the military and law enforcement. They have become successful entrepreneurs, reliable employees, teachers, pastors, and youth counselors. One even became a college professor. Our Christ-centered program based on tough love has changed their lives forever and for good.

One young man, who was a gang leader charged with assault with intent to kill, was brought to our residence home in handcuffs and shackles. He came from indescribably bad circumstances at home. Yet after just eighteen months in our tough-love program, he went on to not only get his college degree but also get married and have children. He and his wife then became house parents at our home, helping other at-risk boys. After getting an advanced degree he now provides counseling services to at-risk children at another facility. So, no, the young men and women who have gone astray and gotten involved in all sorts of criminal activities are not hopeless. They should not be written off. They deserve a chance at forgiveness and redemption.

The great misunderstanding of human nature by the Left leads to all sorts of false conclusions. One afternoon I was talking to my progressive friend and he asked me, "Do you really think you earned the money you make?"

I answered, "Well, I feel that I have been very blessed by God, but, yes, humanly speaking I earn my money."

His rejoinder was, "No, you did not earn your money, you were just lucky in the lottery of life." I was surprised by the fact that he attributed my success to luck when he professed to be a person who lives solely by reason.

I then said, "Don't you believe that risk-taking should be rewarded?"

He answered, "No, risk-taking should not be rewarded."

I was fascinated by this response from someone with a PhD who would argue that he built his life on logic and reason, so I pursued the topic further. I said, "Why do you think that the United States is so prosperous?"

He replied, "Luck." That was his "reasoned and logical" answer!

On another occasion I told him a story about a man who, having graduated high school, got married and while living over a mortuary started a small business installing windows. This man went on to create one of the largest window manufacturing companies in the world and made hundreds of millions of dollars. After telling the story, I said to my progressive friend, "Isn't this a great story? Don't you think this man earned his success?"

My friend responded, "No, he did not earn his success. He should not be rewarded like that." Apparently, in my friend's eyes only those who are intelligent and have advanced degrees like himself deserve to be well-rewarded and serve in important, powerful positions.

At least that was my conclusion following another discussion I had with him. On this particular occasion, I asked him, "How do you define wisdom?"

He responded, "There is no such thing as wisdom." Then he added,

"If there is such a thing as wisdom, it's just a combination of intelligence and education."

Surprised again, I replied, "Don't you think that a man with a limited education can be wiser than a man with a great education?"

My friend was adamant, and perhaps insulted. "No," he said, "that's not possible."

I relate these stories for the purpose of helping you understand how the progressive mind works. But why would progressives believe that risk-taking should not be rewarded? Why would they think that someone with just a high school education who worked hard, took immense risks, and built a company that was hugely successful should not be rewarded with financial success? How can you deny that there is such a thing as wisdom that has little or nothing to do with intelligence and education? My friend is wrong. There is wisdom and it begins with reverence for the Lord. As it says in Proverbs 9:10,

> The fear of the Lord is the beginning of wisdom, and knowledge of the Holy One is understanding.[3]

Isn't an uneducated man who fears the Lord wiser than a PhD who makes up his own moral rules as he goes along? Is it possible that many of those who have PhDs, especially in the soft sciences, are sometimes jealous of those whom they deem to be less smart than they are but have been more successful?

> Leo Tolstoy, the world-famous Russian novelist, was well familiar with the limitations of the intellectual elite. After having been one for a long time, he came to believe that many intellectuals, despite their elaborate programs of self-glorification, were often greedy narcissistic people of bad character. In his *Confessions* [sic], Tolstoy explains that he came to believe that, ironically, the meaning of life is not understood by the people who write the celebrated books of the year on "the meaning of life" for fame and fortune, but by "the poor, the simple, and the

ignorant, the pilgrims, the monks . . . and the peasants."

Whereas, he writes, intellectuals spend their lives "in idleness, amusement, and dissatisfaction with life," the peasants whose lives are filled with "heavy labor . . . live, suffer, and draw near to death in quiet confidence and oftenest with joy." Paradoxically, it is not the more educated who understand the meaning of life but the less educated.[4]

To be sure, this is not a blanket indictment of every professor or everyone with a PhD, but too often college professors closely resemble Tolstoy's description. We need PhDs, of course, but they need to be men and women who are not only smart and well educated, but also possess the wisdom that only faith and humility provide.

I learned much from my friend. Ultimately, I concluded that those with advanced degrees may tend to think that because they have such a degree and are (in their minds) smarter than everyone else, they are the ones who should be running the world. They believe that you and I should not get in their way because they have more intelligence and education than we do. And they insist that the Founders' idea that typical Americans know what is best for themselves and possesses the wisdom to know what is best for their country and their family is simply wrong.

The fact is that progressives/liberals like my friend say the silliest things, such as "there is no absolute truth." But then if you ask them, "Are you married? Do you own a home? How did you get to work? Did you eat breakfast this morning?" they will give you answers and expect you to take those answers as being absolutely truthful.

You are sure to have progressive teachers, progressive professors, and progressive friends who will say some of the same things I have heard from my friend. Don't make them mad, but instead gently ask them questions that will expose the silliness of what they are saying. Ask them how they define wisdom. Ask them where they live, where they were born, what their favorite food is, and then ask them if what they have told you is absolute truth. Ask them if they think that risk-taking should be rewarded. Gently ask them to defend their defenseless views.

You and I know that if our society no longer rewards risk-taking, our country will fail economically. It is a huge risk to start a business. Half of all new business startups fail in the first five years.[5] Becoming an entrepreneur is a high-risk venture, and that is why taking such risk must be rewarded. Of course, if you are successful in business, it means that you are offering a service or product that people want or that other businesses and organizations want. All successful entrepreneurs meet a need or fulfill a craving. But unfortunately, those on the Left don't believe in a meritocracy based on actual accomplishments. Instead, they seek a society that rewards the educated, not the accomplished or the risk-takers. They believe they can achieve what no other group of socialists before them could accomplish: a democratic socialist republic—an oxymoronic phrase because democracy and freedom are completely incompatible with socialism. Ironically, they are chasing a dream that if instituted would instead destroy the American Dream[6] that any American is free to advance through society as far as their talents, ability, and God's blessing take them.

Your freedom to do what you want, when you want to do it may vanish if the socialists have their way. Your personal freedom is not a license to act irresponsibly, to ignore God's morality, to create your own values, but it is the unique, amazing freedom that every American enjoys as a citizen of the United States of America, the greatest nation in the history of mankind. Make the most of it.

8

FREEDOM OR SOCIALISM?

FREEDOM OR SOCIALISM? That's really the choice presented to Americans today, especially young Americans. That's why the second paragraph of the Sharon Statement reminds us

> That liberty is indivisible, and that political freedom cannot long exist without economic freedom.

And, later,

> That the market economy, allocating resources by the free play of supply and demand, is the single economic system compatible with the requirements of personal freedom and constitutional government, and that it is at the same time the most productive supplier of human needs;

That when government interferes with the work of the market economy, it tends to reduce the moral and physical strength of the nation; that when it takes from one man to bestow on another, it diminishes the incentive of the first, the integrity of the second, and the moral autonomy of both.

Nevertheless, in recent years American progressives have moved to the far Left, embracing socialism, communism, and Marxism as the wave of the future. These are not the liberals of twenty or thirty years ago; these are radical, Marxist fanatics, and they have convinced many young people that socialism is good. In fact, according to a Pew Survey, 42 percent of Americans "have a positive view of socialism."[1] This is shocking when you consider that there is no evidence whatsoever of socialism bringing prosperity to any nation. Bernie Sanders cites Sweden as an example of "good" socialism[2] even though Sweden rejected socialism in the 1990s because it was a failure. But is that the kind of socialism that Bernie Sanders and former New York Mayor Bill DeBlasio really want? Bernie didn't take his honeymoon in Sweden, which was then socialist. He and his bride took it in Moscow, the home of the KGB secret police and the center of the Soviet Union, a dictatorship where neighbors were encouraged to spy on each other and all but the government apparatchiks (communist government officials) lived in near or completely abject poverty. Similarly, Bill De Blasio took his wife on a honeymoon in Cuba, another police state that denies freedom of religion, freedom of speech, and suppresses dissidents with their own secret police, the DGI.

You probably know about Vladimir Lenin and Joseph Stalin of the Soviet Union (Union of Soviet Socialist Republics), Fidel Castro of Cuba, Mao Zedong of China, Daniel Ortega in Nicaragua, and Nicolás Maduro in Venezuela. But there are two other socialists you may not have heard about. In fact, let me suggest that you can ask a progressive friend (or your teacher or professor if you are brave/foolish enough) two questions that are sure to stump them or irritate them at the least.

The first question is "What is the full name of the German political party called the Nazi Party?" The answer is National Socialist German Workers Party. The second question is "When was the word 'Socialist' added to the name of that political party?" The answer is after Adolf Hitler took over that party.[3] That's right. Adolf Hitler was, like Lenin and Stalin and Mussolini, a committed socialist; but while Lenin and Stalin were Soviet socialists, Hitler was a National Socialist who said,

> National Socialism derives from each of the two camps the pure idea that characterizes it, national resolution from bourgeois tradition; vital, creative socialism from the teaching of Marxism.[4]

On another occasion, before five thousand loyal supporters, Hitler declared,

> We are socialists, we are enemies of today's capitalist economic system for the exploitation of the economically weak, with its unfair salaries, with its unseemly evaluation of a human being according to wealth and property instead of responsibility and performance, and we are determined to destroy this system under all conditions.[5]

Ideologically, both Hitler and Mussolini differed from Lenin and Stalin only in that they believed in state control of businesses, not state ownership as Lenin and Stalin did. And while Hitler and Mussolini were believers in National Socialism, Lenin and Stalin were believers in international socialism. While this might not seem like a big difference to you and to me, it was a huge disagreement between those on the Marxist Left.

Not surprisingly, Hitler hated Stalin and vice versa, just as the Maoists have violently clashed with Leninists throughout history, even though they are all socialists. In reality, Hitler and Stalin were essentially gang leaders who had each successfully taken over a country, and both were vying to be the top socialist gang leader. They were willing and eager to go to war with each other as gangs often do. Yet prior to World War II, the communists and the Nazis in Germany worked together to overthrow the Social Democrat Party (SPD).[6]

Your teacher or professor may insist that the Nazi Party was a far-right party, using one of the many twisted pretzel-type arguments found on the Internet to argue Hitler was not a socialist but really on the Right, not the Left. But that argument makes no sense whatsoever. Remember that we as conservatives oppose big, powerful government that leads to dictatorships like those of Hitler, Mussolini, Lenin, Stalin, and Mao. We believe in minimum government and maximum personal freedom (including freedom of the press and free speech) under the rule of law. In contrast, Mussolini, Lenin, and Hitler did not want minimal government or individual liberty, as their speeches, writings, and actions show.

They wanted an all-powerful government and opposed freedom of the press and free speech as all socialists do. Remember the meltdown of the Left when it was announced that Elon Musk was going to purchase Twitter and was going to stop the censorship of conservatives on that social network?[7] Free speech is clearly an existential threat to socialism, whether Marxist or Fascist.

If there is any lingering doubt about Hitler being a socialist, consider these planks in the Nazi platform, which he helped write, fully endorsed, and implemented:[8]

Plank 11. *The abolition of all income obtained without labor or effort.* [This means no interest can be paid on savings accounts or investments and certainly no stock dividends.]

Plank 13. *We demand the nationalization of all enterprises.* [Who wants to nationalize the energy industry in the U.S., progressives like Maxine Waters[9] or conservatives like Ted Cruz?]

Plank 17. *We demand land reform in accordance with our national needs and a law for expropriation without compensation of land for public purposes. Abolition of ground rent and prevention of all speculation in land.* [Does the seizure of private property sound like a conservative proposal to you?]

Plank 23. *We demand laws to fight against deliberate political lies and their dissemination by the press. In order to make it possible to create a German press* [a state press that serves as a propaganda tool of the state], *Newspapers which violate the public interest are to be banned.* [This doesn't sound like freedom of the press or free speech but more like the censorship of free speech that the progressives in the U.S. euphemistically call "content modification."]

Plank 25. *To carry out all the above we demand: the creation of a strong central authority in the Reich.* [We conservatives, like the father of the U.S. Constitution, James Madison, favor a weak central government, not a powerful one.[10]]

There is nothing in the platform of Hitler to suggest that he was a man of the Right, nothing. The Nazi platform is a typical leftwing screed that advocates for complete and total control of its citizens by the state. Hitler's platform demands "nationalization of all [business] enterprises." While conservatives seek smaller government, less regulation, and more freedom, progressives/socialists always push for more and bigger government and control of all businesses and industry. To suggest that Hitler was on the Right is not only a calculated lie but also laughable.

Lenin, Stalin, Hitler, Mao, and Mussolini were all on the far, far Left, and each one of them was totally committed to a form of socialism. Let me say it again: we who are on the Right, who believe in limited government and maximum individual freedom, don't support dictatorships, we oppose them. We want minimal government, not a big, powerful government run by radical Left elitists like Alexandria Ocasio-Cortez or the hundreds of thousands of unelected government bureaucrats that make up the deep state. Individual freedom can only exist when government is small, less powerful, less invasive, and very limited in what it can do and what it can order its citizens to do.

The following excerpts from the Sharon Statement point out clearly that our conservative principles are totally consistent with the Founders' view of government and totally inconsistent with that of leftwing dictators like Hitler and Lenin. As the Sharon Statement says, we believe

> That liberty is indivisible, and that political freedom cannot long exist without economic freedom;

> That the purpose of government is to protect those freedoms through the preservation of internal order, the provision of national defense, and the administration of justice;

> That when government ventures beyond these rightful functions, it accumulates power, which tends to diminish order and liberty;

> . . .

> That the market economy, allocating resources by the free play of supply and demand, is the single economic system compatible with the requirements of personal freedom and constitutional government, and that it is at the same time the most productive supplier of human needs;

The beauty of a free society is that its citizens can work where they choose and either run their own business or work for a company or in a profession that maximizes their God-given talents, doing something they want to do. And when that happens, something great takes place: Americans are happy and prosper as they can in no other nation on the face of the earth.

9

THE MIRACLE OF FREE MARKETS

WESTERN EUROPE is an example of socialism coming slowly, with stealth rather than via a violent revolution. Socialism is also threatening the United States today, even faster than it is happening in Europe, and seemingly in a more virulent form. Steadily in our nation, your individual freedom is shrinking.

Ever-expanding social programs, putting us trillions of dollars in debt, not only weaken our economy and drive up inflation but also limit your freedom of choice when it comes to your college education, health care, and social services. Government-run schools that indoctrinate students, rather than educate them, turn out young adults who are less capable of competing in a world marketplace and understanding the pillars of a constitutional republic. When that happens, young men and women become susceptible to the siren song of socialism. Conservatives, on the other hand, understand that prosperity comes not from government guarantees but from free markets that allow free citizens like yourself to maximize your own economic potential.

Free markets work because each party is free, both the seller and the buyer. One is not compelled to sell at a government-set price, nor is the buyer compelled to buy at a government-set price. Instead, both parties are free to sell or not sell, buy or not buy as they choose. Similarly, the job hunter seeks out employment that will pay a salary that he is seeking or that includes an opportunity to be promoted to a job he is pursuing. He is not compelled to take a job he does not like, nor to work at a wage that he deems insufficient. In turn, the employer seeks out employees willing and eager to work for the terms and compensation that they feel they can pay and still be profitable. The employer is not compelled to pay a wage specified by the government, nor is he obligated to hire any individual dictated by the state.

There is a natural and necessary tension between the buyer and the seller, the employer and the employee, each seeking to get the best price or wage respectively. As a firm prospers it has more latitude to increase pay to its employees. Why should an employer pay employees more as they become more productive? Simply put, employee wages must be high enough to keep competitors from hiring them away. Of course, as the employee becomes more skilled at his job, he becomes more valuable to his employer and more marketable to other companies who need his services. In other words, it is in the self-interest of the employer to pay his employees a wage that will keep them in his employ. That means compensation that is satisfactory to them and that still allows him to sell his products or services at a price that enables him to make a profit.

It is competition between companies that drives them to innovate and provide better products and services at market-competitive rates. Competition between business concerns in a free economy not only means better products and services but also the best possible prices for the consumer. If a company falls behind and can't deliver high-quality services and products that its competition can deliver, it loses business, realizes reduced profits, and is in danger of going out of business. This fierce competitive atmosphere exists among businesses everywhere, and it drives innovation that benefits the consumer with lower prices and higher-quality products and services. Running a profitable company that meets the expectations of the people it serves is a very difficult but also rewarding effort.

But under socialism there is no competition. The government owns and runs everything. There is no reason to innovate, and that's why innovation does not happen. That's why the quality of goods and services is poor and shoddy in a socialist state. A German friend told me a story that clearly illustrates this.

Shortly after Ronald Reagan brought sufficient pressure to bring about the collapse of the Soviet Union, Germany was reunited. There was no longer a West Germany and an East Germany (the latter of which was formerly a satellite of the Soviet Union). All the businesses in the former communist East Germany were government owned or totally controlled under both the socialist government of Hitler and later under the socialist government of the Soviet Union. When the Wall fell and Germany was reunited, something had to be done with the approximately 14,000 state-run businesses that were in East Germany.[1] The newly reunified German government wisely decided to sell those that were marketable to the highest bidder. Many of these businesses produced such shoddy products that they were unmarketable, a typical feature of all socialist-run businesses.

My (West) German friend's neighbor owned and ran a machinist business, so he decided to look into purchasing a similar business for sale in the former East Germany. He traveled there and was shocked by what he found. It was as if he had stepped back in time more than fifty years into Hitler's socialist Germany. No improvements had been made to the office equipment, the machine shop equipment, the plumbing, the wiring, or the technology of the company he visited since 1933, when the company had been taken over by Hitler and his socialist Nazi government. Neither had the Soviet socialists made any improvements since they had taken over after World War II. More than that, the phones did not work, the roads were horrible, the sewer system needed repair, and everything was an antiquated mess. In fact, manufacturers and businesses of all kinds were like that across what used to be East Germany and the entire Soviet Bloc. It was a typical socialist disaster. And remember, East Germany was considered to be "the showcase" of the Soviet Union![2] In other words, East Germany was socialism working at its very best!

The lesson is clear. Without free markets and without competition there is no innovation and no incentive to be productive or to create high-quality products by the manager or for the worker. But there is another lesson about free markets. Some objectivists (followers of Ayn Rand) argue that free markets are moral. They argue that a free marketplace will cause the participants, be they workers or owners, to be honest, but that is not true as the record clearly shows. Free markets cannot succeed without the virtues of honesty and integrity being practiced by the vast majority of owners, employees, and customers.

It was the lack of personal integrity that caused the transition from socialism to economic freedom to fail in much of the old Soviet Union. For nearly eighty years the communists in the Soviet Union did their best to destroy faith in God and His moral code as provided in the Bible. The vast bureaucracy and near-universal economic misery they created caused bribery to become firmly embedded into their way of life and into their entire economic system. In the old socialist Soviet Union, the service was so poor that if you needed to purchase a refrigerator from a government-run plant or have a government plumber fix a leak, you had to pay a bribe. The same was true if you wanted to have someone fix your roof or purchase a new stove. That's the only way the system worked at all, according to a good friend who spent many years in Soviet Russia and later in post-Soviet Union Russia. And, sadly, bribery is still a common practice in Russia today.

While free markets are not inherently moral, neither are they immoral. They are simply amoral, and accordingly they do not function well if a high proportion of the general population is not moral. A high level of moral consciousness by both buyer and seller is necessary for free markets to reach a high level of efficiency and for innovation and success to occur.

This takes us back to the importance that America's Founders put on virtue among the people for a free society to survive. A lack of virtue causes free markets to be inefficient and participants to be corrupt. The more corruption there is, the less efficient free markets become, and therefore the entire nation becomes less prosperous.

Similarly, if there is a lack of public virtue, politicians will operate on the basis that the end justifies the means. That outlook causes vote fraud in elections, the rigging of elections, and could lead to the abolishment of the Electoral College and packing of the United States Supreme Court. In short, a lack of virtue breeds distrust, divides Americans, and encourages hatred and revenge. Virtuous men and women are pushed aside, as corrupt and self-serving men and women rise to powerful political positions. The Constitution and the rule of law are then viewed as impediments by those who seek power for themselves. As virtue declines, life itself becomes cheap; babies, the nonproductive elderly, and the infirm are treated as disposables—if they inconvenience the pleasure, opportunity, or lifestyle of others.

The Pilgrims, who arrived in 1620, tried socialism. The original economic plan of the Pilgrims was communal living where everyone would work and put everything they grew, produced, or otherwise obtained into a common pot. But

> since not everyone was pulling the same weight, the colony was constantly running out of food, a typical problem in all the socialist countries, from China to Venezuela.[3]

Realizing that the collectivist approach was not working, William Bradford knew that the Pilgrims needed to make a change if they were to survive. Bradford wrote in his book, *Of the Plymouth Plantation*, what happened:

> So they began to think how they might raise as much corn as they could, and obtain a better crop than they had done, that they might not still thus languish in misery . . .. And so assigned to every family a parcel of land, according to the proportion of their number.[4]

The advent of the private ownership of property, Bradford observed,

> made all hands very industrious, so as much more corn was planted than otherwise would have been by any means . . . and gave far better content[ment]. The women now went willingly into the field, and took their little ones with them to set corn; [Had they been] compelled [they] would have . . . thought [it] great tyranny and oppression.[5]

As a result the Plymouth Colony became one of the most prosperous and successful colonies in America.

> Private property rights and personal responsibility, two pillars of a free-market economy, saved the Plymouth Colony from extinction and laid the economic foundation for the free and prosperous nation that we all enjoy today.[6]

10

CRITICAL RACE HOOEY

CRITICAL RACE THEORY (CRT), which has been taught in America's colleges and universities by Marxist professors for many years,[1] received a big boost with the publication of the 1619 Project[2] in the *New York Times*. Written by Nikole Hannah-Jones, the premise is that the landing of colonists with slaves in 1619 was the defining moment in American history. It defined America as an evil, racist society and suggests that racism continues until this day. In other words, there is nothing good or great about America; it is a bad nation founded by bad people. But is the analysis of Hannah-Jones right and true? In her paper she argues that

> one of the primary reasons the colonists decided to declare independence from Britain was . . . to protect the institution of slavery.[3]

However, the actual history shows that

many of the colonies at the time were in the process of attempting to approve laws limiting, restricting, and reducing slavery when literally no other place in the world was attempting to do so.[4]

In reality, while Patrick Henry and George Washington were serving as delegates to the Virginia House of Burgesses, that body repeatedly passed statutes that would ban the slave trade[5] only to have the statutes vetoed by the king of England, who was greatly profiting from it. In other words, the opposite of what Nikole Hannah-Jones wrote is true. It was the king of England who wanted the slave trade to continue, not the colonists.

In fact, Thomas Jefferson's original draft of the Declaration of Independence included this condemnation of the king's support of slavery:

He [the king of Britain] has waged cruel war against human nature itself, violating its most sacred rights of life and liberty in the persons of distant people who never offended him, captivating and carrying them into slavery in another hemisphere [capturing and transporting slaves from Africa] . . .. Determined to keep open a [slave] market where MEN should be bought and sold, he has prostituted his negative [vetoed colonial laws, thus] . . . suppressing every legislative attempt to prohibit or to restrain this execrable commerce [the slave trade].[6]

Note that Jefferson wrote "MEN" in all capital letters to emphasize that those Africans who had been enslaved by the king were fully men and entitled to the rights of all men, women, and children as defined in the Declaration of Independence. Sadly, the only reason this paragraph was not included in the Declaration of Independence was the refusal of the delegates from Georgia and South Carolina to vote for the Declaration[7] if that phrase were retained in it. It is important to note that delegates from the other colonies (apparently including others from the South) voted for inclusion of the paragraph condemning the slave trade.[8]

While Nikole Hannah-Jones would have us believe that the landing of slaves in 1619 in the Virginia colony defined America, there were other moments in American history that truly defined our nation. One of those took place immediately after the horrific battle between North and South in the American Civil War at the Wilderness. More than 160,000 men were engaged in this battle, which lasted for forty-eight hours, and although the Confederate forces were greatly outnumbered, there was no winner. There were nearly twenty thousand casualties, with the Union forces suffering by far the most losses.[9]

General Ulysses Grant had hoped for a decisive victory, but it was not to be. The Union troops were war weary; each man had already lost countless friends, and the war had dragged on for years. The next morning the Union army broke camp, and as they marched down a road, they came to a junction. They knew that they would either go south toward Richmond or retreat and go north to Washington, DC.

> As Grant came riding to the head of the troops, the blue-coated sol-diers slowly realized they were not in retreat (as had been assumed), and broke into wild cheering.[10]

And, as they were wont to do, these courageous men almost certainly marched along and sang the Battle Hymn of the Republic, which had become the unofficial song of the Union forces.

Read the last verse of the words of the song as it was then written by Julia Ward Howe and see if you can't feel the commitment and resolve of these men, many of them going to their death or to be maimed for life, yet ready to give up their lives to save the union and free Black Americans from slavery:

> In the beauty of the lilies Christ was born across the sea,
> With a glory in His bosom that transfigures you and me;

As He died to make men holy, let us die to make men free!
While God is marching on.[11]

The men in blue who cheered when they realized they were marching on to Richmond was one of the many moments in history that truly define the goodness of United States of America and the bravery and character of its citizens. No, Nikole Hannah-Jones, slavery didn't define the United States of America. The men who gave their lives to free African Americans from slavery was a true defining moment in American history, and there have been many other defining moments when Americans gave up their lives so that we could live free.

Unfortunately, in spite of errors and false conclusions by the author of the 1619 Project, it was immediately embraced by the radical Left teachers' unions, which proceeded to immediately indoctrinate grade school and high school children with critical race theory. Critical theory (from which CRT comes) traces its lineage directly to Karl Marx[12] and from

> several generations of German philosophers and social theorists in the Western European Marxist tradition known as the Frankfurt School.[13]

Not only is CRT wrong, it is dangerous because CRT propagates racism by once again encouraging segregation, exactly as the first progressives did in the late 1800s. Throughout history Marxists have sought any means possible to divide people on the basis of race, income, ethnicity, or any other means to create envy, jealously, hatred, and violence. Communism was and is a

> "tragedy of planetary dimensions" with a grand total of victims variously estimated . . . between 85 million and 100 million.[14]

Karl Marx believed that every person is solely a product of his or her physical, psychological, social, and mental environment. Marx was wrong. The reality is that men and women are imperfect physically, mentally, and in every other respect. Every single person who was ever born lives in a fallen state. We get angry, we hate people, we are self-centered, we lack compassion, we are egotistical, we refuse to forgive others, and we put counterfeit gods before the real God. The best, most compassionate, kindest people in the world are still imperfect sinners. And while the Left denies the fallen state of man, ironically it depends totally on our failings and sins to divide and conquer us. They use our fallen state to set us against each other for the sole purpose of creating the chaos necessary to foment a violent revolution ending in a Marxist communist dictatorship. That is their stated end game.

Today our once great colleges and universities (with a few exceptions you can number on your fingers and toes) have been commandeered by the 1960s Marxist radicals for the sole purpose of advancing their far-Left Marxist cause. To put it in the colloquialism of the day, the vast majority of America's colleges have become "woke," which is essentially a new philosophy of a man-conceived cult that even has its own language, moral code, and certainly its own rules they demand everyone live by.

Long gone are colleges and universities founded by God-fearing men and women who created great universities like Harvard, Yale, Princeton, and William and Mary. Each of the universities named were started by Bible-believing Christians to spread the Gospel and learn about the mysteries of God's creation. Indeed, the original motto of Harvard was "Truth for Christ and the Church."[15] The Yale Charter of 1701 refers to the founders of Yale as men desiring to create a college whose purpose was "upholding & Propagating of the Christian Protestant Religion,"[16] and the original Yale motto was "Christ the Word and Interpreter of the Father, our light and perfection."[17] Similarly, the motto of Princeton was "I restore life to the dead"[18] (referring to Jesus's sacrificial death on the cross and victorious resurrection from the dead).

The founders of Yale and Yale graduates were long known for being active in spreading the Gospel. Both Yale and Harvard students were strongly supportive of the work of the great evangelist D. L. Moody.[19]

But today, these schools and almost all other colleges and universities across the nation are infected with, even dominated by, Marxist professors who hate God and relish the idea of indoctrinating students with CRT. Now they are doing the same thing in our public elementary, junior high, and high schools. In fact,

> In Cupertino, California, teachers forced 8-year-olds to deconstruct their racial and sexual identities, then rank themselves according to a hierarchy of oppression.[20]

Sadly, this is happening in nearly every state, blue or red, across the nation. For instance, in Virginia, a simple Google search shows that public documents from the Virginia Department of Education repeatedly mention the phrase "critical race theory," as well as produces news stories about teacher training by consulting firms associated with CRT.[21]

Any citizen of any state can easily do this search and determine the extent to which CRT is being taught in their state.

Students are taught to view their entire life, their friends, and their values through the prism of race and nothing else. They are taught that they are oppressors if they are White, just as 1890s progressives proclaimed that Black Americans were inferior because they were Black. The intent of CRT is to create anger, hatred, and division by setting one group against another group.

But let there be no mistake: progressives not only seek to label all conservatives as White supremacists and racists, they also monotonously want to remind us that *they* are the repository of all virtue in America, not the average American. They virtue signal at every opportunity, but as Richard McDonough wrote in *American Thinker,*

> Virtue, which, in the real world, is always a hard affair, requiring far more of courage than it does of mere intellect, becomes degraded into virtue signaling, i.e., talking in the safe "politically correct" way mandated by the intellectual "in" crowd.[22]

In reality, it is not virtue that they are signaling but rather their own lack of godly virtue in their daily lives. Instead of trying to fill students with the venom of CRT, Dr. Carol Swain, a former tenured professor at Princeton and Vanderbilt Universities, reminds us that

> we the American people pledged to become a colorblind society in which people would be judged by the content of their character and elevated on their merit through equal opportunity. Equality became the law of the land and it offered a hand up for people—like me—who are the descendants of slaves. It did so within the context of laws protecting all people. Leaders who truly love this country would do well to honor the vision of Civil Rights-era America.[23]

The path forward for our nation is not to spread disunity, but rather teach honest history and learn from those who came before us—and to believe these words from the Declaration of Independence:

> We hold these truths to be self-evident, that all men are created equal, that they are endowed by their Creator with certain unalienable rights, that among these are Life, Liberty and the pursuit of Happiness.

We must now recommit ourselves to the intent of the Declaration of Independence and to those who strove during the Civil Rights movement to make equal opportunity under the law a reality. We must reject CRT and other false Marxist notions such as striving for equity (equal outcomes), which no free society can provide. When all men achieve equal outcomes, there is no freedom, no prosperity, and no harmony—only poverty and universal misery exist. No one wins, except the rulers, and they will rule harshly.

11

FREEDOM OR EQUITY?

CRITICAL RACE THEORY (CRT) is a part of Marxist critical theory and has no place in America. It is about dividing Americans, not unifying them. The United States ended slavery at the price of more than seven hundred thousand American lives, defeated segregation through hard-fought civil rights battles, and today is near to realizing the hope of Dr. Martin Luther King Jr. that his children would be

> judged not by the color of their skin, but rather by the content of their character.[1]

Dr. King's goal was always equal opportunity, but the goal of the radical Left is not equal opportunity; it's equal outcome—what they call "equity." In order to achieve equity, the Left proposes to lower the quality of education by doing away with magnet schools and eliminating AP (advanced placement) courses, including higher math.[2] Dumbing down courses, artificially raising grades, and failing to instill values like hard work and self-discipline won't, of course, help poor Black or Hispanic Americans; it will hurt them.

The less educated and less self-disciplined a child is and the less they are challenged in school, the less chance he or she will have of living out their own American Dream. The lowering of education standards hurts the children of all families but especially the children of new immigrants and the children of the poor. Such an approach sets them back when they try to get into college or obtain a good-paying job. Does the Left really want to keep minorities uneducated and poor just so that they can manipulate them? Is that their goal?

The right solution is the opposite of what the Left proposes. We need good, high-quality schools such as those created through school choice programs. But racist progressive legislators almost universally oppose school choice, not only because they receive millions of dollars from the teachers' unions[3] each election cycle but also because education-focused choice schools do not indoctrinate children with false Marxist propaganda such as CRT.

When we divide our nation into warring camps, the unity that is essential to a free and open society is severely damaged, and of course that is the goal of those on the far Left. For many decades Marxist college and university professors have taught generations of American students to hate each other solely on the basis of race. That is racism pure and simple. But fortunately, upon graduation from college many students realize—after getting a job and living in the real world—that the far-Left propaganda they heard in college is not reality; it does not reflect American society as it actually exists.

This rejection of Marxist claptrap by college graduates has frustrated the radical Left for years. That's why the Left decided to take a different tack. These progressives decided that they needed to start their indoctrination of America's youth much earlier, in elementary, junior high, and high school. That's why they are now pushing Marxist CRT and even sexualist pornography on our youngest children.[4] They are teaching our elementary, junior high, and high school students to hate each other based solely on race or ethnicity.[5] How horrible to encourage young students to despise their fellow classmates on the basis of skin color. Segregation and racial hatred have no place in America!

And if you are White and disagree with and oppose the racism espoused by CRT, they call you a White supremacist. Or the U.S. Department of Justice labels you a potential domestic terrorist.[6] What irony! The progressives of today are emulating their 1890s founders by once again pressing segregation and racism on our nation while at the same time calling conservatives racist.

The Marxists realize that communism can never come to power in a unified, free society. When there is an absence of conflict, but instead harmony and mutual respect, then freedom, not Marxism, flourishes.

Karl Marx said that the entire world was in conflict between the oppressors and the oppressed. This was the foundation of his communist economic theory, and Marx echoed that in the last line of his *Communist Manifesto*, "Workers of the world unite!"[7] Marx forecast that communism would rise first in a highly industrialized state, not a backward non-industrialized state. But the opposite happened. Led by Vladimir Lenin, communism first came to power via a violent revolution in 1917 in Russia, a backward nation far, far behind the industrialized states of Western Europe.

Both Lenin and his successor, Joseph Stalin, created a communist state precisely as Karl Marx described it, promising a "workers' paradise." But building this paradise was to be a no-holds-barred, brutal affair.

> In a 1920 speech to the Komsomol, Lenin said that communists subordinate morality to the class struggle. Good was anything that destroyed "the old exploiting society" and helped to build a "new communist society."[8]

Of course, instead of a paradise, Lenin and Stalin created a nightmare dictatorship of the worst kind, eventually killing tens of millions and enslaving hundreds of millions of people in Eastern Europe and around the globe.[9] And the killings and enslavement continue to this day in Cuba, in China, in Venezuela, in Nicaragua, and in other remaining communist states.

It isn't just the loss of individual freedom and the killings that characterize communism; it is also the imprisonment of those who oppose communism in brutal work camps like the Russian gulags, the inhuman, Siberian work camps into which some *eighteen million* people were placed.[10] It is important to understand that Lenin and Stalin did not fail to create a socialist utopia because they did not do communism right; they failed because they did it exactly as Karl Marx prescribed it.

All we need to do is to look at the entire history of communism in China, Cambodia, Vietnam, Cuba, Venezuela, and Nicaragua. At its core, communism is driven by a hatred of God and the denial of His existence. As a result of this hatred the communist leaders became like the devil himself: evil, cruel, angry, hate filled, envious, mean, dishonest, treacherous, brutal, and murderous. A good example of the homicidal intent of the Chinese Communists is their intentional release of the COVID-19 virus into the rest of the world[11] after its outbreak in China.

The implementation of critical race theory means the end of the American Dream for all races. It means the end of the promise of "life, liberty, and the pursuit of happiness" expressed in the American Declaration of Independence. It also means the end of individual freedom, freedom of speech, freedom of religion, and all the other freedoms we enjoy as American citizens. And historically it has also led to the end of prosperity and opportunity. This Marxist ideology is at war with everything that makes America America.

American history shows that free markets and individual freedom combined with Judeo-Christian virtue create incredible and widespread prosperity that extends to virtually all citizens who get a sound education and work hard. While America is the land of opportunity where everyone is free to seek their dreams no matter where they begin in life, socialism is the exact opposite: no opportunity, no dreams, no prosperity. Socialism makes glowing promises, but the socialist reality is instead a direct path to a bleak life of misery and deprivation except for the elites who run it. It consists of economic shortages, regimentation, the loss of individual freedom, a police state, and the outlawing of faith in God.

When the bloody Soviet dictator Nikita Khrushchev came to America, he was astounded by freeways full of automobiles and the parking lots full of cars, all owned by Americans.[12] He expected to see widespread economic misery; instead he saw widespread prosperity.[13] He knew that in the Soviet "paradise" only the apparatchiks had cars, and instead of widespread prosperity, there was widespread economic misery. It was at this point that Khrushchev obviously knew that the Soviet Union would never triumph over freedom.

Free people never seek socialism unless they have been brainwashed by lies and distortions of the truth. No one with the knowledge of the reality of communism/Marxism would ever willingly seek to be a captive of the state with limited freedom, limited opportunity, and no opportunity to escape from the dreary, prison-like life that is the reality of every Marxist socialist state whether it is located in China, Cuba, or Venezuela.

No country ever peacefully adopted the nightmare that always results from socialism/communism. No one wanted to live in the Soviet Union, which was held together by violence, fear, gulags, torture, and a terrifying middle-of-the-night knock on the door by the KGB. That's why the Soviet Union was surrounded by walls to keep the people from escaping. It was a prison, not a paradise. And that's why people are flooding across our southern border to escape socialism/Marxism/communism. One has only to look at the direction people are crossing our border to understand that freedom and free markets work and socialism/communism/Marxism always fail. There are no exceptions.

Realizing that reality of Marxism/communism, today's advocates have disguised it as critical race theory, based not on its supposed economic benefits (as Karl Marx did) but instead on the Marxist belief that there is always conflict between races and ethnicities. They understood that Marxism had to be applied in a new way in order to set one group against another.

Since division by economic oppressor and victim (the oppressed) was widely rejected across the globe in favor of capitalism, another approach had to be taken as a means of creating hatred and division across our land.

> Decades ago, Marxists ditched class warfare and economics in favor of sexual politics and culture as a vehicle for executing revolution. Ever since, they have been shrewdly redefining marriage, family, sexuality, and gender, to the point where "tolerance and diversity" now means foisting porn, perversion, and predators on our families. Those who won't stand for it are cunningly condemned as bigots.[14]

It is important to remember that it is not necessary for one group to actually oppress the other but only to make one group *believe* that they are being oppressed by the other. When that happens there is division instead of harmony, precisely the goal of the far Left. If the workers refuse to unite because they realize they are not being oppressed, then other groups (always groups, never individuals) must be identified as victims and oppressors.

Marxists always seek to control people, and when they recognized that the original approach of Karl Marx was not working, they devised a new, more comprehensive approach that is today called *wokeism* (accurately described as an oppressive mind virus[15]) based on the idea that

> if you want to control people, you have to control the way they think, you have to control their language . . . [being woke] is a mutated form of Marxism that took "wealth" and replaced it with "power" and switched out the "oppressor" and the "oppressed" with the current identity groups . . . . Instead of distributing wealth to equalize society, the new . . . [woke] Marxism calls for a redistribution of power among the identity groups.[16]

Wokeism ramps up the division between Americans, demanding that the non-woke be treated not just as a political or intellectual opponent but an enemy of society and of our nation. That's what American progressives have done, beginning with President Barack Obama, who characterized his conservative political rivals as enemies,[17] not simply political opponents. That's what President Joe Biden did when he called voters of Donald Trump "dangerous to democracy."[18]

The Marxist progressive agenda across the board is all of one piece with the goal being revolution, not honest political success at the ballot box. So when you wonder why George Soros funded the campaigns of soft-on-crime district attorneys[19] like Kim Foxx in Chicago and George Gascón[20] in Los Angeles, who refuse to prosecute violent lawbreakers (even murderers), it makes total sense if your goal is to incinerate society and impose a socialist dictatorship on our land.

Remember, chaos is their goal. So open borders—letting MS-13 killers, rapists, human traffickers, and drug smugglers cross our southern border—makes sense. Letting Islamic terrorists come across our border and into our nation makes sense. Overwhelming our health care system and making it impossible for it to adequately take care of American citizens makes sense. Destroying the family unit by encouraging sexual perversion beginning in the first grade makes sense. Eliminating bond requirements for those arrested for violent crimes in our cities makes sense.

The politicizing of health issues like COVID makes sense. Demanding that we follow the language of the woke cult makes sense. Dividing our children by teaching them critical race theory makes sense. Urging the destruction of the nuclear family as advocated by the Marxist BLM[21] makes sense. Dividing Americans by kneeling during the National Anthem makes sense. Calling White Americans White supremacists makes sense. Dividing Americans by race, color, ethnicity, sex, location, education, or any other means makes total sense if you wish to roil this nation and turn it into a socialist state.

Although the tactics [of today's progressive Marxists] have changed, the underlying objective is no different from the philosophy of their ideological forebears in Communist hellholes like the Soviet Union and Eastern Europe: the fundamental transformation of society by co-opting and perverting the nuclear family, the most influential societal unit, and the bedrock of Judeo-Christian values.[22]

Today's attacks on the nuclear family and the promotion of CRT were nonexistent in 1960 when the young conservatives met at Sharon, Connecticut, to found Young Americans for Freedom, yet those present were prescient when they declared in the Sharon Statement:

The forces of international Communism are, at present, the greatest single threat to [our] liberties.

While the threat from communism may have shifted to China and to our school classrooms—from grade school to graduate school—communism remains today the greatest threat to our freedom as Americans, just as it was in 1960.

The fruits of Christianity, such as "love your neighbor as yourself,"[23] kindness, forgiveness, peace, reconciliation, generosity, compassion, unity, harmony, are anathema to those who subscribe to the Marxist CRT/woke ideology. Pray for them. Resist them. Convert them. And never give in to them. May love, not hate, triumph.

12

THE DAVOS MAN

HAVE YOU HEARD of the Davos Man,[1] who considers himself to be not really a citizen of his home nation but instead a citizen of the world? This man or woman believes themself to be superior to those they view as the lower classes, who do not possess their sophistication, intellectual prowess, globalist insight, compassion, self-designed and elevated moral compass, or millions or billions of dollars. To be sure, the Davos Man need not be a man or a woman; they can be either provided they hold a globalist outlook. Due to wealth, education, fame, corporate status, and/or viewpoint, they are more concerned about the state of the world than about the state of the United States or any other country.

The so-called Davos Man is transnational in outlook.

Comprising fewer than 4 percent of the American people, these transnationalists have little need for national loyalty, view national boundaries as obstacles that thankfully are vanishing, and see national governments as residues from the past whose only useful function is to facilitate the elite's global operations.[2]

As you can easily perceive, the values and concerns of the Davos Man are in absolute and total conflict with the Sharon Statement and with what the Left might describe as incidental hurdles such as the Declaration of Independence, the Pledge of Allegiance, our National Anthem, the U.S. Constitution, and the rule of law. Accordingly, the Davos Man has little or no commitment to the United States or to the individual freedom of Americans. And the Davos Man likely has no interest in God, for they are now one of the gods in the pantheon of their world. They believe they are the new masters of the universe.

> Over the years, global elites have sought to intervene in what they regard to be "borderless issues." They see matters like climate change, economic disparity, child poverty, the plight of refugees, racism, economic disparity, terrorism and social unrest as international problems that call for extra-national solutions.[3]

They don't reject dictatorships like that of Communist China, they admire them. Canadian Prime Minister Justin Trudeau, a committed Davos Man, said,

> There is a level of admiration I actually have for China because their basic dictatorship is allowing them to actually turn their economy around on a dime.[4]

So while this new Davos Man is seemingly willing to accept and even adopt the dictatorship model of the brutal Communist Chinese government, they still claim moral superiority over their fellow citizens who still believe in individual freedom and in God and His moral precepts.

After discarding their own loyalty to the United States or their home country in favor of loyalty to the world, the Davos Man can rationalize nearly anything. Astute social observer Victor Davis Hansen wrote,

> Legal scholars Jack Goldsmith and Andrew Keane Woods . . . argued that in the debate over free expression and the state's right to censor and control, China, not America . . . had the right idea of censoring internet expression for the greater collective good.[5]

Davos attendee Bill Gates warned against the United States blaming China for the spread of COVID-19:

> He seemed unconcerned that China was a Stalinist-like government: it had interned over one million of its own citizens, caused global havoc due to its incompetence, deceit, and contempt for non-Chinese, and deliberately allowed the virus to spread to others when it knew it could not be contained within China. For Gates and other globalists, there was no reason to pull back from China because it was a communist dictatorship.[6]

Those who attend the annual World Economic Forum in Davos, Switzerland, don't have time to be concerned about human rights or the rule of law; they have gone far beyond those "minor" considerations to deal with world issues such as human-caused climate change. These men and women repeatedly tell us that they are earnestly concerned with climate issues, yet according to Greenpeace,

> private jets flying into the Davos area during the week of the 2022 forum emitted a whopping 9,700 metric tons of carbon dioxide. The study attributed 7,400 metric tons to planes servicing the conference. By comparison, the average person worldwide has an estimated annual carbon footprint of 4 tons.[7]

Just how believable is their earnestness and sincerity about climate change if they eschew far less polluting public transportation in favor of private jets that pour tons of pollution into the atmosphere? Then to emphasize their hypocrisy, they engaged in virtue signaling by announcing at that same Davos gathering that

> to reduce the event's carbon footprint, no paper maps of the town were being distributed.[8]

Who are the transnationalists who attend these exclusive meetings? While the list is not published, these attendees from the business, government, academic, and entertainment world all have one thing in common: they have great wealth or at least access to it. And while they profess to have great concern for humanity, they have little or no regard for the freedom or well-being of the actual people who inhabit the earth. Instead, they have the type of disdain for them personified by comedian Bill Maher, whose arrogance was apparently polished by his attendance at an Ivy League university:

> There are two Americas [the red states and the blue states], where [the blue states have] all the cool jobs [and] people drive Teslas and eat artisanal ice cream [and] have orchestras and theater districts and world-class shopping. We have Chef Wolfgang Puck. They have Chef Boyardee. Our roofs have solar panels. Theirs have last year's Christmas lights. We've got legal bud [marijuana]. They've got Bud[weiser].[9]

Call them what you will—globalists, transnationalists, Davos Men, or post-citizens—these men and women consider it not only their right but also their duty to steer the world toward an interconnected, interdependent, less-free, and less-democratic world where *they* decide what is best for our planet and are willing to use any means necessary to accomplish their goals.

Certainly, in the case of their love affair with Communist China,

These post-citizen authors apparently believe the coercive mechanisms available to a communist and totalitarian dictatorship are superior to the freedoms guaranteed by the U.S. Constitution.[10]

Accordingly, they can easily justify censorship of free speech on the Internet of anyone—no matter their credentials, position, or expertise—if that individual is not aligned with the goals, objectives, and conclusions they seek to advance. Their conceit, their arrogance always goes back to the false foundational belief of the American Progressive movement that they personally have reached a higher ethical plane than have their fellow citizens. It is their extreme hubris that they and they alone, for the first time in the history of the world, have all the solutions to the world's problems.

Let us not forget that it was this same egotistical arrogance that led the 1890s progressives to conclude that Black Americans needed to be segregated from society for their own good.[11] It was the same arrogance that caused early progressives to believe in the "science" of eugenics, which sought to create a superior race by weeding out undesirables through sterilization and abortion.[12]

Sound familiar? No wonder Adolf Hitler found inspiration from the progressive eugenicists to create a master race. Is it surprising that Hitler modeled his mistreatment of the Jews after Jim Crow laws promoted by progressives in the South during the late 1800s and well into the twentieth century?[13] This is not mere speculation. High-ranking Nazi legal experts met on June 5, 1934, and listened to a paper detailing how progressives in the South implemented segregation of Black Americans.[14] It was from this meeting that the idea was developed for the notorious Nuremberg Laws[15] that led to anti-Jewish discrimination and ultimately to the gas chambers. The discussions held at that meeting were captured by a stenographer[16] and there is no doubt about what took place.

Even prior to that meeting,

Hitler himself, took a serious interest in the racist legislation of the United States. Indeed in *Mein Kampf* Hitler praised America as nothing less than "the one state" that had made progress toward the creation of a healthy racist order of the kind the Nuremberg Laws were intended to establish.[17]

The disregard and contempt for the freedom and views of Black Americans and Jewish Germans differs little from the obvious contempt that the Davos Men seemingly have for the rights and freedom of their fellow citizens.

At the beginning of the meeting in Nazi Germany, Justice Minister Franz Gürtner provided a memo on American race law and

> participants returned repeatedly to the American models of racist legislation in the course of their discussion.[18]

Thus it was that the early progressive intellectuals like Edward A. Ross, who had studied in Germany after the Civil War,[19] who ultimately inspired Adolf Hitler and his fellow Nazis to adopt the racist policies that the American progressives had created but this time against the Jews.

The love affair that the Nazis had with the racist policies of progressives in the 1890s was matched by their enthusiasm for the "science" of eugenics promulgated up into the 1940s by progressive activists like Margaret Sanger, the founder of Planned Parenthood. Sanger is, of course, still highly revered by virtually all progressive leaders, including Hillary Clinton, who gushed upon receiving the 2009 Sanger Award from Planned Parenthood,

> I admire Margaret Sanger enormously, her courage, her tenacity, her vision . . . I am really in awe of her.[20]

Margaret Sanger remains today a revered figure in the pantheon of stalwart progressive leaders. She was not only a racist but also enamored with Karl Marx, writing in her book, *The Pivot of Civilization,*

> Every shade of socialistic thought and philosophy acknowledges its indebtedness to the vision of Karl Marx and his concept of the class struggle.[21]

However, until just prior to World War II, Sanger strongly favored the socialism of Hitler over that of Joseph Stalin, maintaining close ties with Dr. Ernst Rudin, a German eugenicist. Rudin authored a long article for her publication, *Birth Control Review,* titled "Sterilization: An Urgent Need," that she published in three parts over successive issues.[22] It is important to note that Rudin wasn't some minor functionary in the Nazi regime but someone whose work had caught the attention of Adolf Hitler.[23]

Hitler's Nazis were also entranced by progressive U.S. President Franklin D. Roosevelt.

> The Nazis frequently praised Franklin Roosevelt and the New Deal government in the early 1930s. FDR received distinctly favorable treatment in the Nazi press until at least 1936 or 1937, lauded as a man who had seized "dictatorial powers" and embarked upon "bold experiments" in the spirit of the Fuhrer.[24]

And,

> The glossy *Berlin Illustrated Magazine* . . . ran heroic photo spreads on Roosevelt.[25]

Racism, segregation, and worse are what happens when progressive elites like the Davos Man are driven by esteem for their self-created moral values, their intellect, and the arrogance that comes with their extreme wealth, to make decisions that negatively affect tens of millions of others. In fact, their fellow citizens have as much right as they do, and likely more common sense, to make their own decisions about how they will live, where they will live, what they will do with their lives, what they will eat,[26] and who should be trusted to lead our nation. Elites like the Davos Man value their own judgments too highly and your freedom too lowly. Your dreams, your aspirations, your desire to live free are simply of no interest to the Davos Man.

13

FATHER OF THE SWAMP

PRESIDENT WOODROW WILSON is known as the father of the administrative state, and rightly so. It is not an exaggeration to say that the problems created during his eight-year term (1913–1921) did more damage to our republican form of government than any other president in American history. It was not just that Wilson was a bitter racist who, in November 1914, arrogantly told Black civil rights leader William Monroe Trotter,

> Segregation is not a humiliation but a benefit, and ought to be so regarded by you gentlemen.[1]

As one historian observed, Wilson

set black progress in the United States back fifty years by insti-
tuting racial segregation throughout the federal government and
greatly empowering the most racist Southern faction within the
Democratic Party.[2]

Wilson's failures were many. Although promising not to get the
United States involved in what was known as the Great War in Europe
(World War I), he did so anyway against the wise counsel of George
Washington and John Quincy Adams, both of whom cautioned
Americans not to get involved in European wars. Not only did 117,000
Americans die in that war, the entry of the Americans eventually broke
the stalemate and resulted in victory over Germany.

It has been plausibly argued that had the United States not entered
World War I, there would have eventually been a negotiated settlement[3]
of the war. And it follows that had that happened, World War II
would likely never have occurred. In fact, the Treaty of Versailles was
so punitive it led to a collapse of the German economy, thereby setting
the stage for the rise of the National Socialist German Workers Party
(Nazi) dictatorship led by Adolf Hitler. If it is true that World War II
would not have happened without U.S. intervention in World War I,
Wilson's decision to enter the Great War was a truly tragic decision of
inestimable proportion.

While Wilson was the first president in American history to
dramatically expand the administrative state (the bureaucracy), there
was little daylight between his views on the power of the state and one
of the men he defeated in 1912, Theodore Roosevelt.[4] Wilson's efforts
to create a powerful bureaucracy have been multiplied many times
by subsequent Democrat and Republican presidents. It is difficult
to argue with Victor Davis Hansen, who sees the nearly all-powerful
unelected high-tech moguls, the ideological corporate news media, and
the administrative state as the greatest threats to freedom and the rule
of law that we face.

Unelected bureaucrats, those who control electronic communications, the media, and the military-intelligence complex of the federal government, all exercise enormous powers over American citizens without being elected to any office and while facing few consequences for their unethical or illegal behavior.[5]

It was the brazen and overt efforts of the bureaucratic state, the corporate media, and the social network moguls that conspired to delegitimize and destroy both the candidacy and the presidency of Donald Trump. The deep state not only promoted a false dossier claiming Trump was backed by Russia[6] but also spied on the Trump campaign[7] and then subsequently lied to Congress about it. This illegal effort was also backed by the media, big tech, and powerful deep state operatives such as FBI (Federal Bureau of Investigations) Director James Comey[8] and former CIA Director John Brennen.[9] These powerful forces nearly succeeded in executing a coup against a sitting American president.

From the beginning, progressives had no fear of a massive government bureaucracy. They had almost childlike faith in the fairness and objectivity of a vast administrative state. Early on,

Progressives believed that administrators, unlike ordinary politicians, could be objective and could focus on the good of the whole people—oddly, their ability to do so rested primarily on being freed from electoral accountability."[10]

Today the U.S. government employs approximately 3.7 million nonmilitary Americans[11] who regulate, monitor, and enforce their nonlegislative dictates to citizens across the United States. The United States Congress may pass laws, but it is the bureaucrats who write tens of thousands of regulations to enforce those laws. These unelected bureaucrats are incredibly powerful, and their reach and impact exceeds that of Congress. And unlike members of Congress who must stand for reelection, they are virtually immune from being fired[12] due to their civil service status.

The administrative state, for the better part of a century . . . has designed policy, made policy, structured policy, implemented policy, and interpreted policy while operating outside the control of Congress, the president, and the judiciary.[13]

Many of these ideological bureaucrats (especially those who were political appointees prior to entering civil service) serve in powerful positions in the bureaucratic state. As such, they use their power to punish (what they regard to be) their political enemies and to reward and protect their political friends.

A good example of this practice was the use of the Internal Revenue Service by Lois Lerner to attack conservative organizations.[14] Another good example is former head of the FBI James Comey, who wrote an exoneration of Hillary Clinton[15] (who infamously destroyed 30,000 subpoenaed emails,[16] illegally used a private server for top secret communications,[17] used bleach bit software to scrub her server,[18] and used hammers to smash her smart phones[19]) before she was even interviewed by the bureau. More recently, United States Attorney General Merrick Garland sicced the FBI on parents, identifying them as domestic terrorists[20] because they complained about their children being indoctrinated with critical race theory and being given pornographic books to read.[21] In a similar vein Garland also used heavily armed FBI SWAT teams to make early morning raids at the homes of those who have peacefully protested abortion, terrorizing their families and leading them away in handcuffs.[22]

Equally shocking was the government's actions taken against journalist James O'Keefe,[23] founder of Project Veritas, who was given access to the diary of President Biden's daughter, Ashley. Although O'Keefe saw the diary, he did not illegally gain access to the diary or disclose any information in it. Nevertheless the FBI raided his apartment, illegally surveilled his communications, and otherwise attempted to destroy Project Veritas. It was another egregious example of illegally using the power of government to harass and destroy political opponents. Most outrageous of all was the air, land, and sea raid on former President Donald Trump's estate, Mar-a-Lago, by heavily armed FBI agents at the behest of AG Garland.

Politicized bureaucracies like the FBI have even changed the entrance exam so that only those on the Left pass and those who are patriotic and conservative fail.[24] Jonathan Gilliam, a former Navy seal who applied, was advised to "think like a liberal" when he answered the questions on the exam.[25]

Even the once great U.S. military has been corrupted by radical Left wokeness. Secretary of Defense Lloyd Austin had the entire U.S. military stand down for sixty days[26] to weed out what he described as "White supremacists." In reality, his target was anyone with traditional patriotic views, especially those who voted for Donald Trump.[27] Racism had absolutely nothing to do with the stand-down; it was all about making sure the military was woke from top to bottom.

And, let's not forget the renegade actions and potential treason of the Chairman of the Joint Chiefs of Staff, General Mark Milley, who personally contacted his Chinese counterpart without notifying President Trump after the 2020 election. In doing so, according to a number of U.S. Senators, he may have committed treason[28] by illegally usurping the constitutional power given exclusively to the president. In taking such a step, he acted explicitly in a way that the Founders of our nation feared: that is the military seizing power from elected civilian authority. Milley's action was illegal, dangerous, and a direct threat to our democracy.

Our military should not be involved in social engineering or any other diversion that potentially weakens our military strength. This extends to the U.S. military academies that train our future military leaders. Unfortunately, our military academies have been infected with woke nonsense for years. For example, through a FOIA (Freedom of Information Act) request, Judicial Watch received a total of 653

Pages of records revealing critical race theory (CRT) instruction at the U.S. Military Academy, West Point. One training slide contains a graphic titled "MODERN-DAY SLAVERY IN THE USA."[29]

This problem is primarily due to the addition of far-Left civilian professors at our military academies who work hard at convincing our military cadets to believe in socialism, reject the principles of America's Founding Fathers, and discourage patriotism. Unfortunately, such radical Left indoctrination has taken place at West Point and the other military academies for decades.

A West Point graduate . . . recently posted photos of himself with pro-communist messages hidden under his graduation uniform.[30]

And,

2nd Lieut. Spenser Rapone posted one image where he is revealing a handwritten message written under his cover [hat] that said "Communism Will Win," while another one showed him revealing a Che Guevara shirt under his uniform.[31]

Shocking as that is, the reality is that today there is a pervading atmosphere in our military academies that is not only friendly to radical views but also hostile to Christianity, something that would have never been tolerated by Revolutionary War General George Washington. As a matter of fact, it was Washington who asked Congress to create the Chaplain Corps and

on July 29, 1775, Congress granted Washington's request and the Chaplain Corps was born.[32]

Almost three years later, emphasizing the importance of faith in the ranks, Washington issued this order at Valley Forge on May 2, 1778:

The Commander-in-Chief directs that divine services be performed every Sunday at eleven o'clock in each bridge which has chaplains . . . . While we are duly performing the duty of good soldiers, we are not to be inattentive to the highest duties of religion.[33]

Unlike in revolutionary times, Christianity is today under attack at our Military Academies,[34] again primarily due to the left-wing bent of civilian professors who now dominate the classrooms of these Academies. The Marxist, pro-critical race theory agenda at the United States Naval Academy[35] is little different than you would find at any public university across the United States.

Radical wokeness is like a cancer that has metastasized throughout our entire federal government, poisoning the minds of our military academy students and causing government bureaucrats to use the vast power of government to thwart the will of the American people. If left to proceed, it will kill freedom and democracy just as cancer left unattended kills a human.

But this need not happen. As a young conservative today, you have the same opportunity and ability as those one hundred young men and women who met at Sharon, Connecticut, over September 9–11, 1960. You have the talent, the ability to roll back the tide of progressivism so that it will never succeed in honest elections or in open debates. The future of our nation is in your good hands.

14

A JUST FOREIGN POLICY

THE LAST WORDS of the Sharon Statement are

> American foreign policy must be judged by this criterion: does it serve
> the just interests of the United States?

What exactly did that mean to the young men and women who founded Young Americans for Freedom?[1] Exactly what were the "just interests of the United States" then and today? What did President George Washington mean when he urged the United States to "observe good faith and justice toward all nations"?[2] Does it accurately describe American foreign policy today?

Merriam-Webster defines "just" as

acting or being in conformity with what is morally upright or good, righteous, as in a just war.[3]

In other words, an action by a government might be considered just if it is not only lawful but also moral, fair, and based on truth. A just foreign policy might logically be one that is based on justice but also fair to the other nations with which we engage in foreign transactions, commerce, military exercises, and legal affairs. Of course, foreign policy covers treaties, as well as trade, military commitments, and warfare as specified under the terms of the United States Constitution. So, has the United States established a history of treating other nations in a just and fair manner?

In fact, the record shows clearly that the United States of America has not only been fair and just but also generous to both allies and enemies after winning a war. While it is not surprising that the United States helped World War II allies get back on their feet after that horrendous war, what is surprising and unprecedented in the annals of world history is that the United States also helped former enemies Japan and Germany to fully recover.

Historically, not only the Sharon Statement but the Conservative movement as a whole have supported a foreign policy that is focused with near exclusivity on protecting and preserving the "just interests of the United States." When Soviet Communism threatened the United States, conservatives embraced the belief that the United States must have clear military superiority over the USSR, and as it says in the Sharon Statement,

> That the United States should stress victory over, rather than coexistence with, this menace.[4]

And, while most Americans, including most conservatives, supported the creation of NATO (North Atlantic Treaty Organization) following World War II to counteract the Warsaw Pact of the Soviet Union, we did not foresee that in doing so (while paying most of the bill, including the cost of stationing U.S. troops in Europe) we would enable Western European nations to largely abandon free enterprise. Although these nations were threatened by a socialist state (the Soviet Union), many, if not most, foolishly embraced a cradle-to-grave nanny state largely made possible by the United States providing for their defense from the Soviet Union. Like well-intentioned individuals who ignore or even enable a friend's drinking problem, the United States enabled the growth and expansion of socialism in Europe.

We further exacerbated the problem after Europe had economically recovered from World War II by continuing to be the primary underwriter of NATO as well as by continuing a lopsided trade arrangement that favored Western Europe. This was done at the expense of American manufacturers, American farmers, and American consumers. Many if not most of the socialist excesses in Europe can be traced directly to the United States treating our European cousins as welfare recipients.

In textbooks and undoubtedly in the classroom you may have been presented with a picture of the United States and the old Soviet Union as being morally equivalent, or worse, that the Soviet Union was morally superior to the United States. The opposite is true.

When World War II ended, the United States was the most powerful nation on earth, in sole possession of the atomic bomb. And our economic might was unequalled across the globe. But for the first time in human history, in stark contrast to the Soviet Union, the United States did not seek to control any land that we had conquered. Even more astoundingly, as previously noted, we spent billions of our own dollars not only rebuilding our wartime allies but also our enemies. It is worth restating: such a compassionate approach as a nation has no match in all of history. Not one. And to put the graciousness and kindness of the United States into clear perspective, just suppose the Soviet Union had acquired the nuclear bomb before the United States. Can you imagine just how they would have used that power for blackmail, to expand their soviet dictatorship across the globe?

Unlike the United States, the Soviet Union took the opportunity of being on the winning side in World War II to enslave every nation in Eastern Europe, including East Germany, Poland, Latvia, Estonia, Romania, Ukraine, Lithuania, Moldavia, Czechoslovakia, Albania, Bulgaria, and Georgia. Tens of millions of men, women, and children were forced to live in a terrorist police state where there was no free speech, no freedom of religion, and no economic freedom. Instead, they were forced to live in the universal economic misery that socialism always brings. And there was always the fear that in the middle of the night the secret police would knock on your door and haul you away to the infamous Lubyanka prison or to a gulag in Siberia without your family being informed of your fate. There were walls around the Soviet Union populated with guards armed with machine guns, not to keep people out but to keep people in.

In all previous wars, from time immemorial, including World War I, which took place just a few years earlier, the victors seized much of the conquered enemy's territory and assets as their booty for winning the war. In addition, they saddled the loser with economic restrictions that held them back from restoring prosperity to their land.

The point is that when the United States eschewed punishing Germany or Japan and took no booty or lands, it was truly following a foreign policy based "on the just interests of the United States." It was just and wise because by restoring prosperity and establishing democratic institutions in those nations, we avoided creating an opportunity for a dictatorship to arise that would lead to yet another war. It was also just and wise because it sustained peace. We did this for Germany and Japan despite the fact that we lost more than four hundred thousand American lives fighting them in World War II. We acted with Christian charity even though our own civilian population lived in drastically reduced economic conditions during the war. Our nation followed policies that were morally and ethically sound, and our decision to not seize territory or take treasure from Germany or Japan was a decision guided by truth, reason, justice, fairness, and common sense. It was a shining example of not only the greatness of the United States of America but also the goodness of our nation.

A just foreign policy means fair and free trade, open seas for trade, and a clearheaded understanding that dangerous enemies such as Communist China use trade with the United States to fund their massive and dangerous military buildup, which threatens the entire world. When Richard Nixon went to China in 1971 and shortly thereafter recognized Communist China, he believed that trade would lead China toward internal freedom for its citizens and make China a more peaceful nation. Nixon's action was most certainly well intentioned, but it produced bad results in more ways than one. By 1990, China's

economy was worth $367 billion, while America's was about $6 trillion. Neither was China a military threat. By 2020, China was a major power. Its economy was worth some $15 trillion to America's roughly $25 trillion.[5]

Thanks to Nixon recognizing Communist China, it is now "the world's premier manufacturing power"[6] upon which the United States and its citizens now depend for essential items such as prescription drugs, electronics, and countless other items. Thanks to Nixon and Henry Kissinger, American citizens are now at the mercy of China, our mortal enemy. But it's even worse.

In 2021, more than 100,000 Americans died from drug overdose,[7] the approximate number of Americans killed in action during the entire duration of the Korean War and the Vietnam War. Most of these deaths are from fentanyl, a drug manufactured in China and trafficked into the United States across our southern border by drug cartels. Make no mistake, those who manufacture fentanyl in China do so with the full approval of the Communist rulers of China who seek to destroy our nation. The drug cartels in Mexico are dangerous and deadly, but not nearly as deadly as the drugs they transport regularly into the United States. These Chicom-manufactured drugs constitute an undeclared war on the United States just as much as their intentional release of the COVID-19 virus into the United States and the world did.[8]

Yes, since we began trade with Communist China, the standard of living for Chinese citizens has increased dramatically, as it has in Communist Vietnam. But Chinese citizens are not free today, and what freedom they have is being further restricted by a new wave of censorship and repression.[9] While the Communist Chinese eased restrictions on Christian churches and other religions for a number of years, a new wave of tyranny has spread across China, bulldozing down churches, locking church doors, and arresting church leaders.[10]

Now is the time for the United States and our weak-kneed European allies to demand that China reduce its military spending, cease threats against Taiwan, and stop all manufacturing of fentanyl as a condition of continued trade. In the absence of that, we should end trade with all nations hostile to the United States, including Communist China and Communist Vietnam. Without American dollars and the theft of American military technology,[11] China would cease to be a threat to our nation. Today, however, we are paying for their military buildup and allowing them to steal military and commercial technology that can be used against us and our allies. China's theft of American technology is estimated to be $300 billion to $600 billion *per year*.[12]

To sum it up, a just foreign policy must be exclusively focused on the well-being and safety of the citizens of the United States and the commercial enterprises of its citizens. We must honor our foreign agreements to the letter as long as all parties do the same. We must protect our nation from Islamic extremists as well as from our primary threat, Communist China, and from Putin's Russia. Moreover, if we are wise and follow the sound advice of George Washington and John Quincy Adams, we will avoid future wars that are not in the just interests of the United States of America.

The United States must have a strategic foreign policy that has the primary goal of protecting and defending the United States, including protecting the sovereignty of our nation from military attacks and border incursions[13] as well as defending American interests around the globe. That policy includes strategic bilateral treaties that are clearly linked to the just interests of the United States and military alliances that serve those goals. Moreover, the United States must have a fighting force that is second to none in preparedness of the men and women who serve, the development of weapons that guarantee the continued military superiority of our nation, and an impenetrable missile defense in the United States.

How then do we define a just American foreign policy? We must conclude that a just foreign policy is neither interventionist nor isolationist but one that is consistently and solely guided by what we believe to be "in the just interest of the United States" and its citizens. It is one that gives primacy to the interests of the United States and does not seek to expand the borders of the United States, nor to intervene in disputes between other nations if the outcome of such disputes neither hurts nor harms the United States or its citizens now or in the future. This approach is totally consistent with the advice that George Washington gave in his Farewell Address[14] to avoid unnecessary foreign entanglements and favoritism, especially those that do not make the United States or its citizens more secure, more safe, or more free.

15

WASHINGTON'S ADVICE

HOW CAN GOOD intentions lead to bad outcomes? Woodrow Wilson provides a good example. But first, let us turn to George Washington's Farewell Address:

> Observe good faith and justice towards all nations; cultivate peace and harmony with all; religion and morality enjoin this conduct, and can it be that good policy does not equally enjoin it? It will be worthy of a free, enlightened, and, at no distant period, a great nation, to give to mankind the magnanimous and too novel example of a people always guided by an exalted justice and benevolence.[1]

This advice from George Washington reveals what he believed to be the character and destiny of America. He argued that the United States should not treat one nation different than another, giving neither preference nor disadvantage. Neither did Washington say that we do not need foreign alliances and treaties. However, Washington made it clear that we should make certain that any alliances or treaties serve the just interest of the United States. And, clearly, Washington did not believe that the United States should arrogantly seek to bring freedom and democracy to the world as well-intentioned presidents of both parties have done since the presidency of Woodrow Wilson. We should not delude ourselves into believing that every society and every culture and nation can sustain a republican form of government, a free society. Rather than impose our values and our principles upon another nation, Washington saw America as a beacon to the world providing an example of freedom that other nations were free to emulate or ignore.

Beginning with the presidency of George Washington, and reinforced by Presidents James Monroe and John Quincy Adams, the United States followed a foreign policy that was not only "in the just interest of the United States" (Sharon Statement) but also first and foremost concerned with advancing the interests of our nation. Washington set the tone in his administration and emphasized it in his Farewell Address, saying,

> The great rule of conduct for us in regard to foreign nations is in extending our commercial relations, to have with them as little political connection as possible. So far as we have already formed engagements, let them be fulfilled with perfect good faith. Here let us stop.[2]

Subsequent American presidents followed Washington's sage advice, especially President John Quincy Adams, who as secretary of state under President James Monroe, wrote the Monroe Doctrine. The Monroe Doctrine was a seminal foreign policy statement that made it clear to foreign nations that any attempts at colonization or other intervention in the affairs of any nation in North or South America would cause the United States to take military action. In other words, the Monroe Doctrine, couched in appropriate diplomatic language, gave notice to nations not in our hemisphere to butt out. Beginning with Monroe, and in his own subsequent presidency, John Quincy Adams codified an American foreign policy that is summed up in this April 28, 1823, letter to U.S. Minister in Madrid Hugh Nelson:

> It has been the policy of these United States from the time when their independence was achieved, to hold themselves aloof from the political system and contentions of Europe . . .. The first and paramount duty of the government is to maintain peace amidst the convulsions of foreign wars and to enter the lists as parties to no cause, other than our own.[3]

Adams's policy, when followed, not only kept America out of war but also minimized problems with the nations of the world. A simple definition of Adams's foreign policy could have been called "America First," but

> Presidents George Washington through Theodore Roosevelt would not have used the term to describe United States policy toward other nations—because they would have deemed any other priority to be mad or criminal.[4]

Regardless of what Adams's policy is called, it was very successful. Nevertheless, the accidental election[5] of Woodrow Wilson in 1912 not only brought an end to that successful foreign policy but also brought about a U.S. foreign policy that was primarily concerned with world issues, and with American priorities only secondarily.[6]

In short, Wilson's foreign policy was a rejection of the proven and successful John Quincy Adams strategy of pursuing a policy that was solely in the "just interests of the United States," putting American interests first and foremost. Instead, Wilson departed from that policy and undertook a goal of spreading democracy across the globe, being at least, and often more, concerned with the objectives of other nations than with those of the United States. Wilson got our nation directly involved in solving international disputes that did not affect us. It was arrogant pie-in-the-sky thinking based on the belief that Americans, at least enlightened and well-educated progressive Americans, had an obligation to bring freedom, democracy, and peace to the world. They believed themselves capable of changing the course of history and eliminating war as a means of resolving disputes between nations. In a public address, Wilson said,

> What are we going to do with the influence and power of this great nation? Are we going to play the old role of using that power for our aggrandizement and material benefit only?[7]

He continued,

> I earnestly believe not only in the democracy of America but of every awakened people that wishes and intends to govern and control its own affairs.[8]

Nice sentiments, good intentions, but it was an unrealistic, high-sounding goal based on fuzzy pseudo-sophisticated thinking that cast reason aside. It rejected the proven successful strategy of George Washington and John Quincy Adams. It was a recipe for countless international problems, unnecessary wars, and the needless loss of life. It was all due to pointless meddling in the affairs of other nations across the globe. It led directly to our uncalled-for intervention in World War I, the victory of which almost surely led to World War II. It also put Americans on the battlefield in the Korean War (President Truman called it a "police action") and in the jungles of Vietnam. Both wars, which cost tens of thousands of lives, were wars the U.S. chose not to win.

And following the Korean War and Vietnam War, there were endless other battles and mini-wars. It was a heavy price to pay for reversing the proven foreign policy of George Washington and John Quincy Adams. And sadly this new rose-tinted glasses strategy seduced not only progressive Democrats but also a long line of progressive Republican presidents, including (but not limited to) Richard Nixon, Gerald Ford, George H. W. Bush, and George W. Bush. This foolhardy approach cost Americans and America dearly in terms of lives, treasure, and respect across the globe.

More important, it has led to weakened and confused presidential leadership that has sacrificed the priorities of Americans and their safety while pursuing unreachable and unrealistic goals such as nation-building in lands where democracy is neither sought nor sustainable. It is not consistent with the wise advice of George Washington, nor with the words of the Sharon Statement. It is a tragedy of great proportions that keeps being repeated by an entrenched, bloated, and misguided foreign policy bureaucracy. It was not until President Donald Trump came along and made a valiant effort to return to the proven, tested, and wise advice of Washington and John Quincy Adams that the United States began to extricate itself from dangerous and unnecessary entanglements with foreign nations.

That brings us to modern conflicts in Europe. Today the GDP (in U.S. dollars) of the European Union nations is $17.1 billion,[9] compared to $1.8 billion[10] for Russia. Similarly, the EU population numbers nearly 450 million, compared to a Russian population of just 145 million. Given this overwhelming advantage in population and economic might by the EU (that does not even include the wealth and population of England), why is it necessary for the United States to bear the burden of defending Europe from Russia? If the European Union is that much wealthier than Russia and that much larger in population, why shouldn't they defend themselves? The EU assuming that burden of defense is not only fair and just, it is in their self-interest to do so. Sharing technological information with those in the European Union is one thing, but becoming directly involved in a war between those in the European Union and Russia not only appears to be but is in direct conflict with the wise and prudent advice of Washington and Adams regarding wars in Europe.

Both Reagan and Trump rebuilt our American military to be superior to any other military in the world. Presidents Reagan and Trump consciously avoided taking unnecessary military action or becoming entwined with disputes between foreign nations except in extreme circumstances where the United States and the lives and property of Americans were threatened. And neither Reagan nor Trump engaged in the foolhardy and fruitless effort of nation-building that cannot and will never succeed. That is especially true in nations that do not have the necessary roots of order, law, peace, liberty, and virtue embedded in them. The best example of such a foolish approach is

President George W. Bush [who] started two wars, expended American blood and treasure in an effort to transform Afghanistan and Iraq into Western democracies, and failed miserably primarily because he broadened the definition of America's interests, and therefore, of victory in both wars. He lost them both.[11]

In sharp contrast, President Ronald Reagan sought victory over communism, defining his policy as "We win, they lose"[12] because he well understood the very real threat to our nation posed by the "evil empire"[13] of the Soviet Union. It is worth noting that while every president from Franklin D. Roosevelt to Jimmy Carter (the immediate predecessor of Reagan) had a similar opportunity to bring down the Soviet Union, only Ronald Reagan did so, and he did it "without firing a shot."[14] It was perhaps the greatest foreign policy triumph in American history.

A just American foreign policy not only entails honoring all existing treaties and agreements that strengthen the security and safety of the United States and its citizens but also withdrawing from all treaties and agreements that do not fulfill this criterion or whose signatories are not trustworthy.

New treaties should be entered into that enhance the safety and security of the United States, and ideally such treaties should be bilateral with individual nations, not multilateral that include a mix of nations with various conflicting interests and concerns. Such multilateral agreements are often written with "creative ambiguity,"[15] a phrase coined by Henry Kissinger to explain that each party to the agreement would interpret it differently and in their own best interest. Of course, this led to meaningless treaties or to treaties that were worse than no treaty at all, especially when dealing with parties that had no intention of honoring them. This is especially true when dealing with communists, who believe that they have no obligation to abide by any treaty that does not benefit them above and beyond the interests of the other parties who sign that treaty. As Vladimir Lenin put it, "Treaties are like pie crusts, made to be broken."[16]

Finally, when it comes to necessary treaties, they *must* be submitted to the United States Senate for ratification as required by the United States Constitution. The requirement by the Constitution that the Senate must approve any treaty with a two-thirds majority indicates the difficulty of approval the Founders sought. Only by ratification of two-thirds can the nation be assured of unity in such important matters. Unfortunately, today that ratification process is often ignored by presidents who make agreements such as the Paris Accords on Climate Change or the Joint Comprehensive Plan of Action (JCPOA). It has been reported by the United Nations that the "the Paris Agreement is a legally binding international treaty on climate change."[17] Except that it is not binding on the United States because it has not been ratified by the U.S. Senate. That enabled President Trump to withdraw from the agreement[18] in November 2017.

It is not the goal or responsibility of the United States to be policeman to the world, nor is it in the interest of the United States to be entangled in conflicts between other nations that do not directly affect the well-being of our nation. Unfortunately, today the U.S. has "some 750 American military facilities . . . in 80 nations and territories around the world."[19]

Those troops and bases that do not serve the just interests of the United States should be closed down. The United States has the right to expect that peace and freedom-loving nations be financially and militarily responsible for their own national defense, to the extent that they are capable of doing so. The EU nations certainly have the GDP and the economies needed to create armies and navies and weapons of war necessary to face down the ambitions of Vladimir Putin. Why then do they demand that the U.S. tax its citizens to defend their freedom?

A just American foreign policy recognizes that warfare comes at the extreme cost of lives and treasure that severely hurt Americans and their families, as well as undermine American unity. Our best course of action is "pursuing what benefits our American character and advances our legitimate interests—in short, fully minding our own business while leaving other people to mind theirs—[which] was the basis of the United States' successful foreign policy from 1815 to 1910."[20]

A foreign policy that concerns "itself primarily with world issues and with American priorities only secondarily"[21] has resulted in countless wars during the past seventy-five years. It is time to return to a just foreign policy as defined by both George Washington and John Quincy Adams, one that is in the sole interest of the United States and its citizens.

16

"THE RIGHT TO LIFE…"

SINCE THE SHARON STATEMENT was written more than twelve years prior to the *Roe v. Wade* U.S. Supreme Court decision legalizing abortion, there was obviously no reference to abortion or the right to life in it. However, it is important to note that the opening words of the Sharon Statement begin, "In this time of moral and political crises . . ." signaling the understanding by the founders of Young Americans for Freedom that the crisis America was facing even then was moral at its foundation. And today there is no issue that is more moral to its core than abortion. Having known a number of YAF founders there is no doubt in my mind that had *Roe* been decided and abortion legalized prior to the signing of the Sharon Statement it would have been firmly condemned in that document. The legalization of abortion was a terrible moral step away from God and a return to ancient paganism.

It is no accident that as America began removing God from its public life, its public squares, its schools, and its culture, what came in to take its place was a revived form of paganism. In every realm, where Christian or biblical values were removed or overturned, what came to fill their place was paganism. Nor is it an accident that the decade that began with the removal of prayer from America's public school system ushered in the practice of abortion on demand in 1970 and then the legalization of abortion across the nation in 1973.[1]

Today, nearly fifty years after *Roe v. Wade,* an estimated 62 million American babies have been killed through the abortion process[2] even though the science clearly supports the proposition that life begins at conception.[3] In fact, the heartbeat of an unborn baby can now be detected at just five-and-a-half to six weeks after conception![4] Only the most skeptical and hardhearted would deny that a heartbeat is clear and irrefutable evidence of life.

In 1973, the United States Supreme Court "discovered" a woman's right to have an abortion without any constitutional validation whatsoever. It was one of the worst rulings in the history of the Court, and Justices appointed by both Republican and Democrat presidents supported that decision. However, after the appointment of Supreme Court Jurists with fidelity to the U.S. Constitution, as well as overwhelming scientific evidence, *Roe* is finally gone. That is a wonderful victory for the unborn, a true watershed event.

However, this Supreme Court reversal does not mean the end of abortion in the United States. The battle now shifts to individual states where abortion continues to be legal and deadly. The current situation is akin to that of the abolitionists prior to the Civil War being temporarily successful in stopping the spread of slavery into new territories of the United States but unable to end slavery in the states where it was then being practiced. The fight for the right to life in the United States has not ended; it has simply shifted to those states in which it continues to be legal.

And make no mistake: the killing of an unborn baby is just as reprehensible as was slavery. And indeed the day will come in the United States when future Americans will look back upon the legalization of abortion with the same contempt and horror that we look back on those who practiced slavery.

Abortion is not only murder; as practiced it is racist and xenophobic. Remember, 22 million Black babies have been aborted[5] since the U.S. Supreme Court declared abortion to be legal. To put that into perspective, the entire Black population of the United States today numbers nearly 44.5 million.[6] In 1973 it was slightly more than 22 million.[7] While it is hard to imagine, today,

> Abortion is the leading cause of death for African Americans, more than all other causes combined, including AIDS, violent crimes, accidents, cancer and heart disease.[8]

Had those aborted Black babies lived and propagated, the Black population today would be at least 50 percent larger than it is today[9] and possibly much larger.

The disproportionate abortion rate for African Americans is not an accident. America's largest abortion provider, Planned Parenthood, which receives more than $1.6 billion from the federal government[10] each year, specifically targets the babies of Black Americans and other minorities for abortion by "locating 79% of Planned Parenthood abortion facilities . . . within walking distance of neighborhoods that have proportionately higher populations of Black or Latina women."[11]

Planned Parenthood also targets Black babies through mass media with radio ads such as this one that aired in New York City:

> If you're a Black woman in America, it's statistically safer to have an abortion than to carry a pregnancy to term or give birth.[12]

Progressive legislators such as Ohio state representative "Janine Boyd . . . proposed Amendment 0291, which provides an exception for black mothers"[13] to the bill outlawing an abortion if there is a heartbeat. Unbelievably, Boyd did not want Black babies to be protected from being aborted! The "heartbeat" bill passed over progressive opposition and was signed into law by Ohio Governor Mike DeWine. Make no mistake: there are pro-abortion office holders on both sides of the aisle as well as pro-life advocates in both parties.

Margaret Sanger was, of course, the founder of Planned Parenthood and

> In her 1922 book, *Pivot of Civilization*, she [Sanger] unabashedly called for the extirpation [elimination] of "weeds . . . overrunning the human garden"; . . . and for the sterilization of "genetically inferior races."[14]

Margaret Sanger made it crystal clear that she was comfortable associating with racists, writing in her autobiography, "I accepted an invitation to talk to the women's branch of the Ku Klux Klan."[15]

The racist practice of abortion that is primarily used to kill off babies that the progressive elites seek to eliminate will continue in individual states so long as the practice of abortion is presented as a clinical practice, not the pagan and barbaric act that it is.

Your voice and your vote count when it comes to detestable immoral practices such as abortion. The reality is that if you justify the elevation of your own choices above the life of an unborn baby and choose to terminate that life for your convenience, you have made a terrible step toward justifying other terrible acts. Based solely on your needs, why not legalize infanticide or the termination of those individuals who no longer bring any benefit (in your mind) to society? Having taken the step to kill an unborn baby, you have, in reality, declared yourself to be god, having life and death power over another human being. You have rejected the true God by violating God's law that says, "Thou shalt not murder."

If we no longer believe that we are created by God but are instead the result of some cosmic accident, our value is as meaningless as are our lives. Life is utterly without any purpose or value if there is no God and if there is no Heaven or Hell. And if life has no value, there is nothing wrong or immoral about taking the life of a baby or taking the life of any other human being.

But life does have value. You have value. I have value. Everyone who was ever conceived has value in the sight of God. It is up to those who are now in high school, college, or recently graduated to not only completely end the scourge of abortion in our land but also to advance the truth that abortion is a heinous crime against humanity. It must be universally realized that abortion is an evil that has placed a shameful moral stain on our nation, exactly as slavery did. As long as we proclaim to be "one nation under God," we cannot and must not allow the killing of the unborn.

17

A SIMPLE TRUTH

LET'S START WITH A SIMPLE TRUTH: the Founders added the Second Amendment to the United States Constitution not for the purpose of self-protection, not for the purpose of hunting, but first and foremost for the purpose of opposing tyranny. Hunting is a great outdoor sport that millions of Americans enjoy. Having a gun for self-protection saves thousands of lives each year. In fact, a 2021 survey showed that Americans used a gun for self-defense nearly 1.7 million times per year.[1]

But as worthy as is the use of guns for sporting and for self-protection, those were not the reason the Founders included the Second Amendment, the right to keep and bear arms, in the Constitution. It was included because more than any other threat to the new United States, the Founders feared big, powerful government. They understood human nature to be frail and as such it made humans susceptible to the lure of gaining power over others. As noted several times earlier, Americans may reject the God of the Bible, but when they do that they either think of themselves as gods or worship something else as their god. That was the devil's temptation that Adam and Eve succumbed to in the Garden of Eden—"You shall be like God"[2]—and throughout history humans have fallen for this lie. When they do, they seek power over the lives of fellow Americans based on their certainty that *they* not only know what is best for themselves but also what is best for others. That's how they justify an all-powerful government, a socialistic government. And in a socialist government there is no room for dissenters, especially a dissenter with firearms.

Virtually all of America's Founders understood that ultimately individual liberty rested upon Americans owning firearms as a means of preserving their freedom. The very presence of firearms in the hands of Americans serves to dissuade would-be tyrants from trying to snuff out individual freedom as the following quotes from America's Founders note.

"A free people ought not only to be armed, but disciplined."—George Washington

"To disarm the people . . .[i]s the most effectual way to enslave them."—George Mason, referencing advice given to the British Parliament by Pennsylvania governor Sir William Keith, June 14, 1788

"Guard with jealous attention the public liberty. Suspect everyone who approaches that jewel. Unfortunately, nothing will preserve it but downright force. Whenever you give up that force, you are ruined . . .. The great object is that every man be armed."—Patrick Henry, Speech to the Virginia Ratifying Convention, June 5, 1778

"And that the said Constitution be never construed to authorize Congress to infringe the just liberty of the press, or the rights of conscience; or to prevent the people of the United States, who are peaceable citizens, from keeping their own arms."—Samuel Adams, Massachusetts Ratifying Convention, 1788

"The right of the citizens to keep and bear arms has justly been considered, as the palladium of the liberties of a republic; since it offers a strong moral check against the usurpation and arbitrary power of rulers."—Joseph Story, *Commentaries on the Constitution of the United States*

"The people are not to be disarmed of their weapons. They are left in full possession of them."—Zachariah Johnson, Virginia Ratifying Convention, June 25, 1788

Of course, an armed citizen does discourage criminals from committing crimes, and the Founders understood that too.

"The laws that forbid the carrying of arms are laws of such a nature. They disarm only those who are neither inclined nor determined to commit crimes . . . .. Such laws make things worse for the assaulted and better for the assailants; they serve rather to encourage than to prevent homicides, for an unarmed man may be attacked with greater confidence than an armed man."—Thomas Jefferson quoting eighteenth-century criminologist Cesare Beccaria, 1774–1776

These and many other quotes from America's Founders make it clear that they believed in the absolute necessity of American citizens being armed as a means of discouraging those in government who might have the goal of enslaving American citizens. Moreover, in subsequent history, the insight of the Founders was confirmed when tyrants in other nations took as one of their very first steps the seizure of all firearms[3] from the citizens of their respective countries. It was Communist Chinese dictator Mao Zedong who coined the phrase "Political power grows out of the barrel of a gun."[4]

And Mao is correct to the extent that when would-be tyrants endeavor to gain absolute power over the citizens of a land, they cannot tolerate the citizens being well armed. It is worth noting that two high-ranking officials of the Obama administration expressed their high regard for Mao, one even favorably quoting Mao's belief that political power comes from the barrel of a gun.[5]

Is it any wonder that progressives on the far Left, who desire to create a socialist state, seek to disarm American citizens? They simply cannot achieve total power over the lives of American citizens as long as those citizens are armed.

Of course, there are those who simply want to restrict firearms and support so-called Red Flag laws that will enable law enforcement to confiscate guns of those they believe are unstable and a potential danger to society. They support these laws in hopes that this will reduce or even eliminate horrific mass murders. That support may grow from a noble desire, but if implemented, such Red Flag laws are actually very dangerous to life and your individual freedom and thus to our republic. The stated intent is to take away guns from individuals whom someone in government deems to be a potential threat and dangerous to society. But as Tucker Carlson pointed out,

Red Flag laws will not end mass shootings, but Red Flag laws will end due process. Due process is a simple concept, but it's the key to everything that is good about America.

In our system of justice, citizens cannot be punished without first being charged with a crime. Politicians cannot just decide to hurt you, throw you in handcuffs, lock you in jail, seize your property simply because they don't like how you think or how you vote. No. Before they punish you, they have to go through a formal process in which they describe which specific law you broke and exactly how you broke it. They have to prove it.[6]

Carlson also noted the case *Caniglia v. Strom*, in which a Red Flag law was used in Rhode Island:

> The Supreme Court sided with the gun owner in that case in a rare nine-zero decision. That means that every justice, liberal and conservative, agreed that authorities cannot just seize your property or throw you in jail because they don't like the way you look or because someone is mad at you. So, Red Flag laws are unconstitutional, period.[7]

Moreover, the problem with such laws is not only the fact that they are unconstitutional but also that they give undue power to the government. That is precisely what happened with the Patriot Act, which was hastily passed by a Congress panicked by the threat from Islamic extremists. Both Red Flag laws and the Patriot Act allow the government to abrogate the constitutional rights of American citizens and monitor their communications.[8] Today the Patriot Act that was supposedly passed to *protect* Americans has now been used by the FBI to spy on parents who protested at school board meetings the unjust treatment of their children.[9] And as recent as January 2023, the FBI continued to arrest peaceful protesters who were waved into the Capitol Building by the Capitol Hill Police on January 6, 2021. Nearly one-thousand arrests have been made.[10]

> You didn't even have to be involved in the Capitol riots to qualify for a visit from the FBI: investigators have reportedly been tracking—and questioning—anyone whose cell phones connected to wi-fi or pinged cell phone towers near the Capitol. One man, who had gone out for a walk with his daughters only to end up stranded near the Capitol crowds, actually had FBI agents show up at his door days later.[11]

The rioters deserved to be arrested, but the peaceful protesters did not deserve to be spied upon and arrested. Nevertheless, the U.S.

Department of Justice was able to do just that by designating the protesters as "domestic terrorists" under the authority of the Patriot Act.

Months later, in 2021, the U.S. Department of Justice used counterterrorism tools against concerned parents[12] who attended school board meetings and suggested the parents, too, were domestic terrorists. Apparently, the Department of Justice once again used the Patriot Act to spy on these parents.[13] If the federal government passes a Red Flag law and it somehow passes muster with the Supreme Court, you can be certain that it will be abused by the bureaucracy to target conservatives who own firearms.

The truth is that Red Flag laws have multiple problems. A federal Red Flag law would be the first time in the history of the United States where someone could be designated dangerous by the government and have their personal property (guns and ammunition) taken away from them simply because some bureaucrat or progressive attorney general decides it should be so. What would keep a radical bureaucrat from disarming any conservative they judged dangerous just for their political views? Red Flag laws are a very slippery slope that would inevitably lead to the disarming of all patriotic Americans.

Americans would be wise to remember the words of Benjamin Franklin: "Those who would give up essential Liberty, to purchase a little temporary Safety, deserve neither Liberty nor Safety."[14]

Passing the Patriot Act and enacting state Red Flag laws in response to violent attacks may attempt to solve one problem, but they will certainly create a far greater problem that will ultimately threaten the preservation of our republic.

There are workable solutions to defending our children from horrific killings by madmen. The first is to keep our schools safe and secure with advanced locking devices that keep killers far away from them. We already know that locked doors deter killers from entering churches and schools. A second and even more powerful deterrent would be to allow voluntary prayer in public schools, thus reintroducing God into our society. The recent ruling of SCOTUS[15] on behalf of high school football coach Joe Kennedy, who was fired because he silently prayed on the football field after football games, is a small step in the right direction. It should not surprise us that when we drive godly virtues out of the classroom and out of society and replace them with manmade morals that men go mad and engage in the slaughter of children.

America's Founders felt so strongly about making sure that Americans had the right to keep and bear arms that they made it the Second Amendment to the Bill of Rights that was added to the Constitution, just after freedom of religion, freedom of speech, freedom to peaceably assemble, and freedom of the press contained in the First Amendment. And they made it a standalone freedom to emphasize its importance to our republic. It must not be surrendered if we are to preserve freedom in our land.

> The constitutional right to bear arms in public…is not "a second-class right, subject to an entirely different body of rules than the other Bill of Rights guarantees," Justice Clarence Thomas wrote in the majority opinion. "We know of no other constitutional right that an individual may exercise only after demonstrating to government officers some special need."[16]

Justice Thomas and the concurring majority was totally right.

The only reason your right to keep and bear arms was not mentioned in the Sharon Statement is that in 1960, the Second Amendment was not under attack by progressives and the corporate media. But had it been under attack, such attacks certainly would have been opposed by those who gathered to found Young Americans for Freedom. In fact, just a few years later, YAF leaders founded Students for the Right to Keep and Bear Arms, later renamed the Citizens Committee for the Right to Keep and Bear Arms, today one of the leading groups defending your Second Amendment rights.

18

CLIMATE OR POLITICAL SCIENCE?

EVERY DECENT AND HONORABLE AMERICAN cares about the health of the earth. We all want clear air, clean water, and a healthy future for ourselves, as well as for our families and for everyone in the world. We believe in science, the scientific method, and accordingly recognize that history shows that no science is settled. It is always subject to debate and intense scrutiny. And as we continue to discover more about our great and extremely complex world, we realize that some of our previous "scientific truths" have limitations of their own.

Sir Isaac Newton postulated his theory of gravity in 1687, and it proved to be quite accurate for that time, but in the twentieth century we learned that his theory had its limitations. Yes, if you throw a ball up in the air, it will come down due to gravity, but if you send a rocket into space, beyond our stratosphere, it will continue on into space.

Similarly, there are several theories that endeavor to explain the travel of light. In 1678 Dutch physicist Christiaan Huygens developed the wave theory to explain the travel of light, and it worked to the extent necessary at that time. But much later, in 1900, the German physicist Max Planck proposed that light is made of finite packets of energy known as a light quanta and it depends on the frequency and velocity of light. Later, in 1905, Einstein proposed that light possessed the characteristics of both particle and wave. He suggested that light is made of small particles called photons. Quantum mechanics gave proof of the dual nature of light.[1]

There are hundreds or even thousands of other examples in the scientific world of one theory being replaced by another as our knowledge expands. The fundamental truth, as the *New York Times* noted, is that "science is never settled. It is, by definition, an ever-evolving body of human knowledge, and climate science is exactly like all the other sciences in that way."[2]

Our knowledge of God's laws of the universe is continually growing. However, the universal reality of science and knowledge is the imperfection of everything in the world. We are imperfect humans living in an imperfect world. Not only do humans live in a fallen state, but also our world exists in a fallen state.

Scientists correctly theorized the potential of man to escape gravity and go to the moon, but it took engineers to actually make it happen. Unlike scientists who live in a world of theory, engineers live in a world of reality. That is not an attack on scientists; the world dearly needs to theorize what we can achieve. It is simply an understanding that it is engineers who turn the proven theories of scientists into real-world applications. This is how one of my engineering professors explained the difference between a scientist and an engineer in an apocryphal story:

There are two individuals in a room, one a scientist and the other an engineer. On the other side of the room is a stack of gold bricks worth ten million dollars. In the center of the room is a bell, and each time it rings the scientist and the engineer can go half the distance to the gold. The question posed to the scientist and the engineer is, "Will you ever get to the gold?" The scientist shakes his head and says firmly, "No, I will never get there." Then the engineer smiles and says, "I'll get close enough!"

Indeed, that is correct. All the engineer has to know when approaching any project or challenge is the acceptable tolerance for his or her calculations, that is, how accurate does my mathematical solution need to be to accomplish the task? Once that acceptable tolerance (an accommodation of imperfection) is identified, it makes it possible for astronauts to fly into outer space, travel to the moon, and to create and build all sorts of other things on this earth. Theory is the critically important starting point, but the reality only happens when those who understand that everything in this world is imperfect accommodate that imperfection into their design calculations.

In contrast to what you may have read or heard, there is no scientific consensus regarding the threat of global warming. In fact, a peer-reviewed paper[3] on the validity and immediacy of this perceived threat revealed that just 36.3% of scientists and engineers (in government and business) surveyed believe that the danger is sufficient to comply with the Kyoto Protocol. Somewhat surprisingly, only 45.2% of government scientists and engineers surveyed believe that it is necessary for the United States to comply with the Kyoto Protocol. More surprising yet, just 24.1% of geoscientists believe that the U.S. should abide by the Kyoto Protocol agreement.

Real science is always subject to debate and challenge. Forecasts based on mathematical models are only as valid as the data input, no matter how powerful the computer used. Every scientist and engineer understands the phrase "garbage in, garbage out."

As Ian Plimer, emeritus professor of earth sciences at the University of Melbourne and professor of mining geology at the University of Adelaide, observed of humans' quest to expand knowledge,

We derive scientific evidence from measurement, observation, and experiment. Evidence must be repeatable and collected over and over again. Computers do not generate evidence: they analyse evidence that should have been repeated and validated. On the basis of the evidence and analysis of evidence, an explanation is given. This explanation is a scientific theory and must be in accord with other validated evidence from diverse sources (this is known as the coherence criterion in science). Unlike in law, there is no inadmissible evidence in science. Science is underpinned by practitioners who must be skeptical of the methodology used to collect evidence, the analysis of evidence, and the conclusions based on the evidence. On the basis of new evidence, scientists must always be prepared to change their opinions.[4]

As shown in Appendix B (page 197), one should be careful about making dramatic doomsday forecasts[5] such as those highlighted on the website of the Competitive Enterprise Institute. From the 1960s to the present day, "scientists" have been making forecasts of catastrophic climate disasters, yet not one of the forty-one doomsday forecasts provided have proven to be even close to being accurate.

Dr. Steven Koonin, who was a professor of theoretical physics at Caltech and also served as vice president and provost of that institution for nearly a decade, and who also served as undersecretary for science at the Department of Energy in the Obama administration, warns that "Climate alarmism has come to dominate U.S. politics, especially among Democrats, where I have otherwise long felt most comfortable politically."[6] Koonin goes on to write,

Humans exert a growing, but physically small, warming influence on the climate. The deficiencies of climate data challenge our ability to untangle the responses to human influences from poorly understood natural changes.[7]

To put the climate change issue into perspective, viewpoints typically fall into three distinct categories:

Catastrophic Climate Change. Those who make claims such as "we only have 12 years to save the planet"[8] or "the seas will rise by 20 feet"[9] or some other extreme, nonscience-based, politically generated exaggeration that fits into this category. The individuals in this category are deemed climate alarmists and rightly so.

Serious Climate Change. This category includes those serious scientists who are concerned about the impact of global warming but not panicked by it. They seek a reduction in CO_2 emissions as desirable, but they recognize that the total solution to the emission problem does not lie only with the United States, but even more so with China, India, and other emerging nations that continue to build coal plants at a record pace.[10] They understand that climate change is a global issue, not solely a national issue.

Incidental Climate Change. This category is comprised of those who are skeptical (skeptics) of the claims of catastrophic climate change and have concluded that a more measured, wait-and-see approach is appropriate. They see no reason to panic or make any dramatic changes in energy generation in the United States at this time. Polling currently indicates that most Americans fit into this category.[11]

Here are just ten of the more than forty false claims made by climate alarmists during the past forty years:[12]

"Scientist predicts new Ice Age by 21st Century," *Boston Globe*, April 16, 1960

"Another Ice Age?" *Time*, June 24, 1974

"No end in sight to cooling trend," *New York Times,* January 5, 1978

"1988: Maldives completely under water in 30 years," RealClimateScience.com

"Rising seas to 'obliterate' nations by 2000," Associated Press, June 30, 1989

"[By 2008] The West Side Highway [in New York City], that runs along the Hudson River, will be completely underwater," James Hansen, NASA scientist. Salon.com, October 23, 2001

"In a few years winter snowfall will become [in Britain] a very rare and exciting event. Children just aren't going to know what snow is," Dr. David Viner, a senior research scientist at the Climatic Research Unit (CRU) of the University of East Anglia, *The Independent,* March 20, 2000

[James] "Hansen echoing work by other scientists, said that in five to 10 years the Artic will be free of sea ice in the summer," Associated Press, June 24, 2008

"U.S. Navy predicts summer ice free Artic by 2016," *The Guardian,* December 9, 2013

These are just a few of the scores of inaccurate forecasts by climate alarmists over the past fifty years. The justification for such exaggerated claims has been rationalized by prominent climate researcher Stephen Schneider:

On the one hand, as scientists we are ethically bound to the scientific method, in effect promising to tell the truth, the whole truth, and nothing but—which means that we must include all the doubts, the caveats, the ifs, ands, and buts. On the other hand, we are not just scientists but human beings as well. And like most people we'd like to see the world a better place, which in this context translates into our working to reduce the risk of potentially disastrous climatic change. To do that we need to get some broad based support, to capture the public's imagination. That, of course, entails getting loads of media coverage. So, we have to offer up scary scenarios, make simplified, dramatic statements, and make little mention of any doubts we might have. This "double ethical bind" we frequently find ourselves in cannot be solved by any formula. Each of us has to decide what the right balance is between being effective and being honest. I hope this means both.[13]

There are three problems with this rationalization by Stephen Schneider. First, it shows the low regard that such scientists have for the intelligence of American citizens that pay for their research. Second, the reality is that if you are a climate scientist, there is no government money for research whose conclusions vary in any way from the mainstream narrative that a climate catastrophe is at hand. Third, once you cross the line and dramatically exaggerate, your exaggeration will inevitably be exposed, thus causing further erosion of the public's confidence in your scientific conclusions. "It is the height of hubris for a scientist even to consider deliberately misinforming policy discussions in service of what they believe to be ethical," said Koonin.[14]

I cannot highly enough recommend reading the book *Unsettled?* by Koonin. His book is filled with tables and charts and data that utilize science to refute many of the conclusions of both climate alarmists and skeptics, yet he makes a very good case for being concerned about the potential long-range impact of humans on the world's environment, particularly the growing concentration of CO_2 in our atmosphere. However, while Dr. Koonin goes into great depth on a number of ways to reduce CO_2 emissions, even the gasification of coal,[15] he dismisses nuclear power[16] even as a partial solution because he does not regard it as a renewable source of energy.

This seems shortsighted and impractical for a number of reasons, including the fact that spent radioactive waste is not large or difficult to store safely.[17] Others, such as Elon Musk and tens of thousands of engineers, believe that nuclear power should play an important role in providing sufficient electrical energy to address future needs.[18] And clearly, neither wind nor solar-generated power provides the reliability necessary to accommodate the growing demand for electricity.

Moreover, we should always be leery of placing too much confidence in the government being able to address any problem, including climate change. The default action of government is always to raise taxes and throw money at a problem. This too often leads to making the problem worse.

The reality is that today, while the U.S. and other European nations spend billions for clean energy,

China is leading the world in new coal power plants, building more than three times as much new coal power capacity as all other countries in the world combined in 2020. It isn't alone in its reliance on coal, however. China and four other countries, India, Indonesia, Japan and Vietnam, account for more than 80% of the coal power stations planned across the world.[19]

China is also the world's largest supplier of the lithium batteries[20] used for electric cars. As such, the amount of pollution put into the atmosphere for the electric power generation from China's coal-powered plants used to produce that battery exceed "by 74%"[21] the lifetime pollution of today's gas and diesel-powered cars and trucks.

Today's [gasoline-powered] vehicles emit only about 1 percent of the pollution than they did in the 1960s, and new innovations continue to improve those engines' efficiency and cleanliness.[22]

And to compound the problem, efforts to develop domestic lithium mines here in the U.S. are often opposed and blocked by environmental and conservation groups[23] that otherwise are supportive of electric automobiles and trucks. Curiously, they are okay with China mining for lithium, but not the United States, as if pollution in China is okay, but not here. That is bizarre since humans in both China and the U.S. draw oxygen from the very same atmosphere.

Equally confusing was President Biden's cancellation of the Keystone Pipeline, blocking fracking, reversing exploration in Alaska's Arctic National Wildlife Refuge (ANWR), and taking other measures that ended the energy independence of the United States (that had been achieved by the Trump administration).

> Canceling the Keystone XL is hugely symbolic . . . it will have only a very small impact on climate change . . .. To give some sense of the scope of this change, it will offset less than eleven days of the increase in China's 2020 December emissions. Similarly, America rejoining the Paris Agreement will by itself reduce temperature rises by the end of the century by just 0.015°F.[24]

Spending billions or even trillions in tax dollars to achieve no or nearly no results in terms of addressing climate change that will result in increased poverty in the United States simply makes no sense.

> The truth is that climate policies hurt the poor everywhere . . . because higher energy prices have a disproportionate negative impact on the poor . . . . One 2019 study showed that U.S. low-income consumers spend 85 percent more on electricity as a percentage of total expenditures than high-income consumers.[25]

This observation confirms the point previously made that artificially raising the price of energy is effectively a racist policy since a disparate share of the poor in our nation is made up of minorities, including Black and Hispanic Americans.

And let us not forget that not all gas and oil is equal when it comes to pollution.

Russian gas piped to Europe has up to 22 percent more greenhouse gas emissions than European coal. U.S. liquefied natural gas (LNG) delivered to the EU, in contrast, has up to 56 percent fewer total emissions than EU coal.[26]

The lesson is that there are no perfect solutions to environmental issues, whether it be powering automobiles or generating electricity. In view of everything *we do not know* about climate change, it is not surprising that a 2020 Pew election poll indicated that U.S. voters ranked their concern about climate change next to last among issues considered.[27] Similarly, according to a USC Dornsife Poll, only 4 percent of American voters in the 2020 election considered climate change to be their top priority.[28] Presumably, voters place concern about man-caused climate change near the bottom of their priorities, not only because there are many unanswered questions regarding the intensity of climate change but also because there are serious issues that they feel are more pressing.

In addition, the outlandish claims by climate alarmists that have already been proven to be untrue are not helpful. In fact, climate alarmists drive away potential supporters and lessen the impact of those who have legitimate concerns about climate issues. In Appendix B (page 197) you will find the American Conservation Ethic,[29] a guide to taking action on the environment based on science, wisdom, and the historic values of the American people. It is an excellent guide to preserving our environment for future generations of Americans.

Whatever steps the United States takes in the future should not impact the personal freedom or the economic opportunity of Americans, especially young Americans.

19

PROGRESSIVE COMPASSION?

WHEN YOU TELL A CLASSMATE or a friend that you are a conservative, one of the first things they may say or assume about you is that you have no compassion. That charge has been made about conservatives for decades. For instance, a University of Pittsburgh professor

> laid out exactly how and why Trump supporters are so awful, and as it turns out, based on polling data, based on conversations with these people, based on tests given to these people and compared to their voting habits, people who support Donald Trump as a whole tend to lack compassion and empathy for their fellow human beings.[1]

According to a review of the study it showed "true sociopathic tendencies among these diehard Donald Trump supporters."[2]

Of course, such attacks on conservatives are nothing new: "One prominent newspaper columnist stated [that Ronald] Reagan was 'the most antipoor, antiblack, and antidisadvantaged [president] in the latter half of the 20th Century.'"[3]

Not to be outdone, soon after Reagan's death, the *Baltimore Chronicle* published an article titled "Killer, Coward, Conman: Good Riddance Gipper!"[4] The article itself said that Reagan declared a "war on the poor and anyone who couldn't buy designer dresses."[5] It added, "It was the New Meanness, bringing starvation back to America so that every millionaire could get another million."[6]

While the corporate media and big tech, along with all progressives, view Reagan, Trump, and all conservatives as mean-spirited and uncaring, is that really true? Do conservatives lack generosity? Are progressives truly compassionate?

What about Americans in general? Are they compassionate and caring? How do average citizens respond to a natural crisis caused by tornados or hurricanes or earthquakes that affect their fellow citizens? How personally generous are they in donating or volunteering to help others in need? How involved are they in organizations and societies fighting diseases, helping the downtrodden, and assisting older people in need? And how do conservatives and progressives objectively measure up when it comes to personal compassion and generosity?

Fortunately, there are reliable, objective yardsticks for measuring the generosity and compassion of conservatives, of liberals, and of all Americans. Thanks to Dr. Arthur C. Brooks and his book *Who Really Cares*, and to the publication *Giving USA*, which tracks all giving on an annual basis, we can ascertain who is compassionate and generous and who is not. While Brooks's book was published a few years back, there is no reason to believe that his survey results are any less accurate today than when his book was published.

Before proceeding to analyze the compassion or lack thereof of both progressives and conservatives, let us look at the generosity of American citizens as a whole. Is the United States of America a generous nation? Yes, compared to the rest of the world, both in terms of the percent of Americans who donate and in actual amounts, this is a very generous nation. In 2021 Americans freely and willingly donated $324 billion dollars.[7] That total is more than the annual budget of Russia, more than the annual budget of Mexico, and more than the budgets of many other nations.

Progressives like to ignore the objective results of the data because it does not put them in a good light. The data not only shows that as a group, progressives are in fact the ones who lack personal compassion, but it also shows that it is conservatives who are the most compassionate and generous members of our society.

To deflect from this objective truth, progressives argue that real compassion is about voting for candidates who will spend tax dollars on social programs, not the dollars freely and willingly donated by Americans to help their fellow citizens in need. This is an odd standard of measurement for sure.

The problem with the progressive argument is that far too often their tax-supported social spending makes the problem worse, as in the case of the failed Great Society.[8] Moreover, the money that is forcefully taken by the government in the form of taxes is too often not provided to those in need out of compassion but rather for the purpose of cynical benefit. Even if your congressman or senator is truly compassionate, government spending is a very ineffective, inefficient way to help fellow citizens, and more often than not the outcome is the opposite of that hoped for. In contrast, individuals voluntarily providing funds, especially at the local level, personifies the true meaning of charity, that is, love.

It is also worth noting that Americans don't pay taxes as an act of compassion; they pay them because they are required to do so by law. If you don't pay your taxes, you will end up paying a huge fine or even going to jail. No one deserves credit for being compassionate because they pay taxes.

True compassion is only about a person spending their time or money in support of those in need. Or to put it another way, if I force you to spend your money and time to help others, you are *not* being compassionate; you are "giving" under duress. On the other hand, if you freely and gladly donate your time and money to help others, that is the very definition of being compassionate. As it says in 2 Corinthians 9:7,

> Each of you should give what you have decided in your heart to give, not reluctantly or under compulsion, for God loves a cheerful giver.[9]

In his book, Brooks argues that "conservative principles are most congenial to the four forces of charity," which he identifies as "religion, skepticism of government in economic life, strong families, and personal entrepreneurism."[10] He goes on to make the case that real charity "has to be consensual and beneficial."[11] Too many times a politician who votes to spend tax dollars ostensibly to help the poor is really voting to make the poor believe he is compassionate so that they will vote for him in an upcoming election. He is, in effect, trying to buy their vote with tax dollars. That's not compassion; that's cynical exploitation. Conversely, charity is an intentional act of the heart, giving time and/or money voluntarily to help someone in need or to benefit a cause deemed valuable to society without the donor receiving any benefit whatsoever.

In addition, Brooks also provides data that strongly suggest that personal "charity is important to our personal prosperity, happiness, health, and ability to express ourselves humanely."[12]

In other words, donating time or money enriches both the recipient and the donor, who is blessed by the good work they have done to help. Giving freely and gladly is the precise description of compassion—giving not because you have to, or because it will help you, but simply out of love to help another human being.

While the corporate media often describe conservatives as being tightwads and progressives as compassionate, the reality, as it turns out, is the exact opposite. When it comes to charitable giving, whether it be to secular causes or to religious-based causes, the data show conclusively that conservatives are more generous than progressives, even though the average income level of progressives is slightly higher than that of conservatives.[13]

> Secular liberals [progressives] are poor givers. They are 19 percentage points less likely to give each year than religious conservatives, and 9 points less likely than the population in general.[14]

Unsurprisingly, this applies not only to financial gifts and volunteering, but also to donating blood. One poll shows that progressives are "12 percent less likely to give money to charities, and one-third less likely to give blood."[15]

Moreover, "People living in conservative states volunteer more than people in liberal states."[16]

Accordingly, the study conducted by Brooks shows that progressives are far less charitable than conservatives, especially Christian conservatives, even when it comes to donating to secular organizations[17] such as the United Way.

Nor is this less-than-compassionate approach to the poor something new to the Progressive movement. It was none other than the "saint" of progressivism, Margaret Sanger (founder of Planned Parenthood), who condemned charitable groups for helping the poor and providing medical services to them, writing,

> Those vast, complex, interrelated organizations aiming to control and to diminish the spread of misery and destitution and all the menacing evils that spring out of this sinisterly fertile soil, are the surest sign that our civilization has bred, is breeding and is perpetuating constantly increasing numbers of defectives, delinquents and dependents. My criticism, therefore, is not directed at the "failure" of philanthropy, but rather at its success.[18]

Do Margaret Sanger's words sound compassionate to you? Of course not. Compassion is caring about every single one of God's children, no matter their problems, their health issues, their race, their economic status, or their ethnicity.

Neither is it compassionate to open our borders to those who refuse to follow the legal immigration process and illegally cross our borders. The Left wants open borders not for reasons of compassion but solely for crass political reasons.

A tweet by progressive Max Lefeld, founder of Casa Venezuela Dallas foundation, a charity that proclaims it is dedicated to helping refugees, accidentally exposed the true "compassion" of the Left. Lefeld referred to the sending of forty illegal border crossers from Venezuela to Martha's Vineyard by Florida Governor Ron DeSantis this way: "It's like me taking my trash out and just driving to different areas where I live and just throwing my trash there."[19]

Referring to border crossers as "trash" doesn't sound like compassion to me. The lack of true compassion by the Left was further exposed by the cold reception the migrants received from the well-connected wealthy progressive elites in Martha's Vineyard (a sanctuary city), who pulled strings to have the Army quickly hustle the migrants off the island to a military base. Some compassion, some sanctuary city!

Progressives ignore the fact that those who illegally cross our border take away jobs from poor American citizens and drive down their wages. So does the evidence show that progressives really care about the welfare of poor Americans or even the illegals who cross our southern border? Sadly, that does not appear to be the case.

By their words and their deeds, the record shows that it is conservatives, not progressives, who support providing the poor with a good education via school choice. It is conservatives, not progressives, who believe in inexpensive energy because we know that high energy costs make it very difficult for the poor to escape poverty. It is conservatives, not progressives, who give of their time and money to help the poor overcome poverty. They do it voluntarily and generously, and that's true compassion.

20

DOING GOOD?

AS CONSERVATIVES we seek not to expand government and its reach over our lives, but to instead shrink it, thus expanding individual freedom for all Americans. As the Sharon Statement says,

> The purpose of government is to protect [individual freedom] through the preservation of internal order, the provision of national defense, and the administration of justice [and that] when government ventures beyond these rightful functions, it accumulates power, which tends to diminish order and liberty.

It is when government goes beyond the limited powers that are specifically enumerated in the United States Constitution "to do good" that our personal freedoms are constricted and the intent of the Founders is violated.

The truth is very few judges (or politicians) understand that when government endeavors to do "good," it more often than not does the opposite. Think of the destruction of the Black family by the Great Society. Think of nation-building. Think of the No Child Left Behind Act. Think of Red Flag laws that violate the due process of law guaranteed to each citizen under the U.S. Constitution. Think of every well-intentioned welfare program ever dreamed up by any president. Think of the Patriot Act that was rushed through Congress and signed into law by President George W. Bush that allows the government to spy on its own citizens.[1] That law that was passed in haste is now a slippery slope toward a police state. Today the Patriot Act has been weaponized by the Left against their political opponents. The Act is a horrible abridgement of your constitutional rights that certainly had a well-intentioned origin but has resulted in a very dangerous outcome. The number of examples of damage done by well-meaning judges, legislators, and presidents is nearly endless.

Clearly, it is not sufficient to have good intentions. If you want to "do good," that is, if you want to actively solve social problems, join with other individuals, faith-based organizations, and charities that are successfully addressing the problems directly. Become a doctor, a nurse, a scientist, an inventor, a police officer, a firefighter, a member of the National Guard, an EMT, work for a nonprofit, or simply be someone who helps those in need by volunteering your time or donating generously to organizations that are making a difference. Government's attempts to "do good" or protect us from ourselves are far less successful than private efforts and always come at the cost of our liberty. The role of government is not to help everyone; it is to preserve freedom and maintain order and justice in society, and when it goes beyond those legitimate functions, the freedom of all Americans is endangered.

Don't use the blunt force of government and other people's money to express your compassion or concern. That's not compassion; that's self-delusion for political gain. Almost every time, the well-intentioned efforts by those in government to "do good"—such as the Patriot Act, Red Flag Laws, nation-building, or Great Society welfare programs—end up doing more harm than good.

And regarding societal problems that must be addressed, in 2008 Barack Obama, in a Father's Day speech, pleaded for Black families to be strong and intact and rightly decried the absence of fathers in Black homes, saying,

> If we are honest with ourselves, we'll admit that what too many fathers also are, is missing—missing from too many lives and too many homes. They have abandoned their responsibilities, acting like boys instead of men. And the foundations of our families are weaker because of it.
>
> You and I know how true this is in the African American community. We know that more than half of all black children live in single-parent households, a number that has doubled—doubled—since we were children. We know the statistics—that children who grow up without a father are five times more likely to live in poverty and commit crime; nine times more likely to drop out of schools, and 20 times more likely to end up in prison. They are more likely to have behavioral problems, or run away from home or become teenage parents themselves. And the foundations of our community are weaker because of it.[2]

But today, Black Lives Matter[3] and many others on the far Left now deny that the preservation of the family unit is essential to the success and prosperity of Black Americans. David Brooks, writing in *The Atlantic*, even called reliance on the nuclear family "a mistake."[4] Today, if you state your belief in the importance of a nuclear family you may be called a racist. But the truth is that this critical foundation of a free society, a nuclear family with a mom, a dad, and children is fast disappearing among all races.

This is frightening because as one who has for more than thirty-five years been involved in a youth home for at-risk boys and girls, I can tell you that to deny the value of an intact family being beneficial to all races is not only wrong but very detrimental to children and thus to our society. Nearly all the boys and girls that come to our home are from broken families. The intact family unit is the essential building block of any successful society. The truth is that progressives who do not support the nuclear family are leading our nation down the path that too often ends in human tragedy and despair.

> Across the United States, the nuclear family is very much in decline. Half a century ago, 42 percent of American families were nuclear; today, that figure has dropped to just 22 percent."[5]

This is truly a human tragedy for millions of boys and girls.

At our residence home we have strong male and female role models for our at-risk boys and girls. In addition, we provide all children with a solid education, instill self-discipline, promote character, and encourage faith in God. We are more often than not rewarded with amazing results.

Children and people of all ages need love and compassion and self-discipline to succeed in life. The decline of the nuclear family and the decline in quality of public education are two of the most serious problems facing this nation.

While progressives give lip service to the idea that a good education is the quickest and most sure route to escaping poverty, they continue to block high performance choice schools in poor areas. Why? Because their support would preclude progressive candidates for public office from receiving funds from the teachers' unions.[6] And it would eliminate much of the Left's ability to indoctrinate school children with their radical ideas such as CRT.

Barack Obama promised to use the power of government for good. In fact, he even complained about the U.S. Constitution, saying in a radio interview before he became president that it is "a charter of negative liberties"[7] that fails because it does not "say what the Federal government or State government must do on your behalf."[8] In other words liberty, as redefined by Barack Obama, Franklin D. Roosevelt, Woodrow Wilson, and those who founded the Progressive movement in the late 1800s, does not mean that every citizen has the right to make their own decisions as to how they will live. Instead, it means that government should not be limited to the specific enumerated powers in the United States Constitution.

Instead, "enlightened" progressives believe they should have the power to go beyond the Constitution and "do good" *for* Americans. But in reality, the best thing any congressman or president can do for the American people is to ensure equal opportunity for all, administer justice fairly, and make sure that every citizen of the United States enjoys maximum individual freedom to follow their dreams and to be able to use their talents and abilities to serve others.

The temptation to do good *for* Americans is very hard for members of Congress, jurists on the Supreme Court, and a president to resist. But we as conservatives must be wary of men and women in government— regardless of political party—who, with the very best of intentions, seek to use government to *do* good. President George W. Bush, a good and patriotic American, succumbed to that temptation when, because he truly cared about the education of the poor, pushed his No Child Left Behind (NCLB) Act through Congress. It sounded good, it even looked like it had a chance of working, but

> Ten years after its implementation, however, research on NCLB suggests that the achievement levels of the nation's students, teachers and school districts remain significantly below established benchmarks.[9]

The failure of NCLB is not surprising for a number of reasons,[10] including the fact that Congress eliminated the school choice option that was in the original draft provided by the Bush administration.

The distortion of the original intent of what the Founders carefully wrote into the U.S. Constitution has led to all sorts of mischief. It has created our welfare state that has only made things worse for the poor and made it harder for them to escape poverty. It has stifled economic growth that, as President John F. Kennedy put it, is like a rising tide that "lifts all boats,"[11] meaning that when the general economy improves, everyone at all income levels benefits—from rich to poor and everyone in between.

But apparently, for today's progressives, America should not be the "land of opportunity" but rather the "land of entitlement." They assert that instead of "equal opportunity" for all we must have "equity," equal outcomes for all, a utopian dream if there ever was one. They believe that they can use the power of government to do good for all even though their record does not substantiate that they have actually used government to do good. The mistake of progressives is that they believe our rights are granted to us by government, not God, as the Founders believed. They are simply wrong. As President Donald Trump put it, "Our rights are not given to us by man; our rights come from our Creator."[12]

When you believe that rights come from the government, you have replaced the power of God with the power of government, and accordingly those who run government become demigods. Those in power then dictate where you will live, what kind of automobile you will drive, how far you can drive it, where you will work, what you will get paid, and every other aspect of your life. But wait. That's a description of socialism, isn't it?

And we know that socialism doesn't mean universal prosperity but rather prosperity for the elites and universal misery for the poor, with no middle class whatsoever. There is no economic ladder of success to climb under socialism. Progressives promise good for all as they define it and as government provides it through socialism. But conservatives understand that big government that seeks to do good is a mirage that inevitably destroys the American Dream and the Pilgrims' vision of our nation as a "shining city on a hill."[13]

21

THEY WANT TO SHUT YOU UP!

TODAY, the big club that the Left uses to silence conservatives is charging conservatives, no matter their race or ethnicity, with being racist, or more recently, with being White supremacists. If you are White, you will be told you have White privilege. And you will be called an Uncle Tom if you are a Black conservative. You will be called a coconut if you are a conservative Hispanic.

The fact is you can never win this argument by simply denying to be a racist or a White supremacist. It won't help to point out your long relationship with Black friends or even that you are yourself Black. The Left's goal is to silence you and to cancel you. Because they reject traditional standards of ethics and morality, progressive teachers and professors won't hesitate to make fun of you in front of the class or mark down your grade because you dared to disagree with them. It is unfair, but that is reality in the twenty-first century.

It wasn't always that way. The principled professor who agreed to be a sponsor of a chapter of Young Americans for Freedom when I was attending college was a self-proclaimed liberal, not a conservative. I knew several conservative professors, but they were intimidated from being a faculty sponsor of our YAF chapter. Liberals/progressives used to pride themselves on being defenders of free speech, and they were—like our YAF chapter sponsor—but those folks are long gone.

They have been replaced by Marxist radicals who identify themselves as progressives. They don't believe that any conservative has a right to free speech, to publish a book, to write a column, to be on the radio, to have a podcast or a blog, to be on the Internet or on television. As NBC anchor Lester Holt put it,

> I think it's become clear that fairness is overrated . . . the idea that we should always give two sides equal weight and merit does not reflect the world we find ourselves in.[1]

Clearly, Holt is worried about giving "equal weight" to conservative speech but not worried at all about the Left's perspective on the issues, which dominates nightly news broadcasts by NBC. The fact is, no matter their lack of honesty or accuracy, the speech of the Left is protected, but conservative speech is not, especially on college and university campuses. Why? The only logical conclusion one can make is that the Left knows that their arguments are so weak and flawed that they cannot survive in an atmosphere of free and open debate. That's why today's Marxist progressives want absolutely nothing whatsoever to do with free speech. They know that they cannot advance their cause or even keep it from shrinking if free speech is allowed. Remember their meltdown when Elon Musk bought Twitter[2] promising to offer free and open speech? Free speech on Twitter or any social media platform terrifies the Left.

So how does a White conservative respond to charges that they are a racist? How does a black conservative respond to a charge of being an Uncle Tom or a Hispanic conservative being called a coconut? I have already shown you how to easily dismantle charges of being a Nazi, but how do you refute the idea that you are a racist or a sell-out?

Surprisingly, it is rather simple, as I have alluded to earlier in this book. The history of the Progressive movement is riddled with racism, cozying up to Nazis, and playing footsie with bloodthirsty communists like Stalin. When you are attacked, don't play defense, go on offense. Point out the fact that the Progressive movement began in racism and is still racist today. Let's reiterate just a few of their current racist policies.

Education is a good place to start. The Left insists that it is conservatives who are keeping poor Black children from getting a good education. But the facts show otherwise. It is progressive politicians (progressives at the state and national level) who have repeatedly blocked high-performance choice schools in poor Black communities. Today most poor Black (and Hispanic) children attend failing public schools that do not provide them with a good education. These children have very little chance of escaping poverty. They can't read at grade level, they can't do simple math, their English comprehension is poor, and they are not prepared to attend and succeed even at a public junior high or high school.

> Twelfth-grade black students are performing at the level of middle school white students. These students are about to graduate, yet they lag four or more years behind in every area including math, science, writing, history, and geography.[3]

Do progressives care? Apparently not. When progressive legislators at the state level have an opportunity to support the creation of a school voucher program (the voucher can be used by minority parents to choose the best school to educate their child), they repeatedly vote against school vouchers in these communities.

Why, why would they do that and harm Black and Hispanic students? The answer becomes clear when you consider that in the

2020 election cycle the teachers unions (National Education Association [NEA] and the American Federation of Teachers [AFT]) donated $129.6 million to progressive candidates for public office.[4] The unions do this on the condition that progressive candidates oppose school choice. The very last thing that teachers unions want is competition. The simple fact is that progressive candidates choose the big dollars from the teachers unions over a good education for poor Black students. The truth is that progressive politicians are captives of the teachers unions, the NEA and the AFT.

I don't believe these progressive politicians really want poor Black (and Hispanic) students to fail. The reality is that they simply can't resist the avalanche of money from these teachers unions, and if they don't take the dollars from the union and block choice schools, they know they will face a well-funded primary opponent in the next election. Sadly, it does not make any difference if the politician is Black, White, or Hispanic: they always take the money. Hypocritically, many self-proclaimed progressive legislators send their children to high-performing private schools. They want the very best education for *their* children, but they block a similarly good education for poor Black and Hispanic children. Point out the hypocrisy of the Left.

When parents are given vouchers by the state government to spend at any school of their choice, they opt out of failing public schools in droves. Such voucher programs empower parents to put their children in schools they believe will give their children the best possible education. And because public schools are so bad in minority communities, parents understandably use their voucher to pay for their child's education at a school where they will actually learn and have a chance to escape poverty.

The good news is that if placed into a situation where public schools must compete with private schools for school voucher money, the public schools would be forced to improve in order to retain students. Competition always brings out the best results, whether in sports, business, or education. It is an undeniable fact that the school voucher programs provide a very big leg up for poor Black students and help them escape poverty. Nevertheless, the Left continues to oppose school choice.

One more reason progressive politicians oppose school choice is the likelihood that a high-quality school voucher program may be sponsored by a church or by a group of Christians, even conservative Christians. And it is likely that school won't use the progressive textbooks and videos that are used in public schools. And these schools certainly won't promote Marxist critical race theory (CRT). Many progressive politicians fear this possibility more than they crave the money from the NEA. They don't want to lose the power to brainwash students with dangerous Marxist CRT nonsense as they do all across our nation in our public schools.

The undeniable truth is that opposition to school voucher programs and continued support for failing public schools for Black Americans is racist. The progressive Left's racism needs to be pointed out. And from an education perspective, their opposition to school choice is foolish. Competition always improves products and services, and when introduced into the education system, it will create better private *and* public schools.

Another issue worth discussing with an open-minded fellow student is abortion. Remind your friend that in America today the number one cause of death for Black Americans is abortion.[5] Also, explain to her that Planned Parenthood intentionally locates more than 70 percent of their abortion facilities near poor Black and Hispanic communities.[6] They also run radio ads promoting abortion over Black radio stations. In the 2020 election, Planned Parenthood donated some $45 million to progressive candidates[7] who were pro-abortion and who voted to fund the organization with your tax dollars.

While Planned Parenthood claims that they do not target Black babies for abortion, that is simply untrue as documented earlier in this book. As previously noted, some 22 million Black babies have been killed[8] since the U.S. Supreme Court made abortion the law of the land. If targeting Black babies for abortion is not racist, what is? If the person you are talking to is even slightly open-minded, he or she will have to think twice about supporting racist politicians.

Regarding women's rights, how can a fair and open-minded person support the destruction of women's sports by transgender biological men? Today, progressives actively support the idea of transgender "girls/women"—that is, men who believe/say they are female—competing against biological girls/women in sports.

Yes, these transgender individuals are required to undergo hormone therapy, but that does not change the fact that their male bone structure and their male muscles, hearts, and lungs are larger than that of women. These facts result in an unfair physical advantage of transgender "women/girls" (biological men) over biological female athletes. For example, "In 2018, 275 high school boys ran the 400 meter faster than the lifetime best of Olympic Team USA member and world-record-holding sprinter Allyson Felix."[9]

For many years young Black female athletes have used their athletic prowess to obtain college scholarships and escape poverty. But now they are being denied this opportunity by progressives who support transgender individuals (biological men) competing against female athletes. This is not only sexist but also racist because a disproportionate number of female athletes are Black, especially when it comes to track and field events as well as basketball. Accordingly, these transgender individuals destroy the one hope that many young Black females have to escape poverty: a college athletic scholarship. Your friend probably does not know these facts, but you can point them out to her.

Jobs for Black and Hispanic Americans is another issue you can use to persuade a friend that progressives are racist. Progressives claim to want jobs for Black Americans, but their policies have failed for years; yet they say that it is conservatives who want to deny Black Americans jobs. As previously noted, the reality is that policies like open borders steal jobs and drive down wages of Black Americans and other minorities by flooding the job market with illegals. Accordingly, it is oxymoronic to call Trump and his supporters racist, considering it was his conservative policies (recommended by the Heritage Foundation, among others) that lifted Black employment rates to the highest levels recorded in American history.[10] In addition, Trump's conservative policies increased Black home ownership for the first time in decades and increased Black wages in real dollars for the first time in thirty years.[11]

On energy prices, on Black nuclear families, on Black self-defense, on peaceful and safe Black communities, progressives always take the racist position. Why is this important? Because you can neutralize the attacks on you and successfully persuade other students by simply and calmly pointing out the truth that the positions that progressives take on these issues are racist.

You can also cite facts and data that prove that free markets work and socialism always fails. No matter the issue—because conservatism is really common sense—you have a chance to persuade others that the Marxist progressive agenda is just one big, uninformed lie.

Don't be conned into playing defense or getting angry. You have the truth and the facts on your side. But you can't win over converts if you don't have the facts straight. That's why it is crucial for you to be well informed on all the issues of the day.

22

HOW TO PERSUADE OTHERS

IT IS IMPORTANT for you and me and every conservative to persuade others who have been duped by the Left to seriously consider our conservative point of view. I know such persuasion is challenging. Truthfully, I fail at this more times than I succeed. Calm persuasion is not my typical default response, and it may not be yours. Too often we want to score points, zing those who disagree with us, make them look foolish, and call out their hypocrisy. That's what we see on TV and hear on blogs and talk radio. But we need converts, not more enemies, and the place to find those prospective converts is among the uninformed who mouth progressive ideas but honestly don't really know what they are talking about. Don't waste your time or breath trying to convince someone who is a strongly committed progressive to change their position. Instead, talk to that fellow student who may be open to hearing what we might call "the other side of the story."

Before you start the conversation, remember that your goal is not to "win" the argument but rather to persuade the person who disagrees with you—or is just questioning—that the conservative approach to culture and to government really works. A good starting point is finding out what your prospective conservative is really interested in and what their current thinking is on a particular issue. It would also help to know how they came to a particular point of view.

> One way to approach people is to ask them questions politely, rather than to confront them with a direct argument. Let them think things through for themselves, rather than create intransigence. If you get a positive result, ask yet another question, but resist the temptation to go too far. You don't want the snail to go back into its shell. When they're by themselves, they'll have something to think about.[1]

By asking questions you will begin to understand where the person you are talking to is on a Left-to-Right scale. This will give you an inkling of what your approach should be and where you might find common ground. The basic idea is to meet the person you want to persuade where they are.

It is advisable to steer clear of unpopular issues and especially issues that your friend feels strongly about. If a fellow student is firm in their views on foreign policy or some domestic issue and you insist on challenging those views, you will not only *not* persuade that student to your perspective but are more likely to drive them further away.

Remember, Ronald Reagan was not only a great communicator but also a great persuader. He had to work with a Democrat-controlled House of Representatives and that meant working with the Speaker of the House, Tip O'Neill. Not only did Reagan not insult him, he had O'Neill over to the White House often and developed a personal friendship with him. Once he did that, O'Neill was less resistant to working with Reagan. Similarly, when you find some common ground with your prospective conservative (sports interest? movie genres? music?), you will have taken a major step toward getting them to listen to you. Moreover, after finding out as much as possible about your fellow student and letting them talk, you will have an opportunity to speak.

And don't forget, Rome wasn't built in a day. Your job as an advocate for freedom is to chip away and plant seeds that will eventually take root. Don't expect a transformation in fifteen minutes. Pride causes a person to cling to their views. It takes time and patience to bring someone over to your point of view. It often takes months or even years for someone to embrace conservatism because the media has told so many lies about conservatives. Be persistent, but do not be obnoxious. Perhaps the second time you talk, you can share an article or newspaper column with your new friend. And don't hesitate to quote from or share articles by those who do not fit corporate media's profile of conservatives—folks like Ben Carson, Shelby Steele, Thomas Sowell, Ben Shapiro, and Candace Owens.

You can also introduce your friends to conservative websites, podcasts, and books by Walter Williams, Milton Friedman, and Frederick Hayek. In fact, Hayek's book *Road to Serfdom* provides a very good understanding of free markets and why they work and why socialism always fails. Walter Williams's book *Race and Economics* might prove to be an eye-opener for those who do not understand that the Left has greatly damaged the economic prospects of Black America. Similarly, *White Guilt* by Shelby Steele provides a perspective on civil rights from Black American intellectuals that is not often heard. And as a former radical leftist and leader of the New Left in the 1960s, David Horowitz's book *Radical Son* is a convincing story of why he left the Marxist Left to become a conservative. Similarly, Thomas Sowell's book *A Personal Odyssey* is a compelling story of his personal journey from being a Marxist-leaning Marine to being one of the greatest intellectual lights in the Conservative movement.

It turns out that it's not sufficient for you to personally understand the conservative approach to foreign policy, economics, and cultural issues. You must be an informed advocate for what you believe in if you are to become an effective member of the freedom generation.

Benjamin Franklin was considered to be the most persuasive of all of the Founders when it came to dealing with an issue of critical importance. Franklin wasn't just well read and thoughtful—although he was both of those things—he was also practiced in the art of persuasion. This was his advice concerning the best way to get someone to consider his point of view:

> [I expressed] myself in terms of modest diffidence; never using when I advanced anything that may possibly be disputed, the words "certainly," "undoubtedly," or any others that give the air of positiveness to an opinion; but rather say, "I conceive or apprehend a thing to be so and so"; "it appears to me," or "I should think so, for such and such reasons"; or "I imagine it to be so"; or "it is so, if I am not mistaken." This habit, I believe, has been of great advantage to me when I have had an occasion to inculcate my opinions, and persuade men into measures that I have been from time to time engag'd in promoting.[2]

What Franklin is saying in today's vernacular regarding persuasion is don't charge into a conversation like a bull in a china shop, acting like a know-it-all who is going to set the other person straight. That won't work no matter how loudly you say it, how emphatic you are, and no matter how right you are. That's one of the reasons the American people no longer trust corporate media. The daily browbeating of patriotic Americans, the talking down to them and insulting them has resulted in a dramatic decline in the media's trustworthiness according to Gallup[3] and justifiably so.

> If all we're interested in is running our mouths and showing our own importance, not in persuading others to adopt our ideas, then we should follow in the media's steps.[4]

The truth of the matter is most of the high school and college students you will encounter who have accepted progressive ideas from their teachers and professors are simply not well informed. They are ignorant of history because much of what they have been told is simply not true. In fact, in many, if not most, cases it is the opposite of the truth.

There is a little paperback book written more than fifty years ago by California conservative leader Bill Richardson[5] called *Slightly to the Right*[6] that provides great advice on persuading others to the conservative cause. In this slim book, Richardson explains that although he had all the facts on his side, he not only lost arguments but also became a pariah at social events due to his boisterous passion for the conservative cause and his unbending instance that he was right on every issue. He was a "know it all," and that's why he was tuned out.

Eventually, he realized that his tactless, bullheaded approach wasn't working, so he redefined and refined his social approach into one that was persuasive, not insistent, and that is what his marvelous book is all about. In the book, Bill humorously describes the various stages of becoming a conservative and eventually an effective conservative. You may even grimace, as I did, realizing that I had too often approached others with a bossy "know it all" approach that Richardson originally did.

Here are a few gems from *Slightly to the Right.*[7]

Knowing your facts and proving your point with documentation doesn't necessarily guarantee a sale.

How many times have you been irrefutably right on a matter and yet unable to convince the other person?

Some [conservatives] are as welcome in social gatherings as the bubonic plague.

Knowledge about ourselves and how we react to given situations can mean the difference between winning converts and chasing people further [away].

Because of our convictions we frequently seem overbearing; in other words we come on like the wrath of God.

Instead of getting mad at [the misinformed person we are trying to win over], we should realize "There but for the grace of God go I."

Bill's point is that sometimes we are our own worst enemy when it comes to persuading others that our commonsense conservative principles really do work. The more we are liked and are likable, the more respected and effective we will be in persuading someone that they are misinformed. (And don't tell them that they are misinformed; that will simply get their dander up.) The more we show kindness and make it clear that we respect and like the person we are talking to, the more they will be open to listening.

So when you are entering a discussion and seek to win over someone to your conservative perspective on a particular issue, try this approach:

- Tone. Take an approach more like Ben Franklin than Ivan the Terrible. Don't offend them, befriend them.

- Know who you are talking to. Think about where they are coming from, what they have been reading, listening to, and so on. Try to learn just how much the person you are speaking to knows about the topic you are discussing. Identify, if you can, something that you have in common with the person you are talking to. It can be something as innocent as a passion for baseball or fishing or reading or cooking or traveling. Be a good listener.

- Be specific. Don't use generalizations or a broad-brush approach that can often backfire or sidetrack you from making the point you wish to make.

- Ask questions. Don't just make declarative statements. Ask questions, and when you do make a statement, then follow it up with another question.

- Stay on track. Don't let yourself get thrown off track. Don't be derailed by an out-of-the blue question. Stay on topic, but do it courteously. And don't keep talking and talking to the point you turn your listener off.

- Compliment. Compliment the person you are speaking to on their knowledge and intelligence. Don't ever give the listener the idea that you think you are smart and they are stupid. If you do, all efforts to persuade will end right there.

- Humor. Do your best to offer a little humor and laugh, even at yourself, to help make the conversation truly enjoyable. Self-deprecation can be helpful in building trust.

- Quote authorities. Quote an authority that you believe is respected by the person you are having an enjoyable conversation with.

- Double standards. Make reference to the double standards practiced by the Left, such as one standard of justice for those on the right and a completely different standard for those on the Left. Memorize a few examples. Be sure to provide an example that the person you are talking to can understand and is likely to agree with. No one likes unfairness, and pointing out that something is clearly unfair is very powerful.

Believe me, too often I don't do what I say, and I offend instead of persuade. These are tough guidelines to follow, but practice will get you closer and closer to being an effective communicator for the conservative cause. Oddly, while I often blow it when trying to persuade others to my political point of view, I was never that way when talking with clients or prospective clients in my business pursuits. I would endeavor to find something I had in common with them, get to know them better, and listen carefully in order to make sure that I understood their concerns, met their needs, served them well, and convinced them that we were the right firm to raise the money they sought. I would have benefitted from taking the same approach when entering a political conversation.

Never underestimate the impact of finding something about which you both are interested in and agree upon, and don't just brush over it. When you find that common ground, you are taking a big step toward gaining credibility when you discuss other topics.

Now, if you really want to be effective in winning over converts to our conservative cause, read this short chapter once more and keep it in mind the next time you come across a prospective conservative convert.

23

WIN! STAY ON OFFENSE!

THE GOAL OF THE CONSERVATIVE MOVEMENT is not only to win politically and triumph intellectually, but the more pressing problem is rolling back the tide of liberal indoctrination and lies. Conservatives want to return to a truly free republic where the size, scope, and reach of the federal government is limited to those important, even crucial responsibilities specifically enumerated in the United States Constitution. As James Madison noted in *The Federalist #45*, "The powers delegated by the proposed constitution to the federal government, are few and defined."[1]

Clearly, the father of the Constitution and those that ratified it never wanted the Constitution to allow federal government intervention into all aspects of the lives of Americans. Its primary goal was to provide for the common defense of our nation, establish order necessary to a free society, administer justice, and (as emphasized in the Bill of Rights) protect the freedom of Americans to go about their lives without the interference of government or of anyone in government.

In a truly free society, the reach and power of government is limited, and the freedom of the people is great. But in order for individual citizens to have such power, they must, as the Founders knew, seek virtue. The citizens of such a land must be honest and have character that does not bend with the wind. They must not be self-serving, but self-giving, as well as generous, compassionate, and thankful for their blessings. Of course, they must exercise self-restraint and be forgiving. In the absence of these virtues, government will, of necessity, be more powerful to constrain law breakers, and curb public vice. As previously noted, in the absence of a consensus of faith in God, there is no public virtue, and when that is lost, we are on the path to the demise of a free society.

In public debate and in discussions with other students, you must not only respond to the bad policies and attacks by those on the Left, but more importantly, you must stay on offense and carry your conservative message to others. Otherwise, you will have no opportunity to succeed in preserving individual freedom in our land. That is really what the Sharon Statement is all about: preserving and extending freedom to future generations of Americans. We cannot expect to receive the blessings of liberty from God if we do not heed His advice and acknowledge His truths. We cannot ignore His moral teachings and expect His blessings. We cannot murder the unborn and expect to be the recipients of His grace. We cannot have a free society if we do not endeavor to live by godly values.

When attacked and called an opponent of democracy, the typical response by a conservative is to go on defense and simply deny the charge. That does not work. For instance, each time a conservative goes on defense after being called an extremist, or fails to respond to that smear, it comes across as being true to others listening. Instead, boldly and honestly tell the truth without abandoning civility. Point out that it is progressives who want to censor and destroy the constitutional guarantee of free speech. It is progressives who want to expand the power of government beyond those powers enumerated in the U.S. Constitution. It is the Left that works to destroy public confidence in the outcome of elections by eliminating the requirement for a government-issued ID in order to vote. It is progressives who want to not only curtail free speech but also such constitutionally guaranteed rights as the right to keep and bear arms. It is the Left that wants to keep Christians from speaking out in the public square and constrict the religious freedom guaranteed in the U.S. Constitution. It is the Left that wants to use the power of the administrative state (the federal bureaucracy) to regulate every aspect of your life. And it is progressives who wish to diminish the power of the individual states and increase the power of the federal government. Those in the progressive Left are not defenders of democracy; they are enemies of democracy.

"You will know the truth, and the truth will set you free."[2]

Conservatives must stop cowering in the corner and instead calmly and truthfully point out the historic fact that it is progressives who by their words and deeds are not only the true racists in our society but also the enemies of limited constitutional government. They falsely accuse conservatives of being the instigators of segregation, Jim Crow laws, literacy tests, and poll taxes—all of which progressives initiated in the late 1890s. And since that time and especially today, they have worked hard to undermine freedom and democracy. Point this out and document it as I have done in this book.

When they call you a Nazi or a fascist, don't let the lie stand in silence. Point out to them in words, in flyers, in articles in the campus newspaper, or in an independent newspaper you help start that they are the ones closest to the Nazis and the fascists. It was the Nazi Nuremberg Laws (which stripped Jews of their citizenship, right to work and marry, and eventually led to the gas chambers) that were modeled after progressive laws in the South to restrict the rights of Black Americans (see books: *Hitler's American Model*[3] by James Q. Whitman and *The Big Lie*[4] by Dinesh D'Souza). Be careful to document and point out that the origin of the Nuremberg Laws is taken directly from the records of the Nazi Party.

Remind those in doubt that the violent and murderous Antifa,[5] whose members dress head to toe in black, ironically act in a manner similar to the Blackshirts of Benito Mussolini and his socialist Fascist Party. Their violence and intolerance of any other point of view also resembles the Brown Shirts of Hitler's Germany. Socialist birds of a feather flock together.

When you are on offense, you must make the Left defend themselves, you must make them play defense. Be proactive in finding ways to keep the Leftists on campus backpedaling and defending their defenseless positions. When you do that and are careful to stick to the facts and document your positions, you will be winning over the fence straddlers, those who are neither on the Right or the Left but who are closely following what is going on and trying to make up their minds.

So when you are under attack and smeared as a White supremacist, a racist, a fascist, or as a Nazi, be aware that progressives don't want to debate the issues because they know they can't win on the issues. Their only hope is to block you and other conservatives from having a platform from which to challenge their Marxist views.

Don't let them intimidate you. Assemble a group of conservatives who share like views, start a YAF chapter, participate in Campus Reform, attend a Turning Point USA meeting, or get involved in some other conservative group on campus. Once you have taken that step, bring a conservative speaker to your campus who will expose their lies, fabrications, and schemes. You can do that by contacting Patrick Coyle at Young America's Foundation.[6] Virtually every conservative speaker on campuses across the United States comes via Young America's Foundation, regardless of the sponsoring campus group.

Never forget that it is progressives who have been and are truly racist and have totalitarian instincts. If you find that one rare leftist who is willing to openly dialogue with you, there are lots of questions you can pose to them that might make them question their beliefs:

Why did progressives lead the charge for segregation in the South? Why do progressive politicians block good schools for poor Black children? Why do progressive groups specifically and disproportionately target the babies of poor Black mothers for abortion? Why do progressives ignore violence in the Black communities and deny law-abiding Black Americans their Second Amendment rights? Why do progressives support transgender men taking away sports scholarships that are often the only path to college for poor but talented Black female athletes? Why do progressives support open borders, causing millions of illegals to steal jobs from poor Black and Hispanic citizens and drive down their wages? Why do progressives want to push up the price of energy that hurts Black families the most? What do progressives have against poor Black Americans? Why do they support policies that hurt Black Americans and cause high unemployment and high inflation, stymie wage increases, and deny them the education and skills to succeed economically? In short, why are progressives so racist?

It is the Left that should be on defense whether the issue is race, freedom, economics, tolerance, jobs, wages, foreign policy, domestic policy, or our culture. The facts are on your side. All you have to do is know the facts, and then start asking your progressive opponents questions that expose the weakness of their positions.

And if you are called a Nazi, you still have all the facts to back you up. For instance, if you are called a Nazi, simply ask, "If that is true, then why did Adolf Hitler add the word 'Socialist' to the name of the National German Workers Party, making it the National *Socialist* German Workers Party?"[7] "Why did the Nazi platform he created call for the control of all major industry and dramatically expand the power of government?"[8]

Ask them to explain how a conservative who believes in small, limited government is somehow similar to tyrants who want big, powerful, total government control like the Nazis, the Fascists, or the Communists. The Left strenuously rejects the idea of small government and maximum individual freedom. All those on the Left are ideological brothers and sisters when it comes to big all-powerful government.

Similarly, if you are called a fascist, ask your accuser to explain why, in 1934, did Benito Mussolini brag that "'three-fourths of [the] Italian economy, industrial and agricultural, is in the hands of the state.'"[9]

As Jack McPherrin of the Heartland Institute explained,

> Despite what many on the political left believe, fascism and socialism share substantial commonality, uniting around centralized economic planning, collectivism over individual rights, and totalitarian ideological control over society. Essentially, fascism can be considered a more effective and advanced form of socialism. Giovanni Gentile, the true author of the original fascist experiment in Italy who ghostwrote "A Doctrine of Fascism for Benito Mussolini," directly stated, "Fascism is a form of socialism, in fact, it is its most viable form."[10]

Then if they protest and say, "That can't be true. That's a lie." Simply ask if they are willing to check it out for themselves. If they won't, why not? Remember, young progressives are often uninformed; all they can do is regurgitate leftist nonsense they heard in the classroom or have been told by another leftist. Don't forget that you have the truth on your side. The entire progressive ideology is built on lies; it's like a house of cards that can be blown over with just a few honest facts.

Conservatives must turn the tables on progressives, no matter the issue. Today, almost anything can be "racist" according to politically correct progressives and the far-Left folks in the mainstream news media. If a conservative suggests a new policy that will put more poor Black people in jobs and thus trim the welfare rolls, that conservative is a racist. If a Black progressive politician breaks the law or commits an immoral or unethical act and a conservative calls them out, the conservative is charged with being a racist. If a conservative supports the police, they are automatically deemed a racist, when the real racist is the progressive politician who says nothing when poor Black areas become war zones where innocents die due to a lack of law and order. If you are White and you disagree with a Black politician on taxes, you are called a racist.

Sadly, the worst and most venomous hatred by progressives is reserved for Black conservatives like Clarence Thomas, Ben Carson, Shelby Steele, Thomas Sowell, and Candace Owens. The attitude of leftist radicals and their allies in the news media is that no Black American can be allowed to think for themselves; they *must* toe the line on all progressive policies. Any Black American who is conservative is automatically smeared as an "Uncle Tom." Nevertheless, Candace Owens has proven that Black conservatives can not only stand up to the radical Left but also make them turn tail and retreat.[11] She always stays on offense. Talking about progressives, she noted that

> They don't want to talk about the illiteracy rates. They don't want to talk about what's actually harming black America, because let me tell you, it's not white supremacy. It's liberal supremacy.[12]

Nevertheless, the lies and smears will continue unless and until conservatives like you and me go on offense and stay on offense. The American people are onto the lies of the Left and the distortions of the corporate news media. In fact, just "17% of Americans overall trust most news organizations."[13]

This is good news because each day, the Left-leaning corporate media continues to spew out lies and falsehoods designed to keep conservatives on defense and intended to advance the progressive agenda. That's why they desperately call conservatives racist, and you can be sure that they will continue to do so. Progressives must do this to maintain their near monopoly of Black support.

Unless and until conservatives start going on offense and point out the extremely racist policies of progressives that continually harm the Black community, they will never create a flood of Black Americans to the Conservative movement. It's not just a matter of courage, it's about telling the truth. The time to go on offense is not tomorrow, it is today. Be bold, be courageous, be forthright, and speak the truth.

24

HAVE THE ANSWERS!

DON'T JUST CALL YOURSELF A CONSERVATIVE; be informed so that you can not only understand the issues of the day in the context of the conservative philosophy but also share this understanding with your friends and your family.

Being informed is more than watching *Fox & Friends,* Tucker Carlson, and Sean Hannity on Fox News or Sean Spicer on Newsmax. It's more than listening to the radio broadcasts of Dan Bonjino, Chris Plante, Mark Levine, Dana Loesh, or another conservative radio host. Those are good steps, but go deeper. Read books by conservative authors such as Victor Davis Hansen, Mark Levin, Thomas Sowell, Dinesh D'Souza, and Shelby Steele as well as those listed in the enclosed bibliography. Listen to podcasts by conservatives like Ben Shapiro, Candace

Owens, and Michael Knowles. And yes, there are still some conservative newspapers worth reading, including dailies like *The Washington Times, The New York Post,* and the *Colorado Springs Gazette,* as well as weeklies such as *The Epoch Times,* to name just a few. Of course, the editorial page of the *Wall Street Journal* is still conservative and worth a read, as is the commentary in *Investor's Business Daily.*

The big treasure of the Conservative movement, however, is in the online publications, many of which have more than a million readers per day. That's right, a number of these online publications have more readers each day than the *New York Times,* the *Los Angeles Times,* the *Houston Chronicle,* or the *Chicago Tribune.* There are some great ones out there, including but not limited to the following:

American Conservative	*The Gateway Pundit*
American Spectator	*Human Events*
American Thinker	LifeZette
The Blaze	*National Review*
Breitbart	YAF's New Guard
CBN News	*New York Post*
Daily Caller	PJ Media
Daily Signal	*RedState*
Daily Wire	*Townhall*
Epoch Times	*Western Journal*
The Federalist	*Washington Times*
Fox News	

There are obviously more conservative websites, but these are some of the high-traffic ones that together reach tens of millions of readers each day. They are both opinion outlets and news organizations with staffs, and as such, most are updated several times daily.

Equally important to the Conservative movement and to being informed are conservative podcasts, of which there are many. Here is a list of fourteen, one or more of which you may already be listening to.

#1 *Ben Shapiro Show*

#2 *Michael Knowles Show*

#3 *Andrew Klavan Show*

#4 *Matt Walsh Show*

#5 *Verdict with Ted Cruz*

#6 *Louder with Crowder*

#7 *Federalist Radio Hour*

#8 *The Derek Hunter Podcast*

#9 *Triggered, Matt Vespa & Storm Paglia*

#10 *Hashing it Out, Siraj Hashmi*

#11 *Guy Benson Show*

#12 *Livin' The Bream, Shannon Bream*

#13 *For Life, Alexandra DeSanctis*

#14 *What the Hell is Going On? Marc Thiessen & Danielle Pletka*

But it's not enough to just be informed; if you are to be an active member of the Conservative movement, you need to be personally involved. That means joining and participating in one of the many conservative youth organizations. It could mean volunteering for a political campaign. Campaigns are always looking for hardworking, reliable volunteers. That's how I got my start in politics. I went to the campaign headquarters, volunteered, and they put me to work immediately. I went day after day, and they kept giving me more responsibility until I was asked to cochair the youth effort for the candidate. Next, I joined Young Americans for Freedom, formed a local chapter, became a state chairman, attended national YAF conventions, and eventually served on the National Board of Directors of YAF.

There are lots of things you can do on your high school or college campus or in your hometown. And there are lots of great conservative youth organizations. One of the very best is Young America's Foundation. Led by former Wisconsin Governor Scott Walker, they work through Young Americans for Freedom and other conservative organizations to bring in speakers like Ben Shapiro, Dinesh D'Souza, Michael Knowles, Star Parker, Matt Walsh, Paul Kengor, Everett Piper, Sean Spicer, Rachel Campos-Duffy, Steven Moore, James O'Keefe, Peter Schweizer, Dana Loesch, and many more.

As previously noted, YAF is the primary source of conservative speakers on thousands of college and university campuses in America. Their emphasis is helping high school and college students understand the foundations of a free society and the current threats to it. As you can see in the chart on page 165, YAF does this through a powerful online presence on YouTube and via conferences for students at their headquarters in Reston, Virginia (just outside of Washington, DC), at the Reagan Ranch Center (Santa Barbara, California), and at the Ronald Reagan Boyhood Home (Dixon, Illinois). Many years ago, Young America's Foundation (today the parent organization of Young Americans for Freedom) saved Ronald Reagan's ranch when no one else was interested in doing so.

When you attend one of the topnotch high school– or college-level YAF conferences at the Reagan Ranch Center, you will have the privilege of touring the Ranch and walking in the footsteps of Ronald Reagan. (the Ranch is not open to the general public). Or you can choose to attend a Foundation conference at the Ronald Reagan Boyhood Home featuring great conservative speakers.

More than any other president before him, Reagan gave meaning to what it means to be a conservative president. It has been said that Reagan was so firm in his conservative principles that he could have governed from inside a closet. President Reagan subdued out-of-control inflation (11.8%),[1] restored prosperity to our land, defeated the Soviet Union, and made America respected again. That's what a principled conservative president does.

If you want to find out how to organize on campus, publish a campus newspaper, raise funds, and obtain publicity, then The Leadership Institute (LI) is the right place for you. Since 1979, LI has trained more than 200,000 conservative activists, leaders, and students. Founded by Morton Blackwell, LI provides training in campaigns, fundraising, grassroots organizing, youth politics, and communications. Today, LI's college campus network extends to more than 1,700 conservative campus groups and newspapers. Similar to Young America's Foundation, LI is easily accessible by Washington, DC, metro. LI also hosts multiday training sessions for those who wish to run for office or to help someone who is running for office. They also have a campus arm called Campus Reform that challenges the Left on campus and defends student rights.

Turning Point USA, another conservative youth group, hosts six national summits and eight regional conferences each year, including the Student Action Summit, the Young Women's Leadership Summit, the Young Black Leadership Summit, and a number of regionally based conferences—all designed to energize and grow the Conservative movement.

There are other great conservative student groups such as the ones shown in the following table, each serving a very good purpose, each with a particular focus. The good news is that Young Americans for Freedom, Campus Reform, Turning Point USA, and other conservative student groups often work together on campus to advance common conservative objectives. That is good for them, good for the conservative cause, and good for America.

This table provides an encouraging picture of the impact that groups like the ones mentioned above are having with millions of young Americans today over YouTube.

GROUP	SUBS	VIEWS
Young America's Foundation	1M	467M
Turning Point USA	710K	229M
Students for Life	84.7K	19.3M
Young Americans for Liberty	9.2Kk	1.2M
Students for Liberty	6.9K	626K
Leadership Institute	6.7K	606K
Intercollegiate Studies Institute	6.2K	888K

Ranked by views January 24, 2023

As you can see, each of these conservative youth groups is effective in reaching out to high school and college students. A recent survey[2] conducted on behalf of Young America's Foundation shows a definite shift in attitudes among younger Americans between high school and college. The results from this survey show that...

66 percent of high school students believe America is exceptional, compared to 47 percent of college students.

55 percent of high school students believe America is a good example for other countries, compared to 37 percent of college students.

70 percent of high school students hold a favorable view of America's history, compared to 44 percent of college students.

63 percent of high school students report feeling proud of America, compared to 40 percent of college students.

While the change in attitude due to the progressive propaganda that college students hear daily is stunning, there is some good news from the same poll.

Overall, among high school and college students, 78% view the United States favorably, which is more favorably than they view Canada, Sweden, Cuba, China, or Russia. More than half—57%—of high school and college students believe America is exceptional, while 82% hold a favorable view of the American flag.[1]

And,

More than three-quarters—79%—of students are glad they live in America. Even more—83%—believe that people around the world would love the opportunity to move to the United States. 74% of students agree that America is a work in progress that is always improving itself.[2]

These viewpoints will continue to move to the right when high school and college students join the workforce and learn that the leftist malarkey that was pushed on them by progressive teachers and professors does not match reality. When these young Americans get their first paycheck and see just how much money the government takes from it, their perspective often changes, just as it does when they learn just how ineffective and wasteful the government is.

When you participate in and join one of the groups mentioned above, you become a part of a rising popular cause that is not only holding off the radical Left but also advancing the conservative agenda. As a member of a conservative youth group, you will be ahead of the learning curve, and you will be able to assist others in understanding the facts. Remember, the conservative agenda is like that of America's Founders that made your freedom and mine possible.

25

THIS IS YOUR TIME!

IT YOU HAPPEN TO READ A NEWSPAPER or articles on the Internet, listen to your teachers or professors, or even turn on Fox News or Newsmax, you soon realize that the deck is stacked against conservatives and patriotic Americans. The Left has a near monopoly on major news media, from CBS to the *New York Times*, to social media, to your local newspaper. Your textbooks are strongly slanted to the progressive point of view; progressives push extreme radical agendas, and justice is applied unequally based on your political beliefs. You are expected to endorse and accept more than fifty different genders, use pronouns demanded by the radical sexualist Left, denounce America's Founders, and remain silent while professors and radical activists tear down statues and rewrite American history. With this kind of near absolute domination of the news media, social media, and the classroom, it may seem like there is simply no chance of returning our nation to sanity. That's what the Left wants you to believe. They want you to shut up and do what they say.

Yet the signs are clear that the radical Progressive movement is in trouble. Even as the Left temporarily dominates politics on the national scene and promotes an even more radical agenda, it becomes ever-more obvious that their drive to turn the United States of America into a socialist state is failing. Clearly, by their language and their desperate tactics, they recognize that they are losing.

Their pagan worship of abortion has crashed and burned in plain sight as the American people rejected their willingness to kill a baby even after it has been born, or kill one right up until the moment of birth. The U.S. Supreme Court did not rule that abortion is illegal, it just ruled that *Roe v. Wade* was made up out of thin air with absolutely no justification in the U.S. Constitution. All SCOTUS did was to send it back to each state to decide, yet the Left went crazy.

If the Left was truly popular, then why are Americans fleeing leftist blue states by the millions to move to conservative red states?[1]

> Caterpillar . . . Tesla, Hewlett-Packard, Oracle and Remington are . . . among the hundreds of companies flocking out of California, Illinois, New York, and New Jersey to business friendly places such as Texas, Arizona, Florida, and Tennessee. Relocating companies have spanned industries including tech, finance, media, heavy manufacturing, autos, and firearms.[2]

And, why is enrollment in most colleges and universities declining?

> Nationwide undergraduate enrollment has dropped by more than 650,000 students in a single year—over 4 percent alone from 2021 to 2022—and some 14 percent in the past decade.[3]

In contrast, conservative Christian college enrollment continues to grow.[4]

Why did the Left totally melt down over the idea of Elon Musk buying Twitter?[5] Why does calling a conservative a "racist" no longer scare Black Americans away from voting for that candidate? Does the Left really think that calling us "White supremacists" will be any more effective in stopping the irreversible movement of Black Americans toward support of conservative candidates and ideas? If more than 50 percent of Hispanic citizens reject progressive policies,[6] why should progressives believe that those crossing the border to flee Marxist socialism won't be conservative? If I were a progressive, I would be in a panic too.

The truth is that the Marxist-inspired Progressive movement is dying in America while the Conservative movement is steadily growing. Let's take a look at a number of crucial areas where conservative ideas are ascendant and Marxist progressive ideas are in decline.

There is no doubt that the Left has executed an effective game plan in our schools, from grade school to graduate school. More than 125 years ago, prior to the turn of the twentieth century, progressives were well underway in their effort to indoctrinate uninformed college students in the lie that socialism not only would bring heaven on earth but that it was also the unstoppable wave of the future.

They understood from the beginning that they could not implement their radical leftist agenda if they did not win over the minds of leaders, so they patiently began a long march through the institutions,[7] initially focusing on America's colleges and universities. By radicalizing the faculties of these public and private colleges and universities, they have been able to virtually shut out all patriotism and free-market economics and substitute their anti-American, anti-God, anti-freedom socialist agenda.

Marxist professors have not only dominated the soft sciences, they have also taken over law schools and made inroads into other departments. In addition, they have shut out conservative professors from being on the faculty candidate selection committees to make sure that only Marxists are hired.

Today senior conservative professors . . . find themselves regularly excluded from search and hiring committees, and [are thus] a dwindling presence on the university faculties.[8]

After their success in colleges and universities, the Left focused their attention on America's elementary and high schools, as we finally discovered due to the COVID-19 pandemic. Now we know they have been subjecting first graders and all students up through their senior year of high school to Marxist CRT and even to leftist sexualist pornography. But despite the radical agenda of the teacher's unions and radical Left school boards, enlightened moms and dads, known as the mama bears and papa bears, are successfully fighting back, recalling school boards, running for school boards, persuading their state legislatures to ban the teaching of CRT, eliminating sexualist pornography, and otherwise fighting to regain control of their children's education. That battle is far from over, but conservatives are making progress in public education and private schools, and home schooling is expanding dramatically.

By far the biggest and best news of all on the education front is that the school voucher program (school choice) has finally made the long-awaited breakthrough that signals its expansion across our nation. In 2022, Arizona enacted a law[9] that lets *all* parents spend their education dollars on behalf of their children as they best see fit in public or private schools, religious or secular. In early 2023, Iowa followed suit and signed into law a universal school choice program. Other states, including Oklahoma, Texas, Indiana, West Virginia, Arkansas, and Florida, are not far behind in passing universal school choice programs.[10]

Instead of the state funds going directly to the public schools, parents will receive a voucher that can be redeemed by either a public or a private school. Parents in school choice states now get to choose where their child will be educated. This will put competition into the education process, and competition always leads to excellence.

As universal school choice inevitably spreads across the landscape of so-called red states, it will inevitably produce a resurgence of quality education in America. Both public and private schools will be forced to compete for students based on the quality of the education they provide. Those offering the best quality will get the students making both the parents and the children the winners.

Choice in education will also mean a return to teaching the values that align with the values that America's parents want for their children. Ultimately, school voucher programs will greatly benefit our society as a whole. The successful schools, both public and private, will return to the basics and turn out students who have real knowledge and are prepared for life. And because states have to compete with other states, eventually, in order to keep up, the so-called blue states will be forced to adopt school voucher programs in order to keep from falling behind. This one step initiated by Arizona can reverse decades of a downward trend in the quality of education in the United States and make American students once again competitive on the world stage.

But what about the political front? The American people aren't fools like the Left believes them to be. They can see with their own eyes and feel in their own pocketbooks that far-Left radical ideas simply do not work. Big spending programs rarely help anyone, and they cause inflation that hurts everyone. American citizens see that the one-sided, unbalanced administration of justice turning violent prisoners free and selectively enforcing the laws leads to danger and chaos. With Americans of all races and ethnicities rejecting the radical leftist agenda, it is clear that the political and policy future of the radical Left looks bleak indeed.

Even on the social media front, the progressive Left has been exposed as biased and one-sided by banning conservative views. The takeover of Twitter by Elon Musk not only terrified the Left[11] but also exposed Twitter as a strongly biased organization that used bots to greatly inflate its impact, and (in violation of freedom of speech guaranteed in the Constitution) it worked with the government and the Democratic Party to block news that might have changed the outcome of the 2020 election.[12] The idea of free speech and letting both liberals and conservatives freely express their views on the Twitter platform aroused all sorts of truly unhinged attacks by the Left on Musk. Free speech terrifies them.[13] That is evident in the way they use "cancel culture" to shut down conservative speakers and to block those speakers from expressing any view that they deem inappropriate.[14] Musk's takeover made them defend their defenseless positions and exposed their collusion with the FBI to cover up the Hunter Biden laptop story.

Even in the entertainment field, patriotism is on the rise. In this politically correct age where the woke U.S. military focuses on the "right" pronouns, weeds out those who are deemed too patriotic, tries to figure out how to build a tank that will run on battery power, waters down the physicality of basic training,[15] and worries about hurting the feelings of those preparing for combat,[16] you would think that an old-fashioned, rah-rah military movie where the United States is the good guy would be a flop, right? You would be wrong.

As a forward indicator of the direction America is moving, consider the success of the Tom Cruise movie *Top Gun: Maverick*[17] (a sequel to the original *Top Gun* released in 1986). Sequels rarely do as well as the original movies, and most sell less theater tickets than the original.[18] So how did *Top Gun: Maverick*, a blatantly pro-America military film, do at the box office? This sequel was a huge box office hit and one of the top-grossing movies of all time, generating nearly $1.2 billion in revenue as of this writing! Can there be any doubt that patriotism in our land is on the upswing?

And, by the way,

> The producers [of *Top Gun : Maverick*] defied another modern entertainment industry requisite—obsequence to China. In the original *Top Gun*, Maverick proudly wears his father's bomber pilot jacket with patches displaying the flags of Taiwan and Japan, nation allies on his old man's missions . . . a 2019 trailer for the sequel showed the jacket patches altered into unrecognizable symbols.
>
> [However] . . .when Tom Cruise dons the famous jacket early in the sequel, you can see the two flag patches digitally restored.[19]

What happened? A Chinese company, Tencent Holdings, objected to the flags and conveyed to the producers that the flags of Taiwan and Japan were not acceptable to them, and if they were used they would withdraw their 12.5 percent stake in the movie, not an insubstantial amount.

Sticking to their guns and showing the patches, the producers effectively told the Chi Coms to take a flying leap. If that's not a sign of the rebirth of American patriotism, I don't know what is. But even better, the powerful reception of this movie makes it clear that those who are patriotic, who believe in the United States, and who revere America's Founders are ascendant today.

While the advances of patriotism, conservatism, and common sense are significant, they won't bring victory overnight. Like those in the Progressive movement, conservatives need to dedicate themselves to making the long march through all of the institutions of society, not just politics or even education, but also our media, our culture, and our places of worship. We need to have both the dedication and the persistence of the Left in restoring our republic to one of limited federal government power. If we are as dedicated to our Founding principles as the Left is to destroying them, we will, by the grace of God, restore our Republic. To be sure, this won't be an easy task, nor always a pleasant one, but as we join the fight shoulder-to-shoulder and spread the conservative message (the same message of freedom espoused by America's Founders), we will repel those who would make us their slaves.

Every generation of Americans must fight for the survival of our nation and for our heritage of freedom, just as our forefathers did. And each generation must pass along the ideas of freedom and liberty so that the next generation is prepared for battle. You must not be the generation that fails.

Together, we must always remember the words of John Hancock (quoted earlier) written during the darkest days of the War of Independence that remind us of who it is that will grant our victory:

All confidence must be withheld from the means we use; and reposed only on that God who rules in the armies of Heaven, and without whose blessing the best human counsels are but foolishness—and all created power vanity.[20]

26

JOIN A GREAT CAUSE

WHEN YOU CHOOSE to be a part of the conservative cause, as I did when I joined Young Americans for Freedom in 1962, you will be joining a great movement that is driven by optimism, a love of freedom, and respect for eternal truths. It is a cause dedicated to the preservation of the rule of law and constitutional government. It involves men and women, young and old, who love their country and love their fellow Americans. They don't hate our nation, nor do they want to silence other Americans who have opinions different from their own. It's a movement that promotes hope and opportunity, not fear or anger. And it is one that is immensely important because as Ronald Reagan reminded us,

Freedom is never more than one generation away from extinction. We didn't pass it to our children in the bloodstream. It must be fought for, protected and handed on for them to do the same, or one day we will spend our sunset years telling our children and our children's children what it was once like in the United States where men were free.[1]

Right now, today, you have the opportunity to be directly involved in that great cause of defending, preserving, and protecting freedom for your own generation and for generations yet unborn. Perhaps you already are. Remember, it is the same cause that America's Founders engaged in when they pledged their lives, their fortunes, and their sacred honor to preserve freedom in our land by breaking off from British tyranny and creating the United States of America. And it is the same cause that generations of Americans before you engaged in to preserve freedom for themselves, their children, and generations yet to come. Without those efforts, neither Reagan nor Trump would have been elected president of the United States, nor would the foundational principles of freedom have a voice on campus.

No, we won't always triumph as we did in 1980 when Reagan was elected or in 2016 when Trump was, but the Conservative movement is not just about political victory or even primarily so. Much more important, this is a mission to win over the hearts and minds of students like yourself—but not just students, we need to reach those in business, those in education, those working in the home, those in the military, and all Americans of good character. Its success depends upon you to pass along the ideas of freedom to those in your area of influence today and to those who will come after you.

When I heard the keynote speech by Brent Bozell Jr. (the brother-in-law of William F. Buckley Jr.), at the World Rally for Victory Over Communism on March 7, 1962, I knew that I wanted to be a part of this great cause. Sponsored by Young Americans for Freedom and held at Madison Square Garden less than two years after the founding of YAF, Bozell began his speech with these words: "We of the Christian

West owe our identity to the entry of God upon the human scene. Not as some supernatural stunt, but a terrestrial event, God in time with us."

Bozell's speech was one of optimism and principle, closing his remarks with the growing roar of the eighteen thousand conservatives packed into the Garden being so loud that he could barely be heard as he concluded,

> . . . and the orders will go out. To our chief of staff in the Congo, change sides! To our commander in Berlin, tear down the wall! And, to the head of CIA, you are under instructions to encourage liberation movements in every nation under communist domination, including the Soviet Union itself. And, let it be known that in the future when men give their lives for freedom, the West will not stand idly by, and communism will be driven from the face of the earth!"[2]

Bozell's speech gave me the conviction that I had to be a part of this great cause of defending and extending freedom to all Americans of all colors and ethnicities. Being a responsible citizen entails more than being passively patriotic; it entails playing an active role as former Vice Mike Pence importuned young Americans,

> America is counting on you to be the leaders our country needs. Now more than ever, America needs young men and women of integrity to take up the mantle of leadership, and keep the torch of liberty burning bright for generations to come! You must be the Freedom Generation![3]

Indeed, I urge you to enjoy the thrill of being a part of the Freedom Generation and of this great cause that brought about the election of one of America's greatest presidents, Ronald Reagan, and then the unlikely conservative champion, Donald Trump.

When you form or join a chapter of Young Americans for Freedom at your high school or on your college campus, you will have taken an important first step in keeping the torch of freedom alive. When you are trained by the Leadership Institute or gain a strong understanding of free enterprise at a Young America's Foundation conference, you will be making yourself a more effective messenger of freedom. When you attend a Turning Point USA event, you will be educating yourself about the foundations of our republic. Similarly, when you attend a Young America's Foundation school at the Reagan Ranch, you will not only walk where Ronald Reagan walked, you will be given a deeper understanding of the principles and values that made the United States the greatest nation in the history of the world. And when the conservative student organization you are a member of sponsors a conservative speaker at your school or on campus, you will be going on offense, sharing the conservative viewpoint with others who are open to hearing the conservative, patriotic point of view.

I promise you that if you let it, your participation in the Conservative movement will become a life-changing event. Due solely to my involvement in Young Americans for Freedom, I had opportunities that I never dreamed possible. I not only raised funds to elect great senators, congressmen, and presidential candidates, I also raised funds for vital conservative organizations that expanded the power and influence of the Conservative movement. In addition, I served as an alternate delegate to the 1980 Republican National Convention that nominated Ronald Reagan to be the GOP's candidate for president. At that convention I also cochaired (along with Jim Roberts) the Jack Kemp for Vice President effort. And, after Reagan became president, my wife, Kathi, and I served as mentors to a Ronald Reagan Scholar at Ronald Reagan's alma mater, Eureka College, who has become a lifelong friend. As such, we spent an amazing evening with a small group of these scholars hosted by President and Mrs. Reagan at the White House. Today we serve as members of the Board of Governors of the Ronald Reagan Ranch.

Had it not been for YAF, I would never have left my career as a mechanical engineer to found a direct-mail fundraising company that raised more than a billion dollars for conservative candidates, political action committees, conservative organizations, and other worthwhile causes. Nor would I have had an opportunity to serve as Ronald Reagan's fundraiser in his first race for the White House.

But even if you never work directly for the conservative cause, as I have been blessed to do, when you participate in a YAF chapter, the Intercollegiate Studies Institute, Turning Point USA, Campus Reform, or some other conservative group, you will indeed be walking in the philosophical shoes of America's Founders. You will be advancing the cause of freedom.

Since 1620 when the Pilgrims landed at Plymouth and John Winthrop envisioned this land as a "shining city on a hill," America was destined to become a great nation. When George Washington, Patrick Henry, John Adams, Thomas Jefferson, Benjamin Franklin, Samuel Adams, and tens of thousands of others fought for our freedom—and when the signers of the Declaration of Independence pledged their lives, their fortunes, and their sacred honor to securing that freedom—they did it not just for themselves but for generations of Americans yet to come, including you and me.

As I mentioned in the first chapter, being an American citizen is not only a great privilege, it also brings with it a great responsibility to pass along the freedom we enjoy to the next generation of Americans. Today, no matter your background, your ethnicity, or your skin color, you have an opportunity to become part of a movement that seeks equal justice, unlimited opportunity, and maximum individual freedom for all Americans.

As a conservative you can actively encourage America to follow a foreign policy that is neither interventionist nor isolationist but, as the Sharon Statement puts it, "in the just interest of the United States." You can be an advocate for free markets, not the soul-numbing socialism of today's would-be totalitarians. You will be on the side of common sense and traditional values, including the protection of life for the unborn. You will be a defender of religious freedom and free speech as provided for in the First Amendment of the Bill of Rights. You will actively affirm that the United States is indeed one nation under God.

You will understand with the Founders that public virtue is absolutely essential to the preservation and survival of our free republic.

Let me strongly urge you to take heart and not despair of the preservation of freedom in our land. Yes, our republic is internally under attack from a Marxist Left that is determined to force socialism upon us, and it is externally threatened by Communist China that seeks our demise. But never forget that every generation that came before us has been faced with seemingly insurmountable challenges—the Revolutionary War, a Civil War, World Wars, and the Cold War to name but a few. Yet by the grace of God, since the time our forefathers, who against all odds, stood up and defeated the world's greatest military power of their day, Great Britain, we too can turn back the tide of socialism and communism in this God-blessed land.

In fact, the Left is weak because their cause is not good, just, or moral. Consider how they act today. You don't need to undermine the integrity of the voting process if you are winning over the hearts and minds of the American people.[4] You don't have to open wide our southern border and allow millions of people to illegally enter our nation and eventually become citizens if you are confident that the people already in America support you. You don't need to spend millions of taxpayer dollars to fly illegals into red states[5] in the middle of the night[6] if you think the American people support your far-Left policies.

You don't need to cover up the Hunter Biden laptop story[7] or cover up the Tony Bobulinski meeting with then–Vice President Joe Biden,[8] the "big guy," if you are confident you will win the presidential election fair and square. You don't need "2,000 Mules"[9] to illegally stuff ballot boxes if you believe you can win in an honest election. You don't need to spread lies about Kyle Rittenhouse[10] or Nicholas Sandmann[11] when you know they are untrue if you are winning. You don't have an emotional meltdown when Elon Musk seeks to buy Twitter and promises that all points of view will be heard[12] if you believe your argument for socialism will triumph in open debate. You don't need to spread lies like the Russian Dossier that falsely accused Donald Trump of collusion with Russia[13] if you believe your candidate will win the election fairly.

And you don't need to prevent conservative speakers such as Ben Shapiro from speaking on campus[14] or turn loose the Antifa goons to block him or another conservative from speaking[15] unless you know that your position won't survive the antiseptic of free speech. You don't need to shout down conservative speakers[16] if you honestly believe your ideas are better. The reality is that the radical Left in America is in full-blown panic mode because they know they are losing in the arena of ideas.

Americans don't like the progressive Left's ideas, and they overwhelmingly reject their policies. And no one knows that better than the progressives themselves. They know that their leftwing lunacy only succeeds when free speech is quashed, the media is controlled, and government is tyrannical. That's why the Left is so desperate today. They know full well that they are far, far from convincing the American people that socialism works or that the abolition of free speech is a good idea. I believe that Americans, especially your generation of Americans, still cherish their freedom.

The progressive Left knows that the vast majority of the American people, including young people,[17] are not taken in by the false promises of Marxist socialism. In their hearts, they know socialism has never worked and never will work. The Left always promises the same thing, "This time we will do it right." It's a con. It's a lie. Marxist socialism *always* ends up as a dictatorship. That's their goal: a dictatorship of the elite. That's why these Marxist socialists admire and praise[18] Fidel Castro, Che Guevara, Nicolás Maduro, Pol Pot, et al. Even Vladimir Lenin and Mao Zedong have come back into fashion[19] with the American Left. Yet, we know that these socialist dictators have killed tens of millions[20] of people in pursuit of a socialist paradise.

The American people won't buy it. The Left doesn't want the American people to know that they are Marxist socialists with the same ideological bloodline as these horrible dictators. That's why they had to disguise their Marxism by running a cognitively impaired man, Joe Biden, as a Trojan Horse moderate to steal into the White House. They could never have elected someone who espoused full-throated Marxist socialism.

The Left today is like the basketball, football, soccer, or baseball team that is getting beat and the game is about over but the players still think they have a chance to win if they can only change the rules of the game or just arbitrarily change the score. And that is precisely what they are trying to do.

The point is that the power of the Left is waning, not accelerating. They are unable to make any permanent gains either politically or intellectually, and they are losing ground with their cultural overreach as the "mama bears" proved in the 2021 Virginia election.[21] Most significant of all, even the deadly and clearly unconstitutional *Roe v. Wade* abortion decision has now been reversed by the U.S. Supreme Court. While this is not a total victory, as the battle will now be fought in the individual states, it is the greatest judicial setback for the radical Left in half a century. And that historic ruling by the U.S. Supreme Court was followed up with a reaffirmation of the right of individual citizens to keep and bear arms,[22] as well as a rejection of efforts by the Left to constrict religious freedom.[23]

The progressive Marxist Left simply does not have the backing of the American people. But, desperate though they may be, they will never surrender or give up. The radical Left, like the devil, will always be with us, trying to subvert our nation and destroy our freedom. And don't think that Marxist professors and those on the Left will take it easy on you if they learn that you are a conservative.

Listen to what happened many years ago to Michelle Easton as a student at Briarcliff College after she started a YAF chapter and passed out flyers showing how radical left George McGovern was:

> Walking down the hall one day, a sociology professor approached me out of nowhere. She was furious. She backed me into a corner and began berating me. "How dare you!" she yelled. "How could you say these things about George McGovern? Why would you make a flyer?" I was shocked into silence. She had assumed the worst about me, as if my views were illegitimate and I had no right to express them . . . I can still see her triggered expression when she stormed away in anger as I started to speak.[24]

Fortunately for us and for America, Michelle was not dissuaded and became one of the outstanding leaders of Young Americans for Freedom as well as the founder and president of the Clare Boothe Luce Center for Conservative Women that prepares young women for leadership in our nation and in the Conservative movement.

As Michelle points out quite accurately in her book *How to Raise a Conservative Daughter,*

> There will be times when raising a hand in class to offer a dissenting point of view will be a courageous decision. Perhaps your daughter will run for student government or assert her principles in a debate setting. Maybe she will bring a conservative speaker to campus and cause a stir. She may have to pick and choose her battles, but standing up at the right time is what activism and leadership are all about. That's how change is created. After all, what's the point of having values if you hide them when they are needed most?[25]

Believe me when I tell you that when you stand up for what you believe is true and then are attacked, it will only strengthen your resolve to stand your ground. As King David said to his son Solomon regarding the seemingly overwhelming task of building the Temple in Jerusalem, "Be strong and courageous, and do the work. Don't be afraid or terrified. The LORD God, my God, will be with you. He will not abandon you before all the work on the LORD's Temple is finished" (1 Chronicles 28:20 GW).

Today, America is engaged in a battle of ideas and values that forces us to take sides. That's why we must not sit idly by and let the Left dominate on campus or in the classroom. There is no doubt that the very underpinnings of our republic are under assault. And our freedom of religion as guaranteed under the Constitution is imperiled. Today, the Left, led by Barack Obama[26] and Hillary Clinton,[27] seeks to redefine freedom of religion as only freedom only to "worship," denying Christians the right to share their faith with others. Nevertheless, if we rise to the challenge and join the battle, with God's blessing we will succeed, just as those who came before us did.

Conservative leaders come from all walks of life and all backgrounds. Ronald Reagan was a struggling actor who was past his prime when he burst onto the national scene. Margaret Thatcher lived above a grocery store her father ran and in which she worked. The great Thomas Sowell was a pro-Marxist Marine who wanted to become a photographer. Rush Limbaugh wanted to be a radio disk jockey playing rock music. Jack Kemp was a football jock. I thought I was going to be an engineer like my brothers, but God had other plans for all of us. Maybe, just maybe, He has a plan for you too—to do something important on behalf of our nation that you never imagined doing.

Don't give up. Don't give in. Join the Conservative freedom movement. And as a reminder of who we are and what we are fighting for, let me close with these inspiring words from President Donald J. Trump:

> We are Americans. We are pioneers. We are the pathfinders. We settled the New World, we built the modern world, and we changed history forever by embracing the eternal truth that everyone is made equal by the hand of Almighty God. America is the place where anything can happen. America is the place where anyone can rise. And, here, on this land, on this soil, on this continent, the most incredible dreams come true. This nation is our canvas, and this country is our masterpiece. We look at tomorrow and see unlimited frontiers just waiting to be explored. Our brightest discoveries are not yet known. Our most thrilling stories are not yet told. Our grandest journeys are not yet made. The American Age, the American Epic, the American adventure has only just begun. Our spirit is still young, the sun is still rising, God's grace is still shining, and my fellow Americans, the best is yet to come.[28]

AUTHOR'S NOTES

AS I HOPE that I made clear in the Preface and throughout this book, this work is not about politics (although many if not most conservatives are engaged in politics). It is rather a book about conservative ideas and the Conservative movement. And despite many references to the necessity of a consensus of citizens seeking to be virtuous in order for a free republic to survive, this is not a book about religion. The fact is that the Conservative movement is made up of all sorts of Americans, a good number of whom are not religious in any way but the overwhelming majority of whom reverence an all-powerful, good, and gracious God and the virtues identified in the Bible.

As for me personally, I fully recognize my imperfection, my sinfulness, and I put my faith in Jesus, my Savior, as my only hope of salvation, my only path to Heaven. My confirmation verse says it best:

> For it is by grace you have been saved, through faith—and this is not from yourselves, it is the gift of God—not by works, so that no one can boast. (Ephesians 2:8–9, NIV)

Pro Gloria Dei.

APPENDIX A

RONALD REAGAN'S FAREWELL ADDRESS

January 12, 1989

MY FELLOW AMERICANS, this is the thirty-fourth time I'll speak to you from the Oval Office, and the last. We've been together eight years now, and soon it'll be time for me to go. But before I do, I wanted to share some thoughts, some of which I have been saving for a long time.

It's been the honor of my life to be your president. So many of you have written the past few weeks to say thanks, but I could say as much to you. Nancy and I are grateful for the opportunity you gave us to serve.

One of the things about the presidency is that you're always somewhat apart. You spend a lot of time going by too fast in a car someone else is driving, and seeing the people through tinted glass—the parents holding up a child, and the wave you saw too late and couldn't return. And so many times I wanted to stop, and reach out from behind the glass, and connect. Well, maybe I can do a little of that tonight.

People ask how I feel about leaving, and the fact is parting is "such sweet sorrow." The sweet part is California, and the ranch, and freedom. The sorrow? The goodbyes, of course, and leaving this beautiful place.

You know, down the hall and up the stairs from this office is the part of the White House where the president and his family live. There are a few favorite windows I have up there that I like to stand and look out of early in the morning. The view is over the grounds here to the Washington Monument, and then the Mall, and the Jefferson Memorial. But on mornings when the humidity is low, you can see past the Jefferson to the river, the Potomac, and the Virginia shore. Someone said that's the view Lincoln had when he saw the smoke rising from the battle of Bull Run. Well, I see more prosaic things: the grass on the banks, the morning traffic as people make their way to work, now and then a sailboat on the river.

I've been thinking a bit at that window. I've been reflecting on what the past eight years have meant, and mean. And the image that comes to mind like a refrain is a nautical one—a small story about a big ship, and a refugee, and a sailor.

It was back in the early eighties, at the height of the boat people, and the sailor was hard at work on the carrier *Midway*, which was patrolling the South China Sea. The sailor, like most American servicemen, was young, smart, and fiercely observant. The crew spied on the horizon a leaky little boat—and crammed inside were refugees from Indochina hoping to get to America. The *Midway* sent a small launch to bring them to the ship, and safety. As the refugees made their way through the choppy seas, one spied the sailor on deck, and stood up and called out to him. He yelled, "Hello, American sailor—Hello, Freedom Man."

A small moment with a big meaning, a moment the sailor, who wrote it in a letter, couldn't get out of his mind. And, when I saw it, neither could I.

Because that's what it has to . . . it was to be an American in the 1980s; we stood, again, for freedom. I know we always have, but in the past few years the world—again, and in a way, we ourselves—rediscovered it.

It's been quite a journey this decade, and we held together through some stormy seas. And at the end, together, we are reaching our destination.

The fact is, from Grenada to the Washington and Moscow Summits, from the recession of '81 to '82 to the expansion that began in late '82 and continues to this day, we've made a difference.

TWO GREAT TRIUMPHS

The way I see it, there were two great triumphs, two things that I'm proudest of. One is the economic recovery, in which the people of America created—and filled—19 million new jobs. The other is the recovery of our morale: America is respected again in the world, and looked to for leadership.

Something that happened to me a few years ago reflects some of this. It was back in 1981, and I was attending my first big economic summit, which was held that year in Canada. The meeting place rotates among the member countries. The opening meeting was a formal dinner for the heads of government of the seven industrialized nations. Well, I sat there like the new kid in school and listened, and it was all Francois this and Helmut that. They dropped titles and spoke to one another on a first-name basis. Well, at one point I sort of leaned in and said, "My name's Ron."

Well, in that same year, we began the actions we felt would ignite an economic comeback: cut taxes and regulation, started to cut spending. Soon the recovery began.

Two years later, another economic summit, with pretty much the same cast. At the big opening meeting, we all got together, and all of a sudden just for a moment I saw that everyone was just sitting there looking at me. And then one of them broke the silence. "Tell us about the American miracle," he said.

Well, back in 1980, when I was running for president, it was all so different. Some pundits said our programs would result in catastrophe. Our views on foreign affairs would cause war, our plans for the economy would cause inflation to soar and bring about economic collapse. I even remember one highly respected economist saying, back in 1982, that "the engines of economic growth have shut down here and they're likely to stay that way for years to come."

Well, he—and the other "opinion leaders"—were wrong. The fact is, what they called "radical" was really "right"; what they called "dangerous" was just "desperately needed."

And in all that time I won a nickname—"The Great Communicator." But I never thought it was my style or the words I used that made a difference—it was the content. I wasn't a great communicator, but I communicated great things, and they didn't spring full bloom from my brow, they came from the heart of a great nation—from our experience, our wisdom, and our belief in the principles that have guided us for two centuries.

They called it the "Reagan Revolution," and I'll accept that, but for me it always seemed more like the Great Rediscovery: a rediscovery of our values and our common sense.

Common sense told us that when you put a big tax on something, the people will produce less of it. So we cut the people's tax rates, and the people produced more than ever before. The economy bloomed like a plant that had been cut back and could now grow quicker and stronger. Our economic program brought about the longest peacetime expansion in our history: real family income up, the poverty rate down, entrepreneurship booming and an explosion in research and new technology. We're exporting more now than ever because American industry became more competitive, and at the same time we summoned the national will to knock down protectionist walls abroad instead of erecting them at home.

Common sense also told us that to preserve the peace we'd have to become strong again after years of weakness and confusion. So we rebuilt our defenses—and this New Year we toasted the new peacefulness around the globe. Not only have the superpowers actually begun to reduce their stockpiles of nuclear weapons—and hope for even more progress is bright—but the regional conflicts that rack the globe are also beginning to cease. The Persian Gulf is no longer a war zone, the Soviets are leaving Afghanistan, the Vietnamese are preparing to pull out of Cambodia, and an American-mediated accord will soon send fifty thousand Cuban troops home from Angola. The lesson of all this was, of course, that because we're a great nation, our challenges seem complex. It will always be this way. But as long as we remember our first principles and believe in ourselves, the future will always be ours.

And something else we learned: once you begin a great movement, there's no telling where it'll end. We meant to change a nation, and instead, we changed a world.

Countries across the globe are turning to free markets and free speech—and turning away from the ideologies of the past. For them, the Great Rediscovery of the 1980s has been that, lo and behold, the moral way of government is the practical way of government. Democracy, the profoundly good, is also the profoundly productive.

When you've got to the point where you can celebrate the anniversaries of your thirty-ninth birthday, you can sit back sometimes, review your life, and see it flowing before you. For me, there was a fork in the river, and it was right in the middle of my life.

I never meant to go into politics: it wasn't my intention when I was young. But I was raised to believe you had to pay your way for the blessings bestowed on you. I was happy with my career in the entertainment world, but I ultimately went into politics because I wanted to protect something precious.

Ours was the first revolution in the history of mankind that truly reversed the course of government, and with three little words: "We the People."

"We the People" tell the government what to do, it doesn't tell us. "We the people" are the driver—the government is the car. And we decide where it should go, and by what route, and how fast. Almost all the world's constitutions are documents in which governments tell the people what their privileges are. Our Constitution is a document in which "We the People" tell the government what it is allowed to do. "We the People" are free.

This belief has been the underlying basis for everything I tried to do these past eight years.

But back in the 1960s when I began, it seemed to me that we'd begun reversing the order of things—that through more and more rules and regulations and confiscatory taxes, the government was taking more of our freedom. I went into politics in part to put up my hand and say, "Stop!" I was a citizen-politician, and it seemed the right thing for a citizen to do.

I think we have stopped a lot of what needed stopping. And I hope we have once again reminded people that man is not free unless government is limited. There's a clear cause and effect here that is as neat and predictable as a law of physics: as government expands, liberty contracts.

Nothing is less free than pure communism, and yet we have, the past few years, forged a satisfying new closeness with the Soviet Union. I've been asked if this isn't a gamble, and my answer is no, because we're basing our actions not on words but deeds.

The detente of the 1970s was based not on actions but promises. They'd promise to treat their own people and the people of the world better, but the gulag was still the gulag, and the state was still expansionist, and they still waged proxy wars in Africa, Asia, and Latin America.

Well, this time, so far, it's different: President Gorbachev has brought about some internal democratic reforms and begun the withdrawal from Afghanistan. He has also freed prisoners whose names I've given him every time we've met.

But life has a way of reminding you of big things through small incidents. Once, during the heady days of the Moscow Summit, Nancy and I decided to break off from the entourage one afternoon to visit the shops on Arbat Street—that's a little street just off Moscow's main shopping area.

Even though our visit was a surprise, every Russian there immediately recognized us, and called out our names and reached for our hands. We were just about swept away by the warmth—you could almost feel the possibilities in all that joy. But within seconds, a KGB detail pushed their way toward us and began pushing and shoving the people in the crowd. It was an interesting moment. It reminded me that while the man on the street in the Soviet Union yearns for peace, the government is Communist—and those who run it are Communists—and that means we and they view such issues as freedom and human rights very differently.

We must keep up our guard—but we must also continue to work together to lessen and eliminate tension and mistrust.

My view is that President Gorbachev is different from previous Soviet leaders. I think he knows some of the things wrong with his society and is trying to fix them. We wish him well. And we'll continue to work to make sure that the Soviet Union that eventually emerges from this process is a less threatening one.

What it all boils down to is this: I want the new closeness to continue. And it will as long as we make it clear that we will continue to act in a certain way as long as they continue to act in a helpful manner. If and when they don't—at first pull your punches. If they persist, pull the plug.

It's still trust—but verify.

It's still play—but cut the cards.

It's still watch closely—and don't be afraid to see what you see.

I've been asked if I have any regrets. Well, I do.

The deficit is one. I've been talking a great deal about that lately, but tonight isn't for arguments, and I'm going to hold my tongue.

But an observation: I've had my share of victories in the Congress, but what few people noticed is that I never won anything you didn't win for me. They never saw my troops; they never saw Reagan's Regiments, the American people. You won every battle with every call you made and letter you wrote demanding action.

Well, action is still needed. If we're to finish the job, of Reagan's Regiments, we'll have to become the Bush Brigades. Soon he'll be the chief, and he'll need you every bit as much as I did.

Finally, there is a great tradition of warnings in presidential farewells, and I've got one that's been on my mind for some time.

But oddly enough it starts with one of the things I'm proudest of in the past eight years; the resurgence of national pride that I called "the new patriotism." This national feeling is good, but it won't count for much and it won't last unless it's grounded in thoughtfulness and knowledge.

An informed patriotism is what we want. And are we doing a good enough job teaching our children what America is and what she represents in the long history of the world?

Those of us who are over thirty-five or so years of age grew up in a different America. We were taught, very directly, what it means to be an American, and we absorbed almost in the air a love of country and an appreciation of its institutions. If you didn't get these things from your family, you got them from the neighborhood, from the father down the street who fought in Korea or the family who lost someone at Anzio. Or you could get a sense of patriotism from school. And if all else failed, you could get a sense of patriotism from the popular culture. The movies celebrated democratic values and implicitly reinforced the idea that America was special. TV was like that, too, through the mid-sixties.

But now we're about to enter the nineties, and some things have changed. Younger parents aren't sure that an unambivalent appreciation of America is the right thing to teach modern children. And as for those who create the popular culture, well-grounded patriotism is no longer the style.

Our spirit is back, but we haven't re-institutionalized it. We've got to do a better job of getting across that America is freedom—freedom of speech, freedom of religion, freedom of enterprise—and freedom is special and rare. It's fragile; it needs protection.

We've got to teach history based not on what's in fashion but what's important: Why the Pilgrims came here, who Jimmy Doolittle was, and what those thirty seconds over Tokyo meant. You know, four years ago, on the fortieth anniversary of D-Day, I read a letter from a young woman writing to her late father, who'd fought on Omaha Beach. Her name was Lisa Zanatta Henn, and she said, "We will always remember, we will never forget what the boys of Normandy did." Well, let's help her keep her word.

If we forget what we did, we won't know who we are. I am warning of an eradication of that—of the American memory that could result, ultimately, in an erosion of the American spirit.

Let's start with some basics—more attention to American history and a greater emphasis of civic ritual. And let me offer lesson number one about America: all great change in America begins at the dinner table. So tomorrow night in the kitchen I hope the talking begins. And children, if your parents haven't been teaching you what it means to be an American—let 'em know and nail 'em on it. That would be a very American thing to do.

And that's about all I have to say tonight. Except for one thing.

The past few days when I've been at that window upstairs, I've thought a bit of the shining "city upon a hill." The phrase comes from John Winthrop, who wrote it to describe the America he imagined. What he imagined was important, because he was an early Pilgrim—an early "Freedom Man." He journeyed here on what today we'd call a little wooden boat, and, like the other Pilgrims, he was looking for a home that would be free.

I've spoken of the shining city all my political life, but I don't know if I ever quite communicated what I saw when I said it. But in my mind, it was a tall proud city built on rocks stronger than oceans, windswept, God blessed, and teeming with people of all kinds living in harmony and peace—a city with free ports that hummed with commerce and creativity, and if there had to be city walls, the walls had doors, and the doors were open to anyone with the will and the heart to get here.

That's how I saw it, and see it still. How Stands the City?

And how stands the city on this winter night? More prosperous, more secure, and happier than it was eight years ago. But more than that: after two hundred years, two centuries, she still stands strong and true on the granite ridge, and her glow has held steady no matter what storm.

And she's still a beacon, still a magnet for all who must have freedom, for all the pilgrims from all the lost places who are hurtling through the darkness, toward home.

We've done our part. And as I "walk off into the city streets," a final word to the men and women of the Reagan Revolution—the men and women across America who for eight years did the work that brought America back:

My friends, we did it. We weren't just marking time; we made a difference. We made the city stronger—we made the city freer—and we left her in good hands.

All in all, not bad. Not bad at all. And so, goodbye.

APPENDIX B

CLIMATE CHANGE INFORMATION

1. Myron Ebell and Steven J. Milloy, "Wrong Again: 50 Years of Failed Eco-pocalyptic Predictions," Competitive Enterprise Institute, September 18, 2019; https://cei.org/blog/wrong-again-50-years-of-failed-eco-pocalyptic-predictions.

2. *Environment*, "The best environmental outcomes are achieved through innovation, economic freedom, respect for private property rights, and the primary role of states in environmental protection," Heritage Foundation; https://www.heritage.org/environment.

3. Becky Norton Dunlop, "Eight Principles of the American Conservation Ethic," The Heritage Foundation, July 25, 2012; https://www.heritage.org/environment/commentary/the-american-conservation-ethic.

The following are excerpted from the Heritage.org website listed above. A deeper understanding of each principle can be found at that website.

PRINCIPLE I: PEOPLE ARE THE MOST IMPORTANT, UNIQUE, AND PRECIOUS RESOURCE
All environmental policy should be based on the idea that people are the most important, unique, and precious resource. The inherent value of each individual is greater than the inherent value of any other resource.

Accordingly, human well-being, which incorporates such measures as health and safety, is the foremost measure of the quality of the environment: a policy cannot be good for the environment if it is bad for people.

PRINCIPLE II: RENEWABLE NATURAL RESOURCES ARE RESILIENT AND DYNAMIC AND RESPOND POSITIVELY TO WISE MANAGEMENT

Renewable natural resources—trees, plants, soil, air, water, fish, and wildlife—and collections thereof, such as wetlands, deserts, forests, and prairies, are the resources upon which we depend for food, clothing, medicine, shelter, and innumerable other human needs. Indeed, human life depends on both the use and conservation of these resources. Such resources are regenerated through growth, reproduction, or other naturally occurring processes that cleanse, cycle, or otherwise create them anew.

PRINCIPLE III: PRIVATE PROPERTY PROTECTIONS AND FREE MARKETS PROVIDE THE MOST PROMISING NEW OPPORTUNITIES FOR ENVIRONMENTAL IMPROVEMENTS

Ownership inspires stewardship: Whether for economic, recreational, or aesthetic benefit, private property owners have the incentive both to enhance their resources and to protect them. Polluting another's property is to trespass or to cause injury. Polluters, not those most vulnerable in the political process, should pay for damages done to others.

PRINCIPLE IV: EFFORTS TO REDUCE, CONTROL, AND REMEDIATE POLLUTION SHOULD ACHIEVE REAL ENVIRONMENTAL BENEFITS

The term "pollution" is applied to a vast array of substances and conditions that vary greatly in their effect on man. It is used to describe fatal threats to human health, as well as to describe physically harmless conditions that fall short of someone's aesthetic ideal.

PRINCIPLE V: AS WE ACCUMULATE SCIENTIFIC,
TECHNOLOGICAL, AND ARTISTIC KNOWLEDGE,
WE LEARN HOW TO GET MORE FROM LESS

Society tends to become more efficient as it accumulates scientific, technological, and artistic knowledge. In the words of economics writer Warren Brookes, "The learning curve is green." Technology promotes efficiency, and through efficiency we substitute information for other resources, resulting in more output from less input—which also means less waste and greater conservation.

PRINCIPLE VI: MANAGEMENT OF NATURAL RESOURCES SHOULD BE
CONDUCTED ON A SITE- AND SITUATION-SPECIFIC BASIS

Resource management should take into account the fact that environmental conditions will vary from location to location and from time to time. A site- and situation-specific approach takes advantage of the fact that those who are closest to a resource or pollution problem are also those who are best able to manage them. Such practices allow for prioritization and the separation of problems into manageable units.

PRINCIPLE VII: SCIENCE SHOULD BE EMPLOYED
AS ONE TOOL TO GUIDE PUBLIC POLICY

Science should inform societal decisions, but ultimately, such decisions should be based on ethics, beliefs, consensus, and other processes. Understanding science's proper role is central to developing intelligent environmental policies.

PRINCIPLE VIII: THE MOST SUCCESSFUL ENVIRONMENTAL
POLICIES EMANATE FROM LIBERTY

Americans have chosen liberty as the central organizing principle of our great nation. Consequently, environmental policies must be consistent with this most cherished principle. Choosing policies that emanate from liberty is consistent with holding human well-being as the most important measure of environmental policies.

WEBSITE RESOURCES

The websites listed below provide access to news and opinion on current issues from a conservative, honest perspective. They are informative and essential to bypass much of the noise, fabrication, and slant of mainstream websites and news media. A number of them have more than a million readers each day. This list is by no means exhaustive.

American Spectator, spectator.org

American Thinker, americanthinker.com

Breitbart, breitbart.com

CBN News, cbn.com

Daily Caller, hdailycaller.com

Daily Signal, dailysignal.com

Daily Wire, dailywire.com

The Federalist, thefederalist.com

Hot Air, hotair.com

Human Events, humanevents.com

National Review, nationalreview.com

NewsMax, newsmax.com

RedState, redstate.com

Townhall, townhall.com

Western Journal, westernjournal.com

CONSERVATIVE PODCASTS

There are a great number of conservative podcasts available today, some of which you may already listen to. Here is a list of just a few of those podcasts and the organization through which they are aired:

Dan Bongino	Daily Breakdown
Steven Crowder	Turley Talks
Candace Owens	Graham Allen
Matt Walsh	Blaze Podcast Network
Michael Knowles	Conservative Daily
Ben Shapiro	Curtis Siwa
Fireside Chat by PragerU	Brian Craig Show
Andrew Klavan	Southern Sense Talk Radio
Mark Levin	Jason Rasntz Show
Whiskey Rebellion	Strident Conservative
Dana Loesch	Townhall Review
American Conservative University	Hugh Hewitt
Daniel Horowitz	"Tapp" into the Truth

BIBLIOGRAPHY

The books in this list are all excellent, but that is not to say that there are not other equally important conservative books. These are simply some of the books I have read and believe to be well written, well researched, and timely.

11 Principles of a Reagan Conservative by Paul Kengor

A Patriot's History of the United States by Larry Schweikart and Michael Allen

America by Dinesh D'Souza

America's Blessings by Rodney Stark

America Transformed by Ronald Pestritto

America's Rise and Fall Among the Nations by Angelo Codevilla

The Big Lie by Dinesh D'Souza

Churchill, Hitler, and the Unnecessary War by Patrick J. Buchanan

Climate Change: The Facts by Institute of Public Affairs

Democracy in America by Alexis de Tocqueville

The Dying Citizen by Victor Davis Hansen

False Alarm by Bjorn Lomborg

The Federalist Papers by Alexander, Hamilton, James Madison, and John Jay

Greatness to Spare by T. R. Fehrenback

How Now Shall We Live by Charles Colson

How the West Won by Rodney Stark

How to Raise A Conservative Daughter by Michelle Easton

If You Can Keep It by Eric Metaxas

The Law by Frederick Bastiat

Liberty & Tryanny by Mark Levin

Liberty's Secrets by Joshua Charles

Myth of the Robber Barons by Burt Folsom

Operation Solo by John Barron

Road to Serfdom by Friedrich Hayek

The Theme is Freedom by M. Stanton Evans

Unsettled? by Steven E. Koonin

Victory of Reason by Rodney Stark

White Guilt by Shelby Steele

Witness by Whittaker Chambers

Who Really Cares by Arthur C. Brooks

ACKNOWLEDGMENTS

FIRST AND FOREMOST, I want to thank my very patient, kind, and tolerant wife, Kathi, to whom I have been blessed to be married for nearly fifty years. She is everything I am not: charming, sophisticated, perceptive, and knowledgeable of the rules of the English language—things that my engineering degree was short on. She not only provided insight and wisdom to the final product but also was the one person I needed to bluntly tell me that something I wrote was incomprehensible. At the same time, throughout the process she was my biggest encourager and friend. Kathi made this book much more readable, and hopefully, she successfully overcame my shortcomings.

A great deal of thanks is due the great folks at Republic Book Publishers who not only agreed to publish this book, but added so much to it in terms of readability as well as marketability. This not only includes Alfred Regnery, someone I first met many years ago in Young Americans for Freedom but also my editor at Republic Book Publishers who knows how to successfully juggle many problems at once, as well as the rest of the team.

I am also in debt to my longtime friend, fellow conservative, and social entrepreneur extraordinaire Ron Robinson. Ron took a tiny foundation acquired long ago by Young Americans for Freedom and turned it into one of the most effective, most successful foundations in the conservative orbit. Young America's Foundation is the success it is today thanks to Ron Robinson, his vision (it was his inspiration to have the Foundation buy the Reagan Ranch), and his immense talent. I leaned on Ron to give me guidance on how to craft a book that would encourage patriotic young Americans to become active in the Conservative movement. The wisdom he shared steered me clear of potholes and miscues that could have easily derailed this book and taken its message off target. Thanks, Ron, for your encouragement and support.

And a special thank you also to Michelle Easton, whose amazing work among young women has created strong leaders who are changing the world. Michelle's insight and encouragement have made me think deeper and hopefully made this a better book.

A special thanks to all the folks who provided testimonials after reading the pre-book manuscript. It takes real friends and committed conservatives to read through yet another conservative book and then write out their thoughts about it. Thank you. I am in your debt.

I would be greatly remiss to not thank my parents who guided me on the path to faith in God and a love of this nation. Your faith and patriotism inspire me daily.

A very big thank you and much gratitude to my copyeditor, Dara Ekanger, who put this book into a format, style, and order that greatly enhanced its readability and comprehension. Dara moved me from the twentieth century into the twenty-first!

Finally, my gratitude is great toward those in the Conservative movement who have inspired and educated me since I joined Young Americans for Freedom in 1962. Thank you, one and all.

ENDNOTES

PREFACE

1   Ronald Reagan, January 5, 1967: Inaugural Address, Ronald Reagan Presidential Library & Museum, January 5, 1967; https://www.reaganlibrary.gov/archives/speech/january-5-1967-inaugural-address-public-ceremony.

2   George Washington Farewell Address, September 19, 1796.

3   Ronald Reagan's Farewell Address, January 12, 1989, Appendix.

4   Ronald Reagan's "shining city on a hill" is a reference to John Winthrop's speech to the Pilgrims prior to landing at Plymouth and exhorting the Pilgrims to be like a shining city on a hill, an example of love, kindness, and virtue to all persons to whom they come in contact with (referring to Matthew 5, 14-16).

5   Staff, "The Sharon Statement," *The New Guard*, Young America's Foundation, May 4, 2016; https://www.yaf.org/news/the-sharon-statement/#:~:text=In%202015%20The%20New%20York%20Times%20recognized%20the,important%20declarations%20in%20the%20history%20of%20American%20conservatism.

6   The one glaring failure of the Sharon Statement was its silence regarding the horrible mistreatment of Black Americans at the time the Sharon Statement was written, even though the young conservative leaders who founded Young Americans for Freedom were overwhelmingly supportive of full citizenship rights and full equality for Black Americans. In fact, numerous Black Americans were early leaders of and participants in Young Americans for Freedom as explained by the book *A Generation Awakes* by Wayne Thorburn. A full explanation of this failure is provided in the book *Coming Home* (Humanix Books) co-authored by Vernon Robinson and Bruce Eberle.

7   William A. Rusher, *Rise of the Right,* (New York: Morrow, 1984), 63.

1: WHY THIS BOOK?

1   Michael Hiban, President, Omega List Company.

2: TODAY'S CONSERVATIVE MOVEMENT

1   These groups included the Student Committee for the Loyalty Oath, Youth for Nixon, and especially the Youth for Goldwater for Vice President Campaign (1960).

2   Wayne Thorburn, *A Generation Awakes* (Ottawa, IL: Jameson Books, 2010), 23.

3   Thorburn, 24.

4   Later renamed the Intercollegiate Studies Institute (ISI).

5   ISI.

6   Clark Woodroe, "Right-Wing Youths Hold Rally in New York," *Harvard Crimson*, March 6, 1961; https://www.thecrimson.com/article/1961/3/6/right-wing-youths-hold-rally-in-new/.

7   M. Stanton Evans, *Revolt on Campus* (Chicago: Henry Regnery Company, 1961), 122.

8   Evans, 123.

9   Lee Edwards, *You Can Make the Difference* (Westport, CT: Arlington House, 1980), 245.

10   Peter Kihss, "18,000 Rightists Rally at Garden," *New York Times*, March 8, 1962; https://www.nytimes.com/1962/03/08/archives/18000-rightists-rally-at-garden-liberals-counter-with-own-mass.html.

11   Lee Edwards, *Goldwater: The Man Who Made a Revolution* (Washington, DC: Regnery Publishing, Inc., 1995).

3: THE SHARON STATEMENT

1   As related to the author by Lee Edwards, who was one of the hundred student leaders at the conference that adopted the Sharon Statement.

2   Benjamin Rush, 1798, upon the adoption of the United States Constitution.

3   George Washington's Farewell Address, September 19, 1796.

4   William J. Federer, quote by John Adams on August 28, 1811, *America's God and Country Encyclopedia of Quotations* (St. Louis: Amerisearch, 1994).

5   Thomas Jefferson, Query XVIII of Notes on the State of Virginia, 1781.

6   Steven F. Hayward, *M. Stanton Evans: Conservative Wit, Apostle of Freedom* (New York: Encounter Books, 2022), 45.

4: THE ESSENTIAL GLUE

1   Alexis de Tocqueville, *Democracy in America* (Chicago: University of Chicago Press, 2000), 517.

2   Larry Schweikart and Michael Allen, *A Patriot's History of the United States* (New York: Sentinel, 2004), 78.

3   M. Stanton Evans, *The Theme is Freedom* (Washington, DC: Regnery Publishing, 1994), 35.

4   Author unknown.

5   William J. Federer, quote by Henry Muhlenberg, founder of Lutheran Church in America, *America's God and Country Encyclopedia of Quotations* (St. Louis: Amerisearch, 1994), 641.

6   William J. Federer, quote by John Hancock, April 15, 1775, *America's God and Country Encyclopedia of Quotations* (St. Louis: Amerisearch, 1994), 275.

7   William J. Federer, quote by John Adams, June 21, 1776, *America's God and Country Encyclopedia of Quotations* (St. Louis: Amerisearch, 1994), 8.

8   William J. Federer, quote by Patrick Henry, May 1765, written on the back of the Stamp Act Resolves passed by the Virginia House of Burgesses, *America's God and Country Encyclopedia of Quotations* (St. Louis: Amerisearch,1994), 287.

9 Larry Schweikart and Michael Allen, *A Patriot's History of the United States* (New York: Sentinel, 2004), xx.

10 Schweikart, xxi.

11 Whitaker Chambers, *Witness*, (Random House, New York, 1952)

12 Chambers, 9.

13 Chambers, 16.

14 Chambers, 17.

15 Ronald Reagan, Ecumenical Prayer Breakfast, Reunion Arena, Dallas, Texas, August 23, 1984

5: THE IRRECONCILABLE DIVIDE

1 Lafayette G. Harter Jr., *John R. Commons: His Assault on Laissez-faire* (Corvallis, OR: Oregon State University Press, 1962), 38–39.

2 Harter, 39.

3 Ronald J. Pestritto, *America Transformed* (New York: Encounter Books, 2021), 20.

4 "The Hegelian Origins of Marx's Political Thought," *The Review of Metaphysics*, Vol. 21, No. 1 (Sep. 1967), 33.

5 Alexandra DeSanctis, "Why Progressivism and Religion Don't Go Together," *National Review*, July 7, 2017; https://www.nationalreview.com/2017/07/democrats-religion-problem-progressivism-faith-inherently-contradictory.

6 Pestritto, 102.

7 Pestritto, 102.

8 James Samson, "DNC Official Suggests Re-Education for Trump Voters—'How Do You Deprogram 75 Million People?'" LifeZette, November 21, 2020; https://www.lifezette.com/2020/11/dnc-official-suggests-re-education-for-trump-voters-how-do-you-deprogram-75-million-people.

9 Samson, "DNC Official Suggests."

10 Charlie Spiering, "Barack Obama Calls for More Censorship: First Amendment 'Does Not Apply to Facebook and Twitter,'" Breitbart, April 21, 2022; https://www.breitbart.com/politics/2022/04/21/barack-obama-calls-more-censorship-first-amendment-does-not-apply-facebook-twitter.

11 Hitler's Nazi platform Plank #13. "We demand the nationalization of all enterprises."

12 Amei Wallach, "Censorship in the Soviet Bloc," *Art Journal*, Vol. 50, No. 3, Censorship I (Autumn, 1991), 75.

13 Jewish Virtual Library, Nazi platform plank #23; https://www.jewishvirtuallibrary.org/platform-of-the-national-socialist-german-workers-rsquo-party.

14 Joseph A. Wulfsohn, "Twitter bans Trump, but Iranian ayatollah, Louis Farrakhan, Chinese propagandists still active," Fox News, January 8, 2021; https://www.foxnews.com/media/twitter-permanently-bans-trumps-but-iranian-ayatollah-louis-farrakhan-chinese-propagandists-still-active.

15 Charles Colson, *How Now Shall We Live?* (Wheaton, IL: Tyndale House Publishers, Inc., 1999), 149.

16 Rush Limbaugh, "My conversation with Ben Shapiro," *The Limbaugh Letter*, April 2019, 8.

17 David W. Southern, *The Progressive Era and Race* (Wheeling, IL: Harlan Davidson, 2005) 46–49.

18 Southern, *The Progressive Era.*

19 William Brooks, "Davos Patricians Want Your Property, Your Country, and Your Freedom," *Epoch Times*, A13.

20 Alexandra DeSanctis, "Why Progressivism and Religion Don't Go Together," *National Review*, July 7, 2017.

21   Genesis 3:5, The Holy Bible.

22   Shalom Auslander, "In This Time of War, I Propose We Give Up God," *New York Times*, April 15, 2022; https://www.nytimes.com/2022/04/15/opinion/passover-giving-up-god.html.

23   Lord John Emerich Edward Dalberg-Acton, "Power and Authority," Acton Institute, "Power tends to corrupt and absolute power corrupts absolutely. Great men are almost always bad men, even when they exercise influence and not authority; still more when you super add the tendency of the certainty of corruption by authority"; https://www.acton.org/research/lord-acton-quote-archive.

24   Isaiah 41:4, The Holy Bible, God's Word Translation.

25   William F. Buckley Jr., *God and Man at Yale* (Washington, DC: Regnery Gateway, 1951, 2021), xvi.

26   Steven F. Hayward, *M. Stanton Evans: Conservative Wit, Apostle of Freedom* (New York: Encounter Books, 2022), 16.

27   Democratic National Committee, San Francisco, August 24, 2019.

28   Franklin D. Roosevelt, "A Mighty Endeavor: D-Day," Franklin D. Roosevelt Presidential Library & Museum; https://www.fdrlibrary.org/d-day.

29   Charles Colson, *How Now Shall We Live?* (Wheaton, IL: Tyndale House Publishers, Inc., 1999), 171.

30   Colson, *How Now Shall We Live*, 171.

31   "America (My Country, 'Tis of Thee)" is an American patriotic song, the lyrics of which were written by Samuel Francis Smith.[2] The melody used is the same as that of the national anthem of the United Kingdom, "God Save the Queen." The song served as one of the de facto national anthems of the United States (along with songs like "Hail, Columbia") before the adoption of "The Star-Spangled Banner" as the official US national anthem in 1931. https://en.wikipedia.org/wiki/America_(My_Country,_%27Tis_of_Thee.

6: THE PROGRESSIVE MOVEMENT'S RANCID ROOTS

1   William F. Buckley Jr., Our Mission Statement, *National Review* first edition, November 19, 1955; https://www.nationalreview.com/1955/11/our-mission-statement-william-f-buckley-jr.

2   Tiffany Jones Miller, "Progressivism, Race, and the Training Wheels of Freedom," *National Review*, November 14, 2011.

3   Lafayette G. Harter Jr., *John R. Commons: His Assault on Laissez-faire* (Corvallis, OR: Oregon State University Press, 1962), 38.

4   Harter, *John R. Commons*, 39.

5   Harter, *John R. Commons*, 131.

6   John R. Commons, *Races and Immigrants in America* (Middletown, DE: Okitoks Press, 2022, Reprint), 17.

7   Commons, *Races and* Immigrants, 18.

8   Commons, *Races and* Immigrants, 21.

9   Miller, "Progressivism, Race," 37.

10   Charlie Kirk, "Barack Obama and the Fear of Modern Philosopher Kings," *Human Events*, April 26, 2022; https://humanevents.com/2022/04/26/barack-obama-and-the-fear-of-modern-philosopher-kings.

11   Kirk, "Barack Obama and the Fear."

12 Lindsay Kornick, "Randi Weingarten slammed for praising op-ed saying parents don't have right to shape school curriculums," Fox News, October 26, 2021; https://www.foxnews.com/media/randi-weingarten-slammed-promoting-piece-trashing-parents.

13 Miller, "Progressivism, Race," 37.

14 Seton Motley, Audio: "FCC's Diversity Czar: 'White People' Need to Be Forced to 'Step Down' 'So Someone Else Can Have Power,'" Media Research Center, News Busters, September 23, 2009; https://www.newsbusters.org/blogs/nb/seton-motley/2009/09/23/audio-fccs-diversity-czar-white-people-need-be-forced-step-down-so.

15 Miller, "Progressivism, Race," 40.

16 James Madison, The Federalist Papers (Liberty Fund, 2001) Number 39, originally published in newspapers in 1787–1788, 194.

17 Sharon Statement, Young Americans for Freedom, adopted September 9–11, 1960

18 Miller, "Progressivism, Race," 37.

19 Miller, "Progressivism, Race," 37.

20 Miller, "Progressivism, Race," 39.

21 Miller, "Progressivism, Race," 38.

22 Mark R. Levin, Unfreedom of the Press (New York: Threshold Editions, 2019) 60.

23 Levin, Unfreedom of the Press, 60.

24 Levin, Unfreedom of the Press, 61.

25 Rachel Elbaum, "Portland Protesters Tear Down Statues of Abraham Lincoln, Theodore Roosevelt," NBC News, October 12, 2020; https://www.nbcnews.com/news/us-news/portland-protesters-tear-down-statues-abraham-lincoln-theodore-roosevelt-n1242913.

26 Tim Fitzsimons, "San Francisco board votes to rename schools named after Washington, Lincoln, and Feinstein," NBC News, January 27, 2021; https://www.nbcnews.com/news/us-news/san-francisco-board-votes-rename-schools-named-after-washington-lincoln-n1255836.

27 Victor Davis Hansen, "The Progressive War against the Dead," Investor's Business Daily, August 25, 2017; https://www.investors.com/politics/columnists/victor-davis-hanson-the-progressive-war-against-the-dead.

28 Hansen, "The Progressive War."

29 Hansen, "The Progressive War."

30 Hansen, "The Progressive War."

31 Hansen, "The Progressive War."

32 Jay Joseph, "Ernst Rüdin: The Founding Father of Psychiatric Genetics," Mad in America, October 19, 2015; https://www.madinamerica.com/2015/10/ernst-rudin-the-founding-father-of-psychiatric-genetics.

33 Bruce Fluery, The Negro Project (Pittsburgh: Dorrance Publishing, 2015), 62.

34 Derek Hunter, "Why 'Progressives' and not 'Liberals'?" Townhall, February 19, 2012; https://townhall.com/columnists/derekhunter/2012/02/19/why-progressives-and-not-liberals-n1012690.

35 Ronald Pestritto, America Transformed (New York: Encounter Books, 2021) 4.

36 Ronald Pestritto, Liberalism, The Heritage Foundation, July 31, 2012; https://www.heritage.org/political-process/report/woodrow-wilson-godfather-liberalism.

37 Susan Ferrechio, "Whistleblowers: FBI probed parents under counterterrorism 'threat tag' for protesting school boards," Washington Times, May 13, 2022; https://www.washingtontimes.com/news/2022/may/12/whistleblowers-fbi-probed-parents-under-counterter/.

38   Kelly Laco, "DHS 'Orwellian' disinformation board should 'shock the core' of American belief system: AG Eric Schmitt," Fox News, April 29, 2022; https://www.foxnews.com/politics/dhs-orwellian-disinformation-board-eric-schmitt.

7: THE ODD PROGRESSIVE VIEW OF REALITY

1   Anne Gearan and Abby Phillip, "Clinton regrets 1996 remark on 'super-predators' after encounter with activist," *Washington Post*, February 25, 2016; https://www.washingtonpost.com/news/post-politics/wp/2016/02/25/clinton-heckled-by-black-lives-matter-activist/?msclkid=08d0edbbcfc411 ecb411ad52c0d50473.

2   Youth for Tomorrow New Life Foundation, Bristow, VA; www.yftva.org.

3   Proverbs 9:10, The Holy Bible, New Internal Version.

4   Richard McDonough, "On the Alleged Moral Superiority of Intellectuals," *American Thinker*, February 20, 2022; https://www.americanthinker.com/articles/2022/02/on_the_alleged_moral_superiority_of_intellectuals.html 2/3.

5   Timothy Carter, "The True Failure Rate of Small Businesses," *Entrepreneur* magazine, January 3, 2021; https://www.entrepreneur.com/article/361350.

6   "American Dream" was a term coined by the historian Truslow Adams in 1931.

8: FREEDOM OR SOCIALISM?

1   "In Their Own Words: Behind Americans' Views of 'Socialism' and 'Capitalism,'" Pew Research Center, October 7, 2019; https://www.pewresearch.org/politics/2019/10/07/in-their-own-words-behind-americans-views-of-socialism-and-capitalism.

2   Carlos Garcia, "Bernie Sanders loves to cite socialist Sweden, but their former prime minister just smacked him down," *Blaze Media*, February 26, 2019; https://www.theblaze.com/news/bernie-sanders-loves-to-cite-socialist-sweden-but-their-former-prime-minister-just-smacked-him-down.

3   Hitler's Nazi Platform, Plank 13. "We demand the nationalization of all enterprises," Platform of the National-Socialist German Workers' Party, Jewish Virtual Library, February 24, 1920; https://www.jewishvirtuallibrary.org/platform-of-the-national-socialist-german-workers-rsquo-party.

4   Adolf Hitler interview with Hanns Johst in Frankforter Volksblatt, January 27, 1934 ; https://der-fuehrer.org/reden/english/34-01-27.htm.

5   John Toland, *Adolf Hitler* (Garden City, NY: Doubleday, 1976), 224–225. Note, some discount this quote and attribute it to someone else; however, based on many other statements by Hitler praising socialism and based on the Nazi platform he helped to draft, it is totally consistent with Hitler's thinking.

6   Billy Moncure, "How Communists in Germany Allied with Nazis to Destroy Democracy," *War History Online*, September 28, 2018; https://www.warhistoryonline.com/instant-articles/communists-allied-with-nazis.html?edg-c=1.

7   Joshua Q. Nelson, "McEnany on liberals' meltdown over Elon Musk buying Twitter: 'They fear a level playing field,'" Fox News, April 26, 2022.

8   Platform of the National-Socialist German Workers' Party, Jewish Virtual Library, February 24, 1920; https://www.jewishvirtuallibrary.org/platform-of-the-national-socialist-german-workers-rsquo-party.

9   Michael Bastasch, "Remember When Maxine Called For 'Socializ-' ... I Mean, 'Taking Over' Oil Companies?" *Daily Caller*, July 26, 2018; https://dailycaller.com/2018/07/26/maxine-waters-oil-companies/

10 James Madison noted in The Federalist #45: "The powers delegated by the proposed constitution to the federal government, are few and defined."

9: THE MIRACLE OF FREE MARKETS

1 "Economic History of the German Re-unification," https://en.wikipedia.org/wiki/Economic_history_of_the_German_reunification.
2 Anna Funder, *Stasiland: Stories from Behind the Berlin Wall* (New York: Harper Collins Publishers, 2022).
3 Helen Raleigh, "Socialism Failed Miserably for the American Pilgrims, Just Like It Does Everywhere," *The Federalist*, November 24, 2020; https://thefederalist.com/2020/11/24/socialism-failed-miserably-for-the-american-pilgrims-just-like-it-does-everywhere.
4 Raleigh, "Socialism Failed Miserably."
5 Raleigh, "Socialism Failed Miserably."
6 Raleigh, "Socialism Failed Miserably."

10: CRITICAL RACE HOOEY

1 Lia Eustachewich, "New website tracks where critical race theory is taught at US schools," *New York Post*, February 5, 2021; https://nypost.com/2021/02/05/website-tracks-where-critical-race-theory-taught-at-us-schools.
2 Nikole Hannah-Jones, "The 1619 Project," *The New York Times*, August 14, 2019; https://www.nytimes.com/.../1619-america-slavery.html.
3 Timothy Barton, "The Revolutionary War and the Origins of Liberty," *Epoch Times*, February 18-22, 2022, A16.
4 Barton, "The Revolutionary War," A16.
5 Bill to Prevent the Importation of Slaves, &c., Virginia House of Burgesses, June 16, 1777; https://founders.archives.gov/documents/Jefferson/01-02-02-0019.
6 Russell Kirk, *Roots of American Order* (LaSalle, IL: Open Court, 1974), 406.
7 Kirk, *Roots of American Order*, 406.
8 Kirk, *Roots of American Order,* 406.
9 "Battle of the Wilderness," *History Net*; https://www.historynet.com/battle-of-the-wilderness.
10 "Battle of the Wilderness," *History.com*, August 21, 2018; https://www.history.com/topics/american-civil-war/battle-of-the-wilderness.
11 Julia Ward Howe, "Battle Hymn of the Republic," verse 5; https://genius.com/Julia-ward-howe-the-battle-hymn-of-the-republic-annotated.
12 Paul Kengor, "Marxism and Critical Race Theory," *The American Spectator*, November 24, 2021; https://spectator.org/marxism-and-critical-race-theory.
13 "Critical Theory," *Stanford Encyclopedia of Philosophy*, March 8, 2005
14 Stephane Courtois, Nicolas Werth, Jean-Louis Panné, Andrzej Paczkowski, Karel Bartošek, and Jean-Louis Margolin, *The Black Book of Communism* (Cambridge, MA: Harvard University Press, 1999), x.
15 Georgia Purdom, "Harvard: No Longer 'Truth for Christ and the Church'" by Dr. Georgia Purdom on October 11, 2011; https://answersingenesis.org/blogs/georgia-purdom/2011/10/11/harvard-no-longer-truth-for-christ-and-the-church.
16 Yale Charter, by the governor and company of his Majesties Colony of Connecticut in New England in America, 1745; https://www.yale.edu/sites/default/files/files/University-Charter.pdf, p. 4.

17 "History of Yale," *All About History*; https://www.allabouthistory.org/history-of-yale.htm.

18 Original Seal of the College of New Jersey; https://www.princeton.edu/frist/iconography/p27.shtml.

19 Kevin Belmonte, *D. L. Moody* (Brentwood, TN: Thomas Nelson, 2010), 156.

20 Christopher F. Rufo, "How to Fight Wokeness," *The American Spectator*, November 3, 2021; https://spectator.org/how-to-fight-wokeness-american-spectator-fall-print-2021.

21 Fred Lucas, "Fact Check: Is Critical Race Theory Taught in Virginia Schools?" *The Daily Signal* published by The Heritage Foundation, November 3, 2021; https://www.dailysignal.com/2021/11/03/fact-check-is-critical-race-theory-taught-in-virginia-schools.

22 Richard McDonough, "On the Alleged Moral Superiority of Intellectuals," *American Thinker*, February 20, 2022; https://www.americanthinker.com/articles/2022/02/on_the_alleged_moral_superiority_of_intellectuals.html 2/3.

23 Carol M. Swain, "CRT: Is It a University-Level Course of a Diet for Our Children?" *Epoch Times*, March 30–April 5, 2022, A16.

11: FREEDOM OR "EQUITY"

1 Dr. Martin Luther King Jr., "I Have A Dream," speech delivered at the March on Washington for Jobs and Freedom on August 28, 1963; Gerard Robinson, "The content of their character: King's theme across the years," *American Enterprise Institute*, January 17, 2020; https://www.aei.org/articles/the-content-of-their-character-kings-theme-across-the-years.

2 Betsy McCaughey, "Racial-equity warriors are hurting the disadvantaged by dumbing down schools," *New York Post*, March 10, 2022; https://nypost.com/2022/03/10/racial-equity-warriors-are-actually-hurting-the-disadvantaged.

3 "Open Secrets," National Education Association, 2020 Election Cycle; https://www.opensecrets.org/orgs/national-education-assn/summary?id=d000000064.

4 "Obscenity in Schools," Parents' Rights in Education; https://www.parentsrightsined.org/obscenity-in-schools.html.

5 John Klar, "Vermont schools use CRT to teach hate against whites," *American Thinker*, June 3, 2021; https://www.americanthinker.com/blog/2021/06/vermont_schools_use_crt_to_teach_hate_against_whites.html.

6 Robby Soave, "A. G. Merrick Garland Tells FBI To Investigate Parents Who Yell at School Officials About Critical Race Theory, School boards want some perturbed parents branded domestic terrorists," *Reason* magazine, October 6, 2021; https://reason.com/2021/10/06/ag-merrick-garland-fbi-critical-race-theory-parents-schools-domestic-terrorists/?msclkid=545261e6b37a11ec989006f35f33f68d.

7 Karl Marx, *Communist Manifesto*, published February 21, 1848.

8 David Satter, "100 Years of Communism—and 100 Million Dead," *Wall Street Journal*, November 6, 2017; https://www.wsj.com/articles/100-years-of-communismand-100-million-dead-1510011810.

9 Satter, "100 Years of Communism."

10 "Gulag," *History.com*, August 21, 2018; https://www.history.com/topics/russia/gulag

11 Seth Lemon, "Chinese whistleblower: COVID-19 was deliberate," first appeared in October 2019, KNX News, September 22, 2021; https://www.audacy.com/knxnews/news/world/whistleblower-china-released-covid-19-on-purpose-in-2019.

12 "Nikita Khrushchev's War on the American Dream," *RedState*, March 20, 2010; https://redstate.com/diary/factapple/2010/03/20/nikita-khrushchevs-war-on-the-american-dream-n218184.

13 "Nikita Khrushchev's War."

14   Carina Benton, "The Left Unmasks Its Desire To Destroy Families-—And The Nation—With Sexual Chaos," *The Federalist*, April 4, 2022; https://thefederalist.com/2022/04/04/the-left-unmasks-its-desire-to-destroy-families-and-the-nation-with-sexual-chaos/?msclkid=8a1ed569b5 aa1leca7a418ce8741ed6d.

15   Wokeism; https://wokeism.org/#:~:text=Wokeism%20is%20an%20oppressive%20mind-virus.%20 Our%20mission%20is,seeks%20to%20silence%20all%20of%20those%20that%20disagree.

16   Matt McGregor, "Former Social Justice Warrior Speaks Out Against 'Cult of Wokeism,'" *Epoch Times*, June 15, 2022, A8.

17   Raven Clabough, "Obama Calls His Critics 'Enemies,'" *The New American*, October 26, 2010; https://thenewamerican.com/obama-calls-his-critics-enemies/.

18   Tyler Olson, "Biden says 'MAGA Republicans' threaten democracy as he and Dems crank up anti-Trump rhetoric ahead of midterms," Fox News, September 1, 2022; https://www.foxnews.com/politics/biden-maga-republicans-threaten-democracy-dems-hammer-trump-emphasize-social-issues-before-midterms.

19   James Varney, "George Soros-funded DAs oversee big cities with skyrocketing crime," *Washington Times*, August 20, 2020; https://www.washingtontimes.com/news/2020/aug/20/george-soros-funded-das-oversee-big-cities-skyrock.

20   Isabel Vincent, "How George Soros funded progressive 'legal arsonist' DAs behind US crime surge," *New York Post*, December 16, 2021; https://nypost.com/2021/12/16/how-george-soros-funded-progressive-das-behind-us-crime-surge.

21   Joshua Rhett Miller, "BLM site removes page on 'nuclear family structure' amid NFL vet's criticism," September 24, 2020; https://nypost.com/2020/09/24/blm-removes-website-language-blasting-nuclear-family-structure.

22   Miller, "BLM site removes page."

23   Mark 12:31, The Holy Bible, God's Word Translation.

12: THE DAVOS MAN

1   Samuel P. Huntington, "Dead Souls: The Denationalization of the American Elite," *The National Interest*, March 1, 2004; https://nationalinterest.org/article/dead-souls-the-denationalization-of-the-american-elite-620.

2   Huntington, "Dead Souls."

3   William Brooks, "Davos Patricians Want Your Property, Your Country, and Your Freedom," *Epoch Times*, A13.

4   Jon Miltimore, "Justin Trudeau Said He Admired China's Dictatorship. Canadians Should Have Believed Him," February 15, 2022; https://fee.org/articles/justin-trudeau-said-he-admired-china-s-dictatorship-canadians-should-have-believed-him.

5   Victor Davis Hansen, *The Dying Citizen* (New York: Basic Books, 2021), 278.

6   Hansen, *The Dying Citizen*, 277.

7   "Thomas Catenacci, Eco group slams Davos summit as global elites arrive in private jets to talk climate policy," Fox News, January 16, 2023; https://www.foxnews.com/politics/eco-group-slams-davos-summit-global-elite-arrive-private-jets-talk-climate-policy.

8   Walter Russell Mead, "All Aboard the Crazy Train," *Wall Street Journal*, January 20, 2020; https://www.wsj.com/articles/all-aboard-the-crazy-train-11579554512.

9   Richard McDonough, "On the Alleged Moral Superiority of Intellectuals," *American Thinker*, February 20, 2022; https://www.americanthinker.com/articles/2022/02/on_the_alleged_moral_superiority_of_intellectuals.html 2/3.

10 Hansen, *The Dying Citizen*, 279.

11 Woodrow Wilson, *Biography* newsletter; https://www.biography.com/us-president/woodrow-wilson.

12 Margaret Sanger, *The Pivot of Civilization* (North Haven, CT: Compass Circle, 2021), 45–51.

13 James Q. Whitman, *Hitler's American Model* (Princeton, NJ: Princeton University Press), 4.

14 Whitman, *Hitler's American Model*, 1.

15 Whitman, *Hitler's American Model*, 1.

16 Whitman, *Hitler's American Model*, 1.

17 Whitman, *Hitler's American Model*, 2.

18 Whitman, *Hitler's American Model*, 2.

19 Tiffany Jones Miller, "Progressivism, Race, and the Training Wheels of Freedom," *National Review*, 37.

20 "Planned Parenthood Honors Hillary Clinton with Margaret Sanger Award," March 27, 2009; https://www.sba-list.org/newsroom/news/planned-parenthood-honors-hillary-clinton-margaret-sanger-award.

21 Sanger, *The Pivot of Civilization*, 62.

22 Bruce Fleury, *The Negro Project* (Pittsburgh: Dorrance Publishing, 2015), 62.

23 Fleury, *The Negro Project* 62.

24 Whitman, *Hitler's American Model*, 6.

25 Whitman, *Hitler's American Model*, 6.

26 Lia Eustachewich, "Bill Gates thinks we should start eating '100% synthetic beef,'" *New York Post*, February 16, 2021; https://nypost.com/2021/02/16/bill-gates-thinks-we-should-start-eating-synthetic-beef.

13: FATHER OF THE SWAMP

1   Woodrow Wilson, *Biography* newsletter; https://www.biography.com/us-president/woodrow-wilson

2   Bruce Bartlett, *Wrong on Race* (New York: Palgrave MacMillan, 2005), 95.

3   Jim Powell, "What If America Never Entered World War I?" *The National Interest*, April 6, 2017; https://nationalinterest.org/blog/the-buzz/what-if-america-never-entered-world-war-i-20056.

4   Ronald J. Pestritto, *America Transformed* (New York: Encounter Books, 2021), 45.

5   Victor Davis Hansen, *The Dying Citizen* (New York: Basic Books 2021), 213.

6   Brian Flood, "Discredited anti-Trump Steele dossier was embraced by liberal media: Here are five of the biggest offenders," Fox News, November 12, 2021; https://www.foxnews.com/media/discredited-anti-trump-steele-dossier-five-biggest-offenders?msclkid=a23c1de9b37d11ec9b3418b7c5bc3e46.

7   Editorial Board, "Trump Really Was Spied On," *Wall Street Journal*, February 14, 2022; https://www.wsj.com/articles/donald-trump-really-was-spied-on-2016-clinton-campaign-john-durham-court-filing-11644878973?mod=hp_opin_pos_4.

8   Editorial Board, "The FBI's Dossier Deceit," *Wall Street Journal*, July 17, 2020; https://www.wsj.com/articles/the-fbis-dossier-deceit-11595027626.

9   Victor Garcia, "Sen. Paul: Source said Brennan, Clapper and Comey pushed discredited dossier, tried to 'bring down a sitting president,'" Fox News, March 28, 2019; https://www.foxnews.com/politics/sen-paul-source-told-me-brennan-clapper-and-comey-pushed-discredited-dossier.

10   Pestritto, 39.

11   USA Facts; https://usafacts.org/annual-publications/government-10-k/part-i/item-1-purpose-and-function-of-our-government-general/employees.

12   Daniel Bier, "In Government, Nobody Quits—And You Can't Get Fired," Foundation for Economic Education, October 15, 2015; https://fee.org/articles/in-government-nobody-quits-and-you-cant-get-fired.

13   Jeffrey Tucker, Climate Depot, a project of the Committee for a Constructive Tomorrow, June 28, 2022; https://www.climatedepot.com/2022/06/28/since-1883-the-administrative-state-has-designed-policy-made-policy-structured-policy-implemented-policy-interpreted-policy-while-operating-outside-the-control-of-congress-president-jud.

14   Victor Davis Hansen, *The Dying Citizen* (New York: Basic Books, 2021), 162.

15   Brooke Singman, "Comey admits drafting Clinton exoneration before interview, defends move as routine," Fox News, April 17, 2018; https://www.foxnews.com/politics/comey-admits-drafting-clinton-exoneration-before-interview-defends-move-as-routine?msclkid=fb2870bab37f11ecad16a0b28415e7aa.

16   Jonathan Zhou, "Hillary Clinton Explains Why She Deleted 30,000 Personal Emails," *Epoch Times*, March 10, 2015; https://www.theepochtimes.com/hillary-destroyed-30000-emails_1278985.html?slsuccess=1.

17   Geoff Earle, "Sensitive spy information found on Hillary's server: report," *New York Post*, January 23, 2016; https://nypost.com/2016/01/23/china-and-russia-likely-hacked-hillarys-emails-robert-gates.

18   "Clinton team used special program to scrub server, Gowdy says," Fox News, August 26, 2016; https://www.foxnews.com/politics/clinton-team-used-special-program-to-scrub-server-gowdy-says.

19   Jessica Chia, "Clinton aide destroyed Hillary's phones by 'breaking them in half or hitting them with a hammer,' FBI documents reveal," Daily Mail, September 3, 2016; https://www.dailymail.co.uk/news/article-3772563/Clinton-aide-destroyed-two-Hillary-s-phones-breaking-half-hitting-hammer-FBI-documents-reveal.html.

20   The Editorial Board, "About Those Domestic-Terrorist Parents," *Wall Street Journal*, October 26, 2021; https://www.wsj.com/articles/about-those-domestic-terrorists-national-school-boards-association-merrick-garland-memo-fbi-11635285900?msclkid=c5bbb808d15311eca99b11365e39804b.

21   Tyler O'Neil, "Fairfax County parents say they're not 'domestic terrorists,' call on school board to condemn DOJ," Fox News, October 8, 2021; https://www.foxnews.com/politics/fairfax-county-parents-school-board-doj-domestic-terrorists.

22   John Rigolizzo, "FBI Team Conducts Early-Morning Raid, Arrests Pro-Life Activist At Pennsylvania Home," *DailyWire*, September 24, 2022.

23   "FBI raids home of Project Veritas James O'Keefe as part of investigation into Ashley Biden's 'stolen' diary," Fox News, November 6, 2021; https://www.foxnews.com/media/fbi-raids-home-james-okeefe-ashley-biden-diary-project-veritas?msclkid=cd92164cb38211ecad9aab4dcf8f52f1.

24   Robert Kraychik, "Former FBI Agent Jonathan Gilliam: Bureau's Top Brass Climb Ladder by Ideology, Not Merit," Breitbart, February 8, 2018; https://www.breitbart.com/radio/2018/02/08/former-fbi-agent-gilliam-bureaus-top-brass-climbs-ladder-ideology-not-merit.

25   Kraychik, "Former FBI Agent."

26 Danielle Wallace, "Pentagon orders 'stand down' across military to investigate extremism in the ranks, Defense Secretary Lloyd Austin issued a 'stand down' for the next 60 days," Fox News, February 4, 2021; https://www.foxnews.com/politics/pentagon-defense-stand-down-military-extremism-in-troops-ranks.

27 "Breaking down Biden's plan to purge military of conservatives," Fox News, May 3, 2021; https://www.foxnews.com/transcript/breaking-down-bidens-plan-to-purge-military-of-conservatives.

28 Caitlin Burke, "Did America's Top General Work Against Trump and Commit Treason? Rubio Calls for Biden to Fire Joint Chiefs Chairman," *CBN News*, September 9, 2021; https://www1.cbn.com/cbnnews/national-security/2021/september/did-americas-top-general-work-against-trump-and-commit-treason-rubio-calls-for-biden-to-fire-joint-chiefs-chairman.

29 "Records Show Critical Race Theory Propaganda at West Point," *Judicial Watch*, June 20, 2022; https://www.judicialwatch.org/crt-propaganda-at-west-point. This information was provided by James J. Bradbury, Freedom of Information/Privacy Act Officer, US Army Garrison—West Point.

30 "West Point, Air Force Academy rocked by scandals, former professors criticize leadership," *USA News*, October 18, 2017; https://www.rt.com/usa/407045-military-academy-investigations-criticism, article includes a photo of West Point graduate 2nd Lieut. Spenser Rapone who on graduation day is displaying what he wrote inside his hat, "Communism Will Win."

31 "West Point, Air Force Academy," *USA News*.

32 Liberty McArtor. First Liberty, July 26, 2019; https://firstliberty.org/news/the-chaplain-corps.

33 Larry Hayden, "A Brief History of American Military Chaplains and their Connection with Methodism in the Anchorage Alaska Community" (Commission on Archives and History, Alaska Missionary Conference' The United Methodist Church), June 2007.

34 Todd Starnes, "Air Force Academy removes Bible verse from cadet's whiteboard," Fox News, March 11, 2014; https://www.foxnews.com/opinion/air-force-academy-removes-bible-verse-from-cadets-whiteboard.

35 Stu Cvrk, "US Naval Academy: Full Speed Ahead on Critical Race Theory," RedState, July 15, 2021; https://redstate.com/stu-in-sd/2021/07/15/us-naval-academy-full-speed-ahead-on-critical-race-theory-n410697.

14: A JUST FOREIGN POLICY

1 "Young Americans for Freedom Celebrates 60 Years," Young America's Foundation; https://www.yaf.org/news/young-americans-for-freedom-celebrates-60-years.

2 George Washington, September 17, 1796, Farewell Address.

3 Merriam-Webster; https://www.merriam-webster.com/dictionary/just

4 The Sharon Statement, adopted by the founding members of Young Americans for Freedom at the family home of William F. Buckley Jr. on September 9–11, 1960.

5 Angelo, M. Codevilla, *The Rise and Fall of America among the Nations* (Encounter Books, New York, 2022), Preface, 19.

6 Codevilla, *The Rise and Fall of America*, 19.

7 Drug Overdose Deaths in the U.S. Top 100,000 Annually, Centers for Disease Control and Prevention; https://www.cdc.gov/nchs/pressroom/nchs_press_releases/2021/20211117.htm.

8 Gordon G. Chang, "China Deliberately Spread The Coronavirus: What Are The Strategic Consequences?" Hoover Institute, Stanford University, December 9, 2020; https://www.hoover.org/research/china-deliberately-spread-coronavirus-what-are-strategic-consequences.

9   Paul Huang, "Censorship in China Turns Social Media into Tool of Repression," *Epoch Times*, March 24, 2018; https://www.theepochtimes.com/censorship-in-china-turns-social-media-into-tool-of-repression_2471548.html?slsuccess=1.

10   Lukas Mikelionis, "Chinese officials burn Bibles, close churches, force Christian to denounce faith amid 'escalating' crackdown," Fox News, September 10, 2018; https://www.foxnews.com/world/chinese-officials-burn-bibles-close-churches-force-christian-to-denounce-faith-amid-escalating-crackdown.

11   Eli Fuhrman, "How China Stole the Designs for the F-35 Stealth Fighter, 1945," July 15, 2021; https://www.19fortyfive.com/2021/07/how-china-stole-the-designs-for-the-f-35-stealth-fighter.

12   Reuters, "China theft of technology is biggest law enforcement threat to US, FBI says," *The Guardian*, US Edition, February 6, 2020; https://www.theguardian.com/world/2020/feb/06/china-technology-theft-fbi-biggest-threat.

13   Laura Hollis, "It Isn't Immigration, It's a Government-Sponsored Invasion," Townhall, August 5, 2021; https://townhall.com/columnists/laurahollis/2021/08/05/it-isnt-immigration-its-a-governmentsponsored-invasion-n2593608.

14   Upon leaving the office of President of the United States after serving two terms, September 19, 1796.

15: AN AMERICAN FOREIGN POLICY FOR AMERICANS

1   George Washington, September 17, 1796, Farewell Address

2   Washington, Farewell Address.

3   Angelo M. Codevilla, *America's Rise and Fall among Nations* (New York: Encounter Books, 2022), 41.

4   Codevilla, *America's Rise and Fall*, vii.

5   When William Howard Taft ran for re-election in 1912, Theodore Roosevelt was extremely unhappy with his policies and decided to run against him in the general election, thus splitting the Republican vote two ways. As a result Woodrow Wilson was elected to the White House with just 41.8% of the popular vote.

6   Codevilla, *America's Rise and Fall*, vii.

7   Edgar E. Robinson and Victor J. West, *The Foreign Policy of Woodrow Wilson, 1913-1917* (New York: Macmillan, 1917), 39.

8   Robinson and West, *The Foreign Policy*, 40.

9   Trading Economics, European Union; https://tradingeconomics.com/european-union/gdp.

10   Trading Economics, Russia; https://tradingeconomics.com/russia/gdp.

11   Robinson and West, *The Foreign Policy*, 40.

12   Terence Jeffrey, "Remember Reagan: We Win, They Lose," *Daily News Record*, January 14, 2017; https://www.dnronline.com/opinion/remember-reagan-we-win-they-lose/article_df55dfb0-d90a-11e6-879c-2face3fbb0fd.html.

13   Ronald Reagan "Evil Empire Speech" to National Association of Evangelicals, Orlando, Florida, March 8, 1983; https://nationalcenter.org/ncppr/2001/11/04/ronal-reagans-evil-empire-speech-to-the-national-association-of-evangelicals-1983.

14   Margaret Thatcher, Eulogy for President Reagan, National Cathedral, Washington, D.C., June 11, 2004.

15   Codevilla, *America's Rise and Fall*, 141.

16   Bradley A. Thayer and Lianchao Han, "China traps the U.S. into negotiations, then breaks its promises," The Hill, February 28, 2015; https://thehill.com/opinion/international/540193-china-traps-the-us-into-negotiations-then-breaks-its-promises/#:~:text=Lenin%20betrayed%20any%20agreement%20when%20it%20no%20longer,treaties%20with%20countries%2C%20but%20hardly%20abided%20by%20any.

17   Climate Action, The United Nations; https://www.un.org/en/climatechange/paris-agreement.

18   Matt McGrath, "Climate change: US formally withdraws from Paris agreement," November 4, 2020.

19   Doug Brandow, "750 Bases in 80 Countries Is Too Many for Any Nation: Time for the U.S. to Bring Its Troops Home," Cato Institute, October 4, 2021; https://www.bbc.com/news/science-environment-54797743.

20   Brandow, "750 Bases in 80 Countries," vii–viii.

21   Brandow, "750 Bases in 80 Countries," vii.

16: "RIGHT TO LIFE, LIBERTY AND THE PURSUIT OF HAPPINESS"

1   Jonathan Cahn, Washington Times, September 8, 2022, B4.

2   Sam Dorman, "An estimated 62 million abortions have occurred since Roe v. Wade decision in 1973," Fox News, January 22, 2021; https://www.foxnews.com/politics/abortions-since-roe-v-wade.

3   Kristi Burton Brown, "It's a scientific fact: Human life begins at fertilization," Live Action, October 30, 2017;| https://www.liveaction.org/news/scientific-fact-human-life-begins-conception.

4   Healthline, "How Early Can You Hear Baby's Heartbeat on Ultrasound and By Ear?" https://www.healthline.com/health/pregnancy/when-can-you-hear-babys-heartbeat.

5   Gary Franks, "Black babies are nearly 40% of U.S. abortions," The Trib, Friday, Jan. 28, 2022; https://triblive.com/opinion/gary-franks-black-babies-are-nearly-40-of-us-abortions.

6   United States Census Bureau; https://www.census.gov/quickfacts/fact/table/US/RHI225219.

7   African American Population; https://www.infoplease.com/us/society-culture/race/african-american-population.

8   Star Parker, editor, "The Effects of Abortion on the Black Community," Center for Urban Renewal and Education, June 2015; https://docs.house.gov/meetings/JU/JU10/20171101/106562/HHRG-115-JU10-Wstate-ParkerS-20171101-SD001.pdf.

9   "Without abortion, the Black American population would be 50 percent higher," California Catholic Daily, June 13th, 2016; https://www.cal-catholic.com/without-abortion-the-black-american-population-would-be-50-percent-higher.

10   Steven Ertelt, "Planned Parenthood Received $1.6 Billion of Our Tax Dollars to Promote Its Abortion Agenda," Life News, January 26, 2021; https://www.lifenews.com/2021/01/26/planned-parenthood-received-1-6-billion-of-our-tax-dollars-to-promote-its-abortion-agenda.

11   Catherine Davis and Bradley Mattes, "Abortion's twisted logic of racism during Black History Month," Washington Examiner, February 28, 2020; https://www.washingtonexaminer.com/opinion/op-eds/since-roe-abortion-has-killed-more-black-babies-than-the-entire-black-population-of-the-u-s-in-1960.

12   Jamie Dean, "Against the Tide," World Magazine, January 19, 2019, 36.

13   "Democrat Legislator Demands Black Babies Be Exempt From Heartbeat Laws," Pulpit & Pen, April 20, 2019; https://pulpitandpen.org/2019/04/20/democrat-legislator-demands-black-babies-be-exempt-from-heartbeat-laws.

14 Steven W. Mosher, "The Repackaging of Margaret Sanger," *Wall Street Journal*, May 5, 1997; https://www.wsj.com/articles/SB862769009690799000.

15 Margaret Sanger, *An Autobiography*, 1938, 366.

17: A SIMPLE TRUTH

1 "How Often Are Guns Used in Self Defense?" American Gun Facts; https://americangunfacts. com/guns-used-in-self-defense-stats.

2 Genesis 3:5, The Holy Bible.

3 Stephen P. Halbrook, "Recalling the Tragic History of Gun Control," *American Spectator*, September 4, 2019; https://spectator.org/recalling-the-tragic-history-of-gun-control.

4 First used by Mao during an emergency meeting of the Chinese Communist Party (CCP) on August 7, 1927, at the beginning of the Chinese Civil War: "Political power grows out of the barrel of a gun," Wikipedia; https://en.wikipedia.org/wiki/Political_power_grows_out_of_the_barrel_of_a_gun.

5 Mark Tapscott, "Another Obama administration czar agrees—'kind of'—with Mao, *Washington Examiner*, October 21, 2009; https://www.washingtonexaminer.com/another-obama-administration-czar-agrees-kind-of-with-mao.

6 Tucker Carlson, "Red Flag laws will not end mass shootings but will end due process," Fox News, June 13, 2022; https://www.msn.com/en-us/news/us/tucker-carlson-red-flag-laws-will-not-end-mass-shootings-but-will-end-due-process/ar-AAYqF19.

7 Carlson, "Red Flag laws will not end mass shootings."

8 Joshua Klein, "GOP Blasts AG Garland After FBI Whistleblower Exposes 'Counterterrorism Tools' Used against Parents: 'Disgrace,'" Breitbart, November 16, 2021; https://www.breitbart. com/politics/2021/11/16/gop-blasts-ag-garland-after-fbi-whistleblower-exposes-counterterrorism-tools-used-against-parents-disgrace.

9 Klein, "GOP Blasts AG Garland."

10 Stephen Dinan, "Two years later, the FBI is still on the hunt for Jan. 6 rioters," *Washington Times*, January 5, 2023; https://www.washingtontimes.com/news/2023/jan/5/two-years-later-fbi-still-hunt-jan-6-rioters/.

11 John W. Whitehead and Nisha Whitehead, "Digital Trails: How The FBI Is Identifying, Tracking, and Rounding-Up Dissidents," State of the Nation, The Rutherford Institute, March 20, 2021; https://stateofthenation.co/?p=56899.

12 Breccan F. Thies, "Department of Justice, Education Bureaucracy Have 'Declared War on Parents' as Whistleblower Reveals Use of Counterterrorism Tools," Breitbart, November 16, 2021; https:// www.breitbart.com/politics/2021/11/16/department-of-justice-education-bureaucracy-have-declared-war-on-parents-as-whistleblower-reveals-use-of-counterterrorism-tools.

13 Bradford Betz, "Whistleblowers: FBI targeted parents via terrorism tools despite Garland's testimony that it didn't happen," Fox News, May 11, 2022; https://www.foxnews.com/politics/ fbi-targeted-parents-via-terrorism-tools-despite-garland-testimony.

14 Benjamin Franklin, "Pennsylvania Assembly: Reply to the Governor," Founders Online, National Archives, November 11, 1755; https://founders.archives.gov/documents/Franklin/01-06-02-0107.

15 Evan Simko-Bednarski, "Supreme Court rules in favor of Washington football coach who prayed on field," *New York Post*, June 27, 2022; https://nypost.com/2022/06/27/supreme-court-rules-in-favor-of-washington-football-coachs-prayer.

16 Thomas Ascik Law and Liberty, Not a Second Class Right, June 27, 2022; https://lawliberty.org/ not-a-second-class-right/.

18: CLIMATE SCIENCE OR POLITICAL SCIENCE?

1 Wave Theory of Light; https://byjus.com/physics/wave-theory-of-light.

2 Justin Gillis, "How Can Climate Science Be Settled?" *New York Times*, December 10, 2015; https://www.nytimes.com/interactive/projects/cp/climate/2015-paris-climate-talks/how-can-science-be-settled.

3 Lianne M. Lefsrud and Renate E. Meyer, Science or Science Fiction? Professionals' Discursive Construction of Climate Change, Sage Journals, November 19, 2012; https://journals.sagepub.com/doi/full/10.1177/0170840612463317.

4 Ian Plimer, *Climate Change: The Facts* (Stockade Books, Woodsville, NH, 2015), 10.

5 Myron Ebell and Steven J. Milloy, "Wrong Again: 50 Years of Failed Eco-pocalyptic Predictions," Competitive Enterprise Institute, September 18, 2019; https://cei.org/blog/wrong-again-50-years-of-failed-eco-pocalyptic-predictions.

6 Steven E. Koonin, *Unsettled?* (Dallas, TX: BenBella Books, Inc., 2021), 5.

7 Koonin, *Unsettled?* 4.

8 John Bowden, "Ocasio-Cortez: 'World will end in 12 years' if climate change not addressed," The Hill, January 22, 2019; https://thehill.com/policy/energy-environment/426353-ocasio-cortez-the-world-will-end-in-12-years-if-we-dont-address.

9 Rachael Rettner, "Al Gore's movie 'An Inconvenient Truth' says sea levels could rise up to 20 feet. Is this true?" Science Line, December 1, 2008; https://scienceline.org/2008/12/ask-rettner-sea-level-rise-al-gore-an-inconvenient-truth.

10 Amy Gunia, "China Is Planning to Build 43 New Coal-Fired Power Plants. Can It Still Keep Its Promises to Cut Emissions?" *Time*, August 20, 2021; https://time.com/6090732/china-coal-power-plants-emissions.

11 US election: Climate crisis struggles to influence voters; https://www.dw.com/en/us-election-climate-crisis-struggles-to-influence-voters/a-55437637.

12 Myron Ebell and Steven J. Milloy, "Wrong Again: 50 Years of Failed Eco-pocalyptic Predictions," Competitive Enterprise Institute, September 18, 2019; https://cei.org/blog/wrong-again-50-years-of-failed-eco-pocalyptic-predictions.

13 Koonin, *Unsettled?*, 8.

14 Koonin, *Unsettled?*, 9.

15 Koonin, *Unsettled?*, 253.

16 Koonin, *Unsettled?*, 253.

17 Storage and Disposal of Radioactive Waste, World Nuclear Association, May 2020; https://world-nuclear.org/information-library/nuclear-fuel-cycle/nuclear-waste/storage-and-disposal-of-radioactive-waste.aspx.

18 Patricia Claus, "Elon Musk Bullish on Future of Nuclear Energy," *Greek Reporter*, September 28, 2021; https://greekreporter.com/2021/09/28/elon-musk-bullish-nuclear-energy.

19 Amy Gunia, "China Is Planning to Build."

20 "China Dominates the Global Lithium Battery Market," Institute for Energy Research, September 9, 2020; https://www.instituteforenergyresearch.org/renewable/china-dominates-the-global-lithium-battery-market.

21 Niclas Rolander, Jesper Starn, and Elisabeth Behrmann, "Lithium Batteries' Dirty Secret: Manufacturing Them Leaves Massive Carbon Footprint," *Industry Week*, Oct. 16, 2018; https://www.industryweek.com/technology-and-iiot/article/22026518/lithium-batteries-dirty-secret-manufacturing-them-leaves-massive-carbon-footprint.

22 Jason Hopkins, "Study: Electric Cars Actually Increase Pollution," *Western Journal*, May 16, 2018; https://www.westernjournal.com/study-electric-cars-actually-increase-pollution/.

23 Scott Sonner, "Judge hears fight over lithium mine on Nevada-Oregon line," *Lahontan Valley News*, July 21, 2021; https://www.nevadaappeal.com/news/2021/jul/21/judge-hears-fight-over-lithium-mine-nevada-oregon.

24 Bjorn Lomborg, *False Alarm* (New York: Basic Books, 2020), 225; "The Paris Agreement is expensive and largely ineffective. It is also going to mean more people left in poverty. A 2019 study found that the massive cost of reducing emissions under the Paris Agreement will lead to an increase in global poverty (compared to what would otherwise be expected) of around 4 percent. The authors issue a stark warning that strong climate change policies could slow efforts to reduce poverty in poor countries," 139.

25 Lomborg, *False Alarm*, 143.

26 This is a summary of a report issued by the National Energy Technology Laboratory (NETL) written by Paul Bledsoe in the June 16, 2021, edition of The Hill titled "Cleaner US gas can reduce Europe's reliance on Russian energy"; https://thehill.com/opinion/energy-environment/558655-cleaner-us-gas-can-reduce-europes-reliance-on-russian-energy. The authors of the NETL report are Selina Roman-White, Srijana Rai, James Littlefield, Gregory Cooney, Timothy J. Skone, Life Cycle Greenhouse Gas Perspective on Exporting, Liquefied Natural Gas from the United States, 2019 Update, National Technology Energy Laboratory, September 12, 2019; https://www.energy.gov/sites/prod/files/2019/09/f66/2019%20NETL%20LCA-GHG%20Report.pdf.

27 US election: Climate crisis struggles to influence voters; https://www.dw.com/en/us-election-climate-crisis-struggles-to-influence-voters/a-55437637.

28 US election: Climate crisis struggles.

29 Becky Norton Dunlop, "The American Conservation Ethic," Heritage Foundation, July 25, 2012; https://www.heritage.org/environment/commentary/the-american-conservation-ethic.

19: PROGRESSIVES COMPASSION?

1 Farron Cousins, "Study Confirms Trump Supporters Completely Lack Compassion For Other Human Beings," Stand Up. Move Forward. The latest Legal and Progressive News, January 13, 2019; https://trofire.com/2019/01/13/study-confirms-trump-supporters-completely-lack-compassion-for-other-human-beings.

2 Cousins, "Study Confirms Trump Supporters."

3 Arthur C. Brooks, *Who Really Cares* (New York: Basic Books, 2006), 19.

4 Brooks, *Who Really Cares*, 19.

5 Brooks, *Who Really Cares*, 19.

6 Brooks, *Who Really Cares,* 19.

7 Giving USA; https://www.bing.com/search?q=How%20much%20did%20American%20donate%20in%202021%20giving%20usa%202021&qs=n&form=QBRE&sp=-1&pq=how%20much%20did%20american%20donate%20in%202021%20giving%20usa%202021&sc=0-52&sk=&cvid=7BEC43BF482A4846915C3AC1FE59C032.

8 Fred Siegel, "The Forgotten Failures of the Great Society," *National Review*, January 10, 2020; https://www.nationalreview.com/magazine/2020/01/27/the-forgotten-failures-of-the-great-society.

9 2 Corinthians 9:7, The Holy Bible, New International Version.

10 Arthur C. Brooks, *Who Really Cares* (Basic Books, New York, 2006), 11–12.

11 Brooks, *Who Really Cares*, 6.

12   Brooks, *Who Really Cares*, 13.

13   Brooks, *Who Really Cares*, 49.

14   Brooks, *Who Really Cares*, 49.

15   Brooks, *Who Really Cares*, 22.

16   Brooks, *Who Really Cares*, 24.

17   Brooks, *Who Really Cares*, 38.

18   Margaret Sanger, Chapter V, "The Cruelty of Charity" (*The Pivot of Civilization*, 1922), 116.

19   Gabriel Hays, "NBC News gutted after deleting tweet with quote comparing Martha's Vineyard migrants to 'trash,'" Fox News, September 17, 2022; https://www.foxnews.com/media/nbc-news-gutted-deleting-tweet-quote-comparing-marthas-vineyard-migrants-trash.

20: DOING GOOD?

1   Polling for YAF's 2020 Youth Patriotism Index.

2   Polling for YAF's 2020 Youth Patriotism Index.

3   Surveillance Under the USA/Patriot Act, American Civil Liberties Union; https://www.aclu.org/other/surveillance-under-usapatriot-act.

4   Text of Obama's fatherhood speech, *Politico*, June 15, 2008; https://www.politico.com/story/2008/06/text-of-obamas-fatherhood-speech-011094.

5   Joseph A. Wulfsohn, Black Lives Matter removes "What We Believe" website page calling to "disrupt . . . nuclear family structure," Fox News, September 21, 2020; https://www.foxnews.com/media/black-lives-matter-disrupt-nuclear-family-website.

6   David Brooks, "The Nuclear Family Was a Mistake," *The Atlantic*, March 2020; https://www.theatlantic.com/magazine/archive/2020/03/the-nuclear-family-was-a-mistake/605536/?msclkid=4eed7d4cd16511ec89c25e524cd269de.

7   John MacGhlionn, "The Demise of the Nuclear Family Has Marxist Roots," *Epoch Times*, May 11, 2022, A16.

8   https://www.opensecrets.org/orgs/national-education-assn/summary?id=d000000064

9   Paul Roderick Gregory, "Why the Fuss? Obama Has Long Been on Record in Favor of Redistribution," *Forbes*, September 23, 2012; https://www.forbes.com/sites/paulroderickgregory/2012/09/23/why-the-fuss-obama-has-long-been-on-record-in-favor-of-redistribution/#1ca3a675593a.

10   Gregory, "Why the Fuss?"

11   Margaret Weigel, "No Child Left Behind and education outcomes: Research roundup," *The Journalist's Resource*, August 25, 2011; https://journalistsresource.org/politics-and-government/nclb-no-child-left-behind-research.

12   Anton Batey, "The Trouble with No Child Left Behind," Mises Institute, March 23, 2010; https://mises.org/library/trouble-no-child-left-behind.

13   Robert Palmer, "A rising tide lifts all boats," *The Times Daily*, May 18, 2013, 1963 Speech by President John F. Kennedy; https://www.timesdaily.com/archives/a-rising-tide-lifts-all-boats/article_683b4189-c348-54e3-93c6-d822ed0120e3.html.

14   Remarks of President Donald Trump at the 2018 National Prayer Breakfast held at the Washington Hilton Hotel, Washington, D.C., on February 8, 2018; https://www.whitehouse.gov/briefings-statements/remarks-president-trump-66th-annual-national-prayer-breakfast.

15   Evita Duffy, "Why We Must Preserve John Winthrop's Vision Of America As 'A Shining City Upon A Hill,'" *The Federalist*, December 17, 2020; https://thefederalist.com/2020/12/17/why-we-must-preserve-john-winthrops-vision-of-america-as-a-shining-city-upon-a-hill.

21: THEY WANT YOU TO SHUT UP!

1 Anthony Buckley, "Free Speech and Fairness? The Left Thinks They're Overrated," April 8, 2021; https://redtea.com/america-now/free-speech-and-fairness-the-left-thinks-theyre-overrated.

2 Matt Vespa, "The Hilarious Angle of the Whole Liberal Meltdown Over Elon Musk's Push to Buy Twitter," Townhall, April 15, 2022; https://townhall.com/tipsheet/mattvespa/2022/04/15/the-rather-hilarious-angle-of-the-whole-liberal-meltdown-over-elon-musks-push-to-buy-twitter-n2605916.

3 Lindsey Burke, PhD, and Matthew Ladner, "Closing the Racial Achievement Gap: Learning from Florida's Reforms," Heritage Foundation, quote from Professor Lawrence Stedman of the State University of New York at a Brookings Institute Conference; https://www.heritage.org/education/report/closing-the-racial-achievement-gap-learning-floridas-reforms.

4 Eliana Miller, "Educators set donation records, back Biden over Trump nearly 6-1," Open Secrets, September 29, 2020; https://www.opensecrets.org/news/2020/09/educators-break-records-920.

5 Karen Schuberg, "In the 2020 election Planned Parenthood donated $45 million to progressive candidates who are pro-abortion," CNS News, October 22, 2009; https://www.cnsnews.com/news/article/abortion-kills-more-black-americans-seven-leading-causes-death-combined-says-cdc-data.

6 Protecting Black Life, 2010 Census; https://www.protectingblacklife.org/pp_targets/index.html.

7 Kate Smith, "Planned Parenthood launches $45 million investment in 2020 elections," CBS News, January 16, 2020; https://www.cbsnews.com/news/planned-parenthood-45-million-we-decide-2020-elections-investment-today.

8 Gary Franks, "Black babies are nearly 40% of U.S. abortions," The Trib, Friday, Jan. 28, 2022; https://triblive.com/opinion/gary-franks-black-babies-are-nearly-40-of-us-abortions.

9 Andi Davis, "Should male athletes be allowed to compete in female sports?" Super Talk, February 23, 2020; https://www.supertalk.fm/should-male-athletes-be-allowed-to-compete-in-female-sports.

10 Jason L. Riley, The Trump Boom Lifted Black Americans, Wall Street Journal, January 28, 2022; https://www.wsj.com/articles/the-trump-boom-lifted-black-americans-unemployment-rate-education-real-wages-upward-mobility-economic-growth-biden-equity-11643389476

11 Patrice Onwuka, "Election 2020: A vote for Trump is a vote for economic progress for African Americans," *USA Today*, November 1, 2020; https://www.usatoday.com/story/opinion/2020/11/01/donald-trump-african-american-black-economic-progress-vote-column/6081310002.

22: PERSUADE OTHERS TO YOUR POINT OF VIEW

1 Roger L. Simon, How to Be Happy in 2023—Make Saving the Republic Your New Year's Resolution, Epoch Times, p. A13

2 Benjamin Franklin, *The Autobiography of Benjamin Franklin*; https://www.goodreads.com/quotes/7971222-i-retained-only-the-habit-of-expressing-my-self-in

3 Megan Brenan, "Americans' Confidence in Major U.S. Institutions Dips," Gallup, July 14, 2021; https://news.gallup.com/poll/352316/americans-confidence-major-institutions-dips.aspx

4 Annie Holmquist, "How to Change the Minds of Those You Disagree With," *Epoch Times*, January 26–February 1, 2022, B4.

5 L.A. Paredes, "Senator H.L. 'Bill' Richardson, Political Maverick and GOC Founder, Passes Away at 92," Gun Owners of California, January 14, 2020; https://www.gunownersca.com/2020/01/14/senator-h-l-bill-richardson-political-maverick-and-goc-founder-passes-away-at-92.

6 Bill Richardson, *Slightly to the Right* (Whittier, CA: Constructive Action, 1965).

7 Richardson, *Slightly to the Right*.!

23: WIN! STAY ON OFFENSE!

1 James Madison, *The Federalist*, edited by George W. Carey and James McClellan (Liberty Fund, 2001), 241.

2 John 8:32, The Holy Bible, God's Word Translation,

3 James Q. Whitman, *Hitler's American Model* (Princeton, NJ: Princeton University Press, 2017).

4 Dinesh D'Sousa, *The Big Lie* (Washington, DC: Regnery Publishing, 2017).

5 Antifa is supposedly and oxymoronically against fascism, but Benito Mussolini was a dedicated socialist until the day he died.

6 Pat Coyle is the one to speak with about putting a conservative speaker on your college or university campus. He knows all the challenges and obstacles the Left will put in your way and how to overcome them. He is practical, knowledgeable, and reliable. Give him a call at 703-318-9608 or 800.USA.1776. You can e-mail Pat at pcoyle@yaf.org.

7 In April 1920, Hitler advocated that the party should change its name to the National Socialist German Workers Party (NSDAP). "The Nazi Party: Background & Overview," Jewish Virtual Library; https://www.jewishvirtuallibrary.org/background-and-overview-of-the-nazi-party-nsdap.

8 Nazi Party Plank #13: We demand the nationalization of all businesses which have been formed into corporations; Plank #14: We demand profit-sharing in large industrial enterprises; Plank #16: We demand . . . the immediate communalizing of big department stores; Plank #17: We demand a land reform suitable to our national requirements, the passing of a law for the expropriation of land for communal purposes without compensation; Plank #25: We demand the creation of a strong central state power for the Reich. Holocaust Encyclopedia; https://encyclopedia.ushmm.org/content/en/article/nazi-party-platform.

9 Lawrence K. Samuels, "The Socialist Economics of Italian Fascism," EconLib; https://www.econlib.org/library/Columns/y2015/Samuelsfascism.html.

10 Jack McPherrin, "American Fascism," *Washington Times*, September 30, 2022, B3.

11 Debra Heine, "Turning Point USA's Candace Owens Smacks Down Black Lives Matter," PJ Media, April 22, 2018; https://pjmedia.com/trending/tpusas-candace-owens-smacks-black-lives-matter-kanye-likes-sees.

12 Melanie Arter, "Candace Owens: White Supremacy Isn't What's Harming Black America—'It's Liberal Supremacy,'" CNS News, August 9, 2019; https://www.cnsnews.com/article/national/melanie-arter/candace-owens-white-supremacy-isnt-whats-harming-black-america-its.

13 Jennifer Harper, "How Americans really feel about the mainstream media," *Washington Times*, September 12, 2018; https://www.washingtontimes.com/news/2018/sep/12/how-americans-really-feel-about-mainstream-media.

24: KNOW THE FACTS–HAVE THE ANSWERS!

1 Jonathan Kyle, DebtInflation; https://debtinflation.com/how-much-did-inflation-increase-during-president-carters-term.

2 Polling for YAF's 2020 Youth Patriotism Index—released in partnership with Townhall—was conducted by Echelon Insights from June 21 to June 25, 2020, from a sample of 800 current high school students and 800 current college students aged 13–22.

25: THIS IS YOUR TIME!

1   Brad Polumbo, "Americans fled blue states in droves in 2021. Here's one big reason why," *Washington Examiner*, January 6, 2022; https://www.washingtonexaminer.com/opinion/americans-fled-blue-states-in-droves-in-2021-heres-one-big-reason-why.

2   Kevin Stocklin, "More Companies Join the 'Great Migration' to Red States," *Epoch Times*, July 6, 2022, p. 1 and 6.

3   Victor Davis Hansen, Are Universities Doomed?, The Epoch Times, December 28, 2022, A18

4   The author serves on the Board of Regents of Wisconsin Lutheran College, a conservative Christian college whose enrollment continues to grow in a manner similar to other conservative Christian colleges.

5   Derek Hunter, "What Really Scares the Left About Musk Buying Twitter," *Townhall*, April 26, 2022; https://townhall.com/columnists/derekhunter/2022/04/26/what-really-scares-the-left-about-musk-buying-twitter-n2606319.

6   Nicole Silverio, "Biden's Support Among Hispanics Collapses, Spelling 'Nightmare Scenario' for Democrats," Daily Caller, April 13, 2022; https://dailycaller.com/2022/04/13/quinnipiac-poll-biden-support-hispanics-collapses.

7   The long march through the institutions (German: der lange Marsch durch die Institutionen) is a slogan coined by communist student activist Rudi Dutschke around 1967 to describe his strategy for establishing the conditions for revolution: subverting society by infiltrating institutions such as the professions. https://en.wikipedia.org/wiki/Long_march_through_the_institutions.

8   David Horowitz, *The Professors* (Washington, DC: Regnery Publishing, 2006), xxxvii.

9   Christine Stanwood, "Arizona Governor to sign bill expanding school voucher," ABC 15, June 28, 2022; https://www.abc15.com/news/state/arizona-governor-to-sign-bill-expanding-school-voucher.

10 Keri Ingraham, "Two States Now Have Universal School Choice—and Yours Could Be Next," The Federalist, January 27, 2023; https://thefederalist.com/2023/01/27/two-states-now-have-universal-school-choice-and-yours-could-be-next/

11 Joe Hildebrand, "The Left's apocalyptic reaction to the Elon Musk Twitter takeover shows they oppose accountability and transparency," Sky News, April 27, 2022; https://www.skynews.com.au/world-news/joe-hildebrand-the-lefts-apocalyptic-reaction-to-the-elon-musk-twitter-takeover-shows-they-oppose-accountability-and-transparency/news-story/2957bd22238902f875aadbc84be45b06.

12 Alex Hammer and Keith Griffith, "Musk says Twitter was 'acting under orders from the government to suppress free speech' as he releases Hunter Biden laptop files that show execs replying 'handled' to requests from 'Biden team' to delete tweets," Daily Mail, December 3, 2022; https://www.dailymail.co.uk/news/article-11498015/Musk-says-Twitter-acting-orders-government-suppress-Hunter-Biden-laptop-story.html

13 Gregory Hoyt, "Musk Twitter Deal Shows Free Speech Terrifies The Left—The Breakdown: Free speech is dangerous?" Red Voice Media, April 27, 2022; https://www.redvoicemedia.com/2022/04/musk-twitter-deal-shows-free-speech-terrifies-the-left-the-breakdown.

14 "UMKC Chancellor Appeases Leftist Thugs Following Left Attack on Knowle's YAF Lecture," New Guard, April 12, 2019; https://www.yaf.org/news/umkc-chancellor-appeases-leftist-thugs-following-attack-on-knowles-yaf-lecture.

15 The author spoke directly with a former drill instructor, known as a DI, who said the DIs can no longer yell at recruits, submit them to rigorous physical training, or prepare them effectively for the trauma of combat.

16 Evalyn Homoelle, "Navy Training Video Tells Sailors How to Use 'Correct' Pronouns and Create 'Safe Spaces,'" The Daily Signal, June 22, 2022; https://www.dailysignal.com/2022/06/22/navy-training-video-tells-sailors-how-to-use-correct-pronouns-and-create-safe-spaces.

17 https://www.topgunmovie.com/home/.

18 Amen Oyiboke, "19 Sequels That Made Much More Than the First Film," August 28, 2020; https://www.gobankingrates.com/money/business/sequels-made-more-money-first-film.

19 Lou Aguilar, "Top Gun, a Cinematic Maverick," The American Spectator, May 30, 2022; https://spectator.org/top-gun-a-cinematic-maverick/#.

20 William J. Federer, quote by John Hancock, April 15, 1775, *America's God and Country Encyclopedia of Quotations* (St. Louis: Amerisearch, 1994), 275.

26: JOIN A GREAT CAUSE

1 1964 Republican National Convention remarks by Ronald Reagan.

2 Closing remarks of Brent Bozell Jr., March 7, 1962, Madison Square Garden speech titled "To Magnify the West," "Brent Bozell's Triumphs," The American Conservative, June 12, 2014. As remembered by Bruce Eberle; https://www.theamericanconservative.com/articles/brent-bozells-triumphs.

3 Mike Pence post, Twitter, April 30, 2022.

4 Mollie Hemingway, *Rigged, How the Media, Big Tech, and the Democrats Seized Our Elections* (Washington, DC: Regnery Publishing, 2021).

5 Trent Baker, "Mo Brooks: Biden Admin Spent Over $2 Billion to Transport Illegal Aliens Across U.S., Breitbart," February 3, 2022; https://www.breitbart.com/clips/2022/02/03/mo-brooks-biden-admin-spent-over-2-billion-to-transport-illegal-aliens-across-u-s.

6 Emily Crane, "Flights carrying illegal immigrants now landing in Pennsylvania: reports," *New York Post*, January 4, 2022; https://nypost.com/2022/01/04/flights-carrying-illegal-immigrants-land-in-pa-reports.

7 Jonathan Turley, "Media and Biden administration cover up these three scandals in 'scandal-free' year," Fox News, January 4, 2022; https://www.foxnews.com/opinion/media-biden-administration-journalism-scandal-hunter-biden-jonathan-turley.

8 Michael Goodwin, "Hunter biz partner confirms email, details Joe Biden's push to make millions from China: Goodwin," *New York Post*, October 22, 2020; https://nypost.com/2020/10/22/hunter-biz-partner-confirms-e-mail-details-joe-bidens-push-to-make-millions-from-china.

9 Miranda Devine, "Are Democrats and Joe Biden up to their old election tricks?" *New York Post*, April 24, 2022; https://nypost.com/2022/04/24/biden-is-up-to-old-election-tricks.

10 Miranda Devine, "10 heinous lies about Kyle Rittenhouse debunked," *New York Post*, November 17, 2021; https://nypost.com/2021/11/17/10-debunked-heinous-lies-about-kyle-rittenhouse-devine.

11 Tré Goins-Phillips, "Nick Sandmann Wins Another Legal Victory Against Four Major Media Outlets," CBN News, October 3, 2020; https://www1.cbn.com/cbnnews/us/2020/october/nick-sandmann-wins-another-legal-victory-against-four-major-media-outlets.

12 Joshua Klein, "Liberals Fume over Elon Musk Twitter Purchase: 'It's About White Power,'" Breitbart, April 26, 2022; https://www.breitbart.com/tech/2022/04/26/liberals-fume-over-elon-musk-twitter-purchase-its-about-white-power.

13 "Brooke Singman Durham says CIA found data alleging Trump-Russia connection not 'technically plausible,' was 'user created,'" Fox New, April 16, 2022; https://www.foxnews.com/politics/durham-cia-concluded-data-alleging-trump-russia-connection-not-technically-plausible-user-created.

14   Spencer Brown, "Berkeley Blocks Ben Shapiro," New Guard, July 19, 2017; https://www.yaf.org/news/berkeley-blocks-ben-shapiro.

15   Jonathan Turley, "Conservatives Attacked by BLM and Antifa Supporters in Effort to Hold Free Speech Rally in San Francisco," October 18, 2020; https://jonathanturley.org/2020/10/18/conservatives-attacked-by-blm-and-antifa-supporters-in-effort-to-hold-free-speech-rally-in-san-francisco.

16   "11 times campus speakers were shouted down by leftist protesters this school year," The College Fix, April 24, 2018; https://www.thecollegefix.com/11-times-campus-speakers-were-shouted-down-by-leftist-protesters-this-school.year.

17   Sam Abodo, "Why do so many young people like communism?" *Washington Examiner*, July 20, 2021; https://www.washingtonexaminer.com/opinion/why-do-so-many-young-people-like-communism.

18   David Harsanyi, "Why Bernie Sanders's Praise of Fidel Castro Matters," *National Review*, February 25, 2020; https://www.nationalreview.com/2020/02/bernie-sanders-praise-fidel-castro-why-it-matters/#slide-1.

19   Steven Santana, "Lenin, Mao sculpture kicks off downtown San Antonio art enclave," MySanAntonio, March 23, 2022; https://www.mysanantonio.com/entertainment/arts-culture/article/Lenin-Mao-sculpture-San-Antonio-downtown-17023655.php.

20   David Satter, "100 Years of Communism—and 100 Million Dead, The Bolshevik plague that began in Russia was the greatest catastrophe in human history," *Wall Street Journal*, November 6, 2017; https://www.wsj.com/articles/100-years-of-communismand-100-million-dead-1510011810.

21   Asra Nomani, "'Hopping Mad' mama and papa bears elect Youngkin," *Fairfax County Times*, November 5, 2021; https://www.fairfaxtimes.com/articles/fairfax_county/hopping-mad-mama-and-papa-bears-elect-youngkin/article_c675c506-3d8b-11ec-a454-1b6ff223b791.html.

22   Brittany Bernstein, "Supreme Court Strikes Down New York Concealed-Carry Restriction," *National Review*, June 23, 2022; https://www.nationalreview.com/news/supreme-court-strikes-down-new-york-concealed-carry-restriction.

23   Virginia Allen, "Touchdown! Supreme Court Rules in Favor of Football Coach's Right to Prayer," *Daily Signal*, June 27, 2022; https://www.dailysignal.com/2022/06/27/touchdown-supreme-court-rules-in-favor-of-football-coachs-right-to-prayer.

24   Michelle Easton, *How to Raise a Conservative Daughter* (Regnery, Washington, DC, 2021), 128.

25   Easton, *How to Raise a Conservative Daughter*, 127–128.

26   Randy Sly, "Obama Moves Away From 'Freedom of Religion' Toward 'Freedom of Worship,'" Fox News, May 7, 2015; https://www.foxnews.com/opinion/obama-moves-away-from-freedom-of-religion-toward-freedom-of-worship.

27   Gary Lane, "Hillary Clinton, Progressives and the Freedom to Worship," CBN News, November 11, 2016; https://www1.cbn.com/globallane/archive/2016/11/11/hillary-clinton-progressives-and-the-freedom-to-worship.

28   Farewell Address of Donald J. Trump, The White House, 45th President of the United States of America; https://trumpwhitehouse.archives.gov/farewell-address.

INDEX